Imaginative Teaching through Creative Writing

Imaginative Teaching through Creative Writing

A Guide for Secondary Classrooms

Edited by
Amy Ash, Michael Dean Clark, and Chris Drew

BLOOMSBURY ACADEMIC
LONDON • NEW YORK • OXFORD • NEW DELHI • SYDNEY

BLOOMSBURY ACADEMIC
Bloomsbury Publishing Plc
50 Bedford Square, London, WC1B 3DP, UK
1385 Broadway, New York, NY 10018, USA
29 Earlsfort Terrace, Dublin 2, Ireland

BLOOMSBURY, BLOOMSBURY ACADEMIC and the Diana logo are trademarks of
Bloomsbury Publishing Plc

First published in Great Britain 2021
Paperback edition published 2022

Copyright © Amy Ash, Michael Dean Clark, Chris Drew and contributors, 2021

Amy Ash, Michael Dean Clark, Chris Drew and contributors have asserted their right under the Copyright, Designs and Patents Act, 1988, to be identified as Authors of this work.

For legal purposes the Acknowledgments on p. xv constitute an extension of this copyright page.

Cover design by Namkwan Cho
Cover image © Getty Images

All rights reserved. No part of this publication may be reproduced or transmitted in any form or by any means, electronic or mechanical, including photocopying, recording, or any information storage or retrieval system, without prior permission in writing from the publishers.

Bloomsbury Publishing Plc does not have any control over, or responsibility for, any third-party websites referred to or in this book. All internet addresses given in this book were correct at the time of going to press. The author and publisher regret any inconvenience caused if addresses have changed or sites have ceased to exist, but can accept no responsibility for any such changes.

A catalogue record for this book is available from the British Library.

A catalog record for this book is available from the Library of Congress.

ISBN:	HB:	978-1-3501-5268-7
	PB:	978-1-3502-1659-4
	ePDF:	978-1-3501-5269-4
	ePUB:	978-1-3501-5270-0

Typeset by Integra Software Services Pvt. Ltd.

To find out more about our authors and books visit www.bloomsbury.com and sign up for our newsletters.

The editors would like to dedicate this volume to our own secondary English teachers, who helped teach us how to teach. We offer our sincere thanks and appreciation to Marlis Day, Donna Dyer, Sue Fuhrman, Karen Hill, Mary Huckstep, Tom Milbery, Carol Patton, Alice Sims, Roger Stuckey, Steve Thompson, and Patti Wallingford.

Contents

List of Figures	x
List of Tables	xi
Foreword	xii
Acknowledgments	xv
Introduction	1

Part One

1. Finding Our Angels in Ourselves: Overcoming Lore and Myth to Teach Creative Writing — 7
   Stephanie Vanderslice

2. Creativity and "Common" Sense: The Standardization of Creative Writing in the Secondary Classroom — 17
   Chris Drew

3. The Creative Writing Process: A View from the Classroom — 37
   Alexa Garvoille

4. "Workshop" as Verb and Environment: Imagining New Possibilities and Approaches — 51
   Amy Ash

5. Collaborative Worldbuilding: Bridging Critical Thinking and Creative Production — 61
   Trent Hergenrader

6. Our Hidden Prime Directive: How Classism Teaches People to Leave Spaceships and Wizards out of the Classroom — 73
   Jennifer Pullen

7. Break Stuff: The Necessity of Mistakes and the Risks That Cause Them in Creative Writing — 85
   Michael Dean Clark

8. Freedom in Limits: Using Demi-Rubrics to Evaluate Creative Work — 99
   John Belk

Part Two

9   Creative Foundations: The Benefits of Prioritizing Creative Nonfiction in the Secondary Standards-Based Classroom   113
Sara C. Pendleton

10   Unruining Poetry   123
Tim Staley

11   The Poetry of Math and Science   131
Kelli Krieger

12   Making Writers Out of Readers: Using Creative Writing to Deepen Literary Analysis in Secondary Settings   143
Heather J. Clark

13   Responsive Freedom: Creative Writing in the Advanced Placement English Literature and Composition Classroom   153
Amanda Clarke and Nan Cohen

14   From Queen to Court Jester: Writing Multigenre Papers alongside My Students   165
Oona Marie Abrams

15   Crafting Online Worlds as Literary Response   175
Stacy Haynes-Moore

16   Capturing Flash Fiction: Utilizing Graphics, Family, and Friends to Engage ELL Students   185
Mark Esperanza

17   Yours, Mine, Ours: Collaboration and Differentiated Learning in the Creative Writing Classroom   195
Tanya Perkins and Josh Tolbert

18   NaNoWriMo and Young Writers: Using a Novel Approach to Push Students' Writing   205
Erik Burgeson and Tom Strous

19   Beyond Brick Walls and Computer Screens: The Story of a University/Middle School Writing Partnership   217
Erica Hamilton and Dana VanderLugt

20   Beyond the Desk: Fostering Community Engagement through Authentic Writing Experiences in and out of the Classroom   231
Justin Longacre

Appendices
Appendix 3.1: Workshop Procedure 241
Appendix 3.2: Flash Fiction Assignment 244
Appendix 8.1: Sample Materials 246
Appendix 16.1 250

Notes on Contributors 251
Index 255

Figures

11.1 Sample page from Newton's *Philosophiæ Naturalis Principia Mathematica*, 1687	135
11.2 Student illustration of Newton's word choices	137
18.1 The individual class tracking sheet providing information for each student and a status for the total school word count	209
18.2 Tracking class and student progress using a shared spreadsheet	211
19.1 Erica's Google slideshow model page	221
19.2 Dana's Google slideshow model page	221
19.3 M&Ms for mentors and mentees (beginning of the semester)	222
19.4 M&Ms for mentors (end of the semester)	223
19.5 Excerpt from "Directions from Dana" (October 17, 2017)	224
19.6 Mentee questions and mentor responses on a poetry-based creative writing experiment	225
A8.1 Frontispiece, *Late Poems, 1968–1993*, Kenneth Burke	247

Tables

8.1	Sample Rubric	101
13.1	For *Song of Solomon* by Toni Morrison	157
13.2	For *Wide Sargasso Sea* by Jean Rhys	157
15.1	Language arts standards that frame the role-play	178
18.1	NaNoWriMo writing timeline	210
19.1	GVSU Preservice teachers' majors/minors	218
19.2	University/secondary school partnership logistical considerations	228
A8.2	Narrative Self-Portrait Assignment Requirements	248

Foreword

This book has been completed at a marked moment in time. It is April 2020, mid-semester, and I haven't been in a classroom with my students in over forty days. Around the globe, school doors are locked with signs that warn students and teachers away from the buildings where we once taught and learned. Inside, students' work still hangs proudly on bulletin boards in our hallways. Now their work is submitted to us online. If we write together as a class, it is only from a distance. I can no longer hear the thrilling scrape of twenty-five pens moving across the page in concert.

On the last day that my university campus was open to us, my students and I lingered in our classroom. We didn't know how things would go or what would happen next. We lingered there because we enjoyed each other's presence and valued what we had been able to make together in the small space. We talked for a long while, and then we wrote.

Our basement-level classroom had no window, only a wallpapered mural of a rather generic mountain scene. In that space, day after day, we made stories and poems and illustrated broadsides, and we talked about what it means to make. Our making made us more attentive readers. We could look more closely at this particular sentence and that particular choice of phrase because we had each tried to write sentences like that too.

By D. G. Myers's account in *The Elephants Teach*, creative writing was, from the start, a mode of learning together and a discovery of how to read. It was, in Myers's words, "the concrete representation of an idea about the best way to teach literature."[1] As Myers tells the story, creative writing emerged from a shared desire for "literature to be taught in a more *literary* manner—from within, from the standpoint of literary creation."

This book is a space where theory converses with activity, where educational standards are met with unpredictable creative play. It is in this space where we can invite each student to be at once poet, reader, theorist, co-creator, worldbuilder, and thinker. In this space we can have conversations that value complexity and uncategorizable experience; we can share in meaning-making that values the suspended ending, the refusal to resolve matters into a tidy, once-and-for-all argument.

In an educational milieu that emphasizes "productivity," this book considers what it means to produce new forms, modes of engaging, and all that comes with the arts. If educational policy prompts us to make ourselves and our students more productive, better able to meet predetermined outcomes, this book is a welcome moment to see the essential role of art and literary writing as a form of cultural production.

Common educational discourses of productivity are often structured by false divisions: separating the critical and the creative, the functional and the artistic, expository and literary writing. These discourses neglect what Jacques Derrida calls the "overrun" of one category into another.[2] As Derrida teaches us to expect, the creative is already inside of the critical; the critical is already inside of the creative, just as truth is already in fiction.

We need a robust vocabulary for thinking through modes of producing, receiving, and teaching texts—and their possibilities. The essays in this collection supply that lexicon and framework.

This is a teacher's book. It brings together university faculty and K–12 educators, creating important conversations that are too rarely provided a space to flourish. Here, we can talk about what we can do in the classroom. In this volume, secondary and postsecondary teachers come together to envision a future for education that values what art-making can uniquely provide.

The changes our globe most needs will be written firmly in the imagination first. I think of Walidah Imarisha's words in the introduction to the short story collection *Octavia's Brood*, inspired by the genius of novelist Octavia Butler: "We believe in that right Butler claimed for each of us—the right to dream as ourselves, individually and collectively. But we also think it is a responsibility she handed down: are we brave enough to imagine beyond the boundaries of 'the real' and then do the hard work of sculpting reality from our dreams?"[3]

We know we need art. Stories are told and retold. Poems are passed between friends. Neighbors share in lyrics sung from apartment balconies. Art sees us through moments of intensified uncertainty; art stays with us and responds to long-standing vulnerability and precarity. We want our students to know literature, to look toward it. We want our students to make more of it.

This morning I wrote to my students. I thanked them for the strength they've shown in moving through this unprecedented and tumultuous semester. And I thanked them for making art because it is necessary.

I thank the authors and imaginative teachers of this collection because they know that to be true.

Janelle Adsit, Humboldt State University

Notes

1 D. G. Myers, *The Elephants Teach: Creative Writing since 1880* (Englewood Cliffs, NJ: Prentice Hall, 1996), 12.
2 Jacques Derrida, *Demeure: Fiction and Testimony*, translated by. Elizabeth Rottenberg, (Palo Alto, CA: Stanford University Press, 2000), 20.
3 adrienne maree brown and Walidah Imarisha, *Octavia's Brood* (Oakland, CA: AK Press, 2015), 5.

Acknowledgments

Amy wishes to thank the English Language Arts teachers who have had a lasting influence on her life and career, as well as her former colleagues and students at Vista Middle School in Las Cruces, New Mexico, who taught her what it means to be a secondary teacher. She also thanks her friends and colleagues at ISU, especially the creative writing faculty—Mark Lewandowski, Emily Capettini, Chris Drew, Brendan Corcoran, and Matthew Brennan—as well as her fabulous creative writing students, who are all a dream to work with. Many thanks, also, to editors Michael and Chris for their vision, their dedication, and their friendship. Finally, she would like to express abundant gratitude and love for her husband, Daniel, and their daughter Ryan—for everything, always.

Michael would like to acknowledge his family for allowing him the space to work and write, his department at Azusa Pacific for enabling him to follow his more unconventional ideas, the faculty and students of Whittier High School where he learned the ropes of secondary English instruction, and his coeditors for taking this book from a conversation over dinner to publication.

Chris would like to thank Michael and Amy for their ceaseless hard work and tolerance of his micromanaging tendencies; his colleagues in the ISU Department of English for their support and guidance in helping him find his scholarly footing; his English teaching and creative writing students at ISU for inspiring him daily; the faculty and students of Jasper High School, Heritage Hills Middle School, and Mater Dei High School for helping him understand what a secondary English teacher should (and could) be; and most especially his family—Brooke, Savannah, and Esme—for their unflagging encouragement and patience.

All of the editors would like to express their gratitude to Lucy Brown at Bloomsbury Academic for believing in this project and for her patience and guidance throughout the process of shaping this book for publication. They also thank all of the contributors to this collection for their insightful, inventive, and inspiring work.[1] Finally, they would like to thank the Creative Writing Studies scholars who have laid the groundwork for this book, as well as the dedicated, determined, and creative teachers at both the secondary and postsecondary levels committed to imaginative teaching in their classrooms.

Note

1. It should be noted that the final sixty days of this manuscript's creation fell in March and April of 2020. While everyone involved with the project worked diligently throughout a nearly three-year process, nothing could have prepared any of them for the effort it would take to complete this book in the midst of a life-altering global pandemic. Somehow, while hurriedly converting classrooms to online-only formats and learning how to collaborate in quarantine, everyone found a way to see it through to completion. The editors would like to amplify their thanks for a final effort made under such unprecedented circumstances.

Introduction

Sometimes it seems like the art of language has been muted in English Language Arts classrooms. Creative writing, a powerful generative force in students' acquisition of and comfort with their communication skills and analytical abilities, has been marginalized by increasingly narrow utilitarian views of what students "need" to learn. Functional texts and forms easily aligned with uniformly testable skills have supplanted the more difficult and less concrete art of self-expression intrinsically involved in writing poetry and prose. Put another way, standards-based frameworks have given way to standardized curricula that privilege argumentative and expository writing as *the* central need for students and suggest, by implication, that creative writing cannot teach these necessary language skills.

However, those of us who teach creative writing understand that the process of exploring ideas by writing creatively is often the *most* effective path to learning the lessons valued in ELA standards. Furthermore, unlike many more prescriptive forms of composition, creative writing can convey lessons on empathy and personal connection to issues of cultural, racial, sexual, and socioeconomic difference when students are tasked with accurately exploring situations unlike their own and people unlike themselves.

Some might argue that the study of literature in English Language Arts classrooms adequately addresses these sorts of personal, interpersonal, and cultural concerns and that many students aren't and shouldn't have to be creative writers. However, merely appreciating the works of others isn't enough. Students must create their own poems and stories to better understand and appreciate the ones they read, in the same way an architect can't only and forever pore over others' blueprints to fully master that discipline. If students aren't given license and space to explore their own creativity in the one required subject of their secondary education that should allow such work, where will they gain this necessary training in the variety and possibility of the language they're learning?

Of course, even teachers who recognize the importance of creative exploration in ELA writing can face a variety of implementation challenges—perhaps none more pervasive than the assumption that it will not fit into a course calendar already straining under formidable constraints such as required standards-based lessons, standardized testing and its accompanying preparation, and limited access to new materials. Add to all of this the dearth of reliable sources on the effective teaching of creative writing and implementation of its accompanying pedagogies at the secondary level—especially when compared to the flood of resources on other types of writing available from educational publishers—and these barriers can feel insurmountable, especially when combined with a general sense that grading creative work is difficult, inherently subjective, and prohibitively time-consuming.

With these needs in mind, *Imaginative Teaching through Creative Writing* seeks to connect pedagogical scholarship from the postsecondary field of Creative Writing Studies with innovative and practical creative writing activities implemented daily by talented and forward-thinking secondary ELA teachers. Structured around these dual components, this book provides a justification of creative writing as much more than just an enjoyable diversion in the standards-driven secondary classroom, while also offering teachers pedagogically sound examples of classroom lessons and activities from their peers that can either be imported directly into classrooms or used as starting points for planning related units and materials.

Using this schema, the collection is divided into two parts, providing readers with two distinct entry points. For those looking to orient themselves to the theory of teaching creative writing before delving into particular classroom practices, Part One offers a number of different views on some of the "big picture" issues in Creative Writing Studies today. The first three chapters act as a collective framework for considering the role of creative writing in secondary settings, beginning with Stephanie Vanderslice's exploration of the value of creative writing as a pedagogical structure and accompanying rationale for why *any* student will benefit from creative work. Then, Chris Drew examines how creative writing pedagogies are not only warranted in a standards-based environment but are also uniquely suited to address over half of Common Core and other similar ELA standards. Finally, Alexa Garvoille offers a consideration of the ways existing secondary pedagogies can be adapted for creative writing assignments and mindsets. Together, these three chapters offer a clear and concise justification for creative writing in secondary ELA classrooms.

Subsequent chapters in Part One delve into key design elements and pedagogies that can be critical in creating successful and manageable writing experiences for students. Amy Ash explains the central pedagogical tool of the traditional creative writing classroom—the workshop—and offers ideas on its implementation, limitations, and potential. Trent Hergenrader and Jennifer Pullen explore, respectively, the benefits of collaborative worldbuilding for engaging student imagination and arguments for including the types of genre fiction loved by many students but too often devalued by secondary curricula. Part One ends with chapters that articulate a shift from product-based to process-oriented evaluation: Michael Dean Clark discusses the notion of building productive failure into collaborative processes, and John Belk details how to counteract assumptions about the challenges of grading creative work by using precisely designed demi-rubrics to help young writers better understand their craft while keeping time commitments manageable for teachers.

For those who prefer jumping straight into practical models and sample lessons, Part Two offers a collection of tangible classroom activities from the secondary instructors who created and taught them. Each approach spotlights creative work while connecting it to a variety of specific curricular and standards-based requirements from broader ELA frameworks, whether Common Core or other state/district standards.

First, Sara C. Pendleton describes her work combining creative nonfiction and intellectual hospitality to broaden students' perceptions of expository writing and themselves. Two more chapters focus on the place of poetry in secondary environments, with Tim Staley exploring how he seeks to "unruin" the form for students by demystifying the writing process through accessible and collaborative projects and Kelli Krieger detailing activities that engage concepts of math and science through poetry to help students understand both more fully.

The next three chapters evaluate different ways creative writing can augment Advanced Placement (AP) courses. Heather Clark guides readers through a progressive series of projects designed to teach students literary analysis through creation rather than identification. More broadly, Amanda Clarke and Nan Cohen detail a variety of ways creative writing can help students meet demanding AP requirements while maintaining more choice in how they do so. Finally, Oona Marie Abrams tells the story of learning how multigenre creative projects can act as important counterprogramming to the rote test preparation that dominates much of the AP experience.

The next chapters revolve explicitly around classroom models that emphasize collaborative creative experiences. In Stacy Haynes-Moore's chapter, a class of improving readers takes on a collective worldbuilding project patterned on the *Hunger Games* series, while Mark Esperanza combines small groups, personal photos, and flash fiction to help English language learners move from prior knowledge to language acquisition. Through the lens of a digitally facilitated classroom, Tanya Perkins and Josh Tolbert describe collaborative work that allows students to generate ideas for a creative project together while maintaining the ability to create unique individual texts.

The final three chapters revolve around partnerships that allow students more opportunities to create art in standards-based curricula. Librarian Erik Burgeson and middle school teacher Tom Strous discuss leveraging the momentum of the NaNoWriMo structure and student competitiveness to foster a school culture of creativity while addressing Common Core standards. Dana VanderLugt and Erica Hamilton explore the benefits of a program partnering high school creative writers with preservice teachers at a nearby college for more immediate and useful feedback on their work. And finally, Justin Longacre traces the ways he designs experiences connecting students with their school and the broader literary community through public readings and journal submissions of their creative work.

Taken together, these two parts of the book provide both the practical experience and theoretical knowledge needed to maximize the role of creative writing in the secondary classroom and justify its inclusion throughout the ELA curriculum. We, the editors, believe this structure not only provides the most versatility and flexibility for readers, but also offers an introduction to the value and practice of creative writing in the secondary classroom that is too often missing from teacher training programs. Prior to our current positions, we each taught secondary ELA at varying grade levels, from middle school students to seniors, and in reflecting on those experiences, we've attempted to create here the kind of teaching resource we wish we'd had in our own classrooms. We sincerely hope it fills that role for current teachers.

More generally, *Imaginative Teaching* seeks to spur a necessary and productive conversation about best practices in the ELA classroom and provide a bridge between secondary and postsecondary educators that will benefit both groups. It is also an instigation of sorts, drawing creative writing back into its rightful place at the center of pedagogical conversations about how we can best help students learn to read and write in ways that will wholly prepare them for whatever they imagine might come next.

Amy Ash, Indiana State University
Michael Dean Clark, Azusa Pacific University
Chris Drew, Indiana State University

Part One

1

Finding Our Angels in Ourselves: Overcoming Lore and Myth to Teach Creative Writing

Stephanie Vanderslice
University of Central Arkansas

Creative learning and creative writing are important in virtually any education curriculum from kindergarten through university because they are essential to the working lives people will lead in the twenty-first century. As Patrick Blessinger articulates in "Transforming Higher Education's Creative Capacity," creative learning is important because "jobs that do not require some form of creativity are more likely to be outsourced or automated. Creative industries contribute significantly to gross economic output and that contribution is likely to increase in the future."[1] In other words, we must prepare our students for a future in which they are able to respond to a constantly changing economy that will demand their creative response.

Incorporating creative writing into the classroom and addressing standards at the same time is not difficult; it just requires a little, ahem, creativity. In the next chapter of this book, Chris Drew makes an abundant, detailed case for the ways in which the Common Core standards correspond to teaching creative writing in the K–12 classroom, calling for secondary ELA teachers to "further refine and communicate how creative writing pedagogy and practice serve as powerful tools in reimagining and expanding the ways secondary English educators can help their students succeed."

But even if those of us who teach English agree that creative writing belongs in the ELA classroom, there are still obstacles to teaching it. One of these is the persistence of myths about writers and creative writing. At the postsecondary level, the discipline of Creative Writing Studies has been trying to debunk these myths for years. But because, through no fault of their own, as Drew notes, "many teachers have neither been taught creative writing pedagogy nor participated in a creative writing workshop, since such activities are not usually part of their required training," they are at risk for reinscribing these myths in their own classroom instead of providing their students with a more authentic creative writing experience. Before describing what the authentic creative writing experience is, let's take a look at what some of these creative writing myths are and how they came to be.

Myth Magic

There are many myths—ideas about creative writing that are not grounded in research or fact—that surround the practice of creative writing in Western culture, from the idea that creative writers require illegal substances to stimulate their creativity to the idea that writers can only write in a garret when inspired. For the purposes of this chapter, however, I am going to focus on the myths that are most inhibiting to secondary ELA teachers and that may not only prevent them from incorporating creative writing in their classroom but, importantly, from seeing themselves as writers and empowering their students as writers. These myths are:

1. Creative writers are "born," not made, and we must be rigorous in our gatekeeping because our society can only support a very few of these "born" creative writers.
2. Good creative writing just naturally springs from the pen of these "born" writers with little attention to process and revision.

Indeed, from where I stand, after twenty-five years of teaching and working with teachers, it is the first myth that is the most damaging. In that time, I have encountered dozens of people—some of them my own students, some already teaching ELA whom I encountered through the National Writing Project—who felt they were "not" writers, and many who were actually (and undeservedly) ashamed of their writing. They were victims of a cultural conception that a writer either "has it or they don't," and either they didn't believe they had "it," or they had actually been told by another gatekeeper along the way, often early in their education, that they didn't. Some of them had even become gatekeepers themselves, eager to pronounce who among their students seem to have "it" and who did not, as if it was their cultural responsibility.

The truth is, and the research shows, people are not actually "born" writers. Writers progress at different rates over the course of their development. One writer who appears to have "it" in your classroom may simply be someone who has read extensively and written for pleasure for many years, and so they have more experience than the student at the desk next to them who did not have those advantages and has never considered writing much before but is interested in it now. Our culture loves to "anoint" writers and artists, to proclaim one person among a group or class as the "one," but the fact is, most beginning creative writing classes are simply collections of people at different stages of practice and experience. Some writers who may end up being successful are only getting started and are making the same mistakes that the more practiced reader and writer got to make in the privacy of their own home when they read past bedtime and wrote page after page in their journals.

As Vicki Spandel notes in *The 9 Rights of Every Writer*, none of us are born walking, yet when we watch a toddler practice cruising, stumbling, and falling, we don't say, "He's no walker." We all learn to walk at different rates, but we eventually learn to walk.[2] Likewise, when my younger son walked a month earlier than my older son did (partly because he was extremely motivated to catch up with his brother), I didn't say, "Look at that kid. He's a natural. He's going to be a great walker someday." That's because walking is something we assume that most of us—at least those who don't have a disability that affects them in this way—will be able to achieve with practice. But because creative writing is considered one of the arts, Westerners view it differently. We think we should limit the number of people who can see themselves as artists. We gatekeep. And that gatekeeping starts as early as elementary school. Each year when I teach creative writing pedagogy, a course I have been teaching for seventeen years, I usually get a variation on the following question from one of my students—often a preservice teacher: "What if I have a student who just doesn't have 'it' as a writer? When should I tell them? What's the best way to break it to them?"

The scary thing about this question and the fact that it keeps occurring is that many of the students who ask it will be teaching either elementary or secondary language arts. Basically, they are assuming that they should single one writer out of a group of, say, ten-year-olds or fifteen-year-olds, who they believe has "it" and encourage them, and that it is their responsibility as teachers to gently discourage the rest. They are also assuming that they are the ones who should be making this distinction and that they will simply "know" creative writing talent when they see it—a dubious assessment method if I ever saw one. Today, even most university writing teachers will tell you they never discourage people from writing, because "making it" as a writer has just as much to do with perseverance and determination as it does talent or anything else.

These kinds of assumptions are not the fault of these preservice teachers or even those currently teaching elementary and secondary ELA who might also hold them. Creative writing myths have been reinscribed generation after generation in a way that leaves no one unaffected. Current ELA teachers may have been celebrated for their writing, for being the most talented writer in the classroom, at the expense of others, or disdained and told, "Hate to break it to you kid, but you're no Shakespeare." Nobel prize-winning author Toni Morrison once famously wrote, "The function of freedom is to free someone else."[3] Not surprisingly, many teachers fear writing, teaching creative writing, or even calling themselves writers because they too are caged by these myths. They don't feel free to be writers, so they cannot free their students to aspire to be writers either.

Where did this myth come from? It's difficult to pinpoint the exact origin of the myth, but the Romantics of the nineteenth century have a lot to answer for. As Joshua Wolf Shenk explains, in the eighteenth century, "as the feudal and agrarian gave way to the capitalist and industrial, artists needed to be more than entertaining; they needed to be original, [in order] to profit from the sale of their work."[4] It became more important for artists to set themselves apart, to be seen as "geniuses," "lit up by an inner light," and during the Romantic era, "the true cult of the natural genius emerged."[5] Shakespeare was a "signal example; so little biographical material existed that his story could be made up."[6] While the story of Shakespeare according to the Romantics dominates—that one individual genius gave birth to dozens of brilliant plays with a talent that sets him light years apart from anyone else—the actual history is somewhat different. Playwriting in the Renaissance was a collaborative effort in which dramatists, according to Shenk, made "compelling work from familiar materials. Shakespeare, for example, did not typically dream up new ideas for plays whole cloth but rewrote, adapted, and borrowed from the plots, characters, and language of previous works." In fact, *Romeo and Juliet* is an "episode-by-episode dramatization of a poem by Arthur Brooke."[7]

Fast forward to today and the Romantic genius myth continues to suffuse our culture, as Shenk points out, where posters paying homage to the individual genius—think Martin Luther King, Jr., Richard Feynman, Thomas Edison, Marie Curie, Walt Disney, and so forth—decorate classrooms around the country, failing to mention that most of these individuals collaborated with others or, at the very least, like Shakespeare, drew from the context of their time and the work that preceded it.[8]

So, while the genius myth originated with the Industrial Revolution and the Romantic era, artists in the two hundred years since have done much to perpetuate it, often because it serves them as well. If there are actual steps to developing as a writer—reading, studying, practicing—the individual artist might become less important than the process. Less unique. Less saleable.

Concurrent with the myth of the genius, then, is the myth that the best creative writing arrives close to fully formed, borne on the wings of angels to the lucky few. As Wendy Bishop notes in *Released into Language: Some Options for Teaching Creative Writing*, however, writers are notoriously unreliable narrators of their own writing processes—often misremembering their process in ways that make them appear (surprise!) special, unique, or chosen.[9] Romantic writer William Blake, for example, likened his writing process to "taking dictation from angels."[10] Certainly, there are times when writers experience a kind of "flow"— the state that psychologist Mihaly Csikszentmihalyi named and described "as a state of concentration or complete absorption with the activity at hand and the situation"[11] where their writing feels divinely inspired. But what writers often leave out are all the times they struggle to put words on the page as well as all the different prewriting strategies they develop, through time and experience, in order to achieve any writing at all. As a result, when beginning writers sit down to write and discover, "Wow, this is really hard, where are my angels?," their next step is often to assume: "If there are no angels, I must not be a real writer." Likewise, if their teacher also believes that "real" writers get it right more or less the first time, with only a little editing, they will fail to teach the writing process or teach it in such a way that they imply that "process" is really only for those who struggle with writing, not those who, you guessed it, have been given the elusive "it"—the golden "Congratulations, you are a real writer" ticket from the literary gods.

So How Did We Get Here?

Although aspects of the history of creative writing pedagogy have been described in other chapters in this book, it's worth connecting the rise of creative writing as a teachable subject to the ways in which, even *as* a teachable subject, it has resisted theory and research to ultimately explain why a lot of these myths continue to persist in creative writing classrooms at all levels. Traces of the inclusion of creative writing in higher education begin as far back as the early verse-making courses at Harvard and the University of Iowa in the 1890s. In the following decades, the University of Iowa began to take this idea further, first allowing creative theses in the English department and later founding the first graduate creative writing program in the country, the Iowa Writers' Workshop, which recruited advanced writers to study creative writing and improve their craft in a workshop setting (a signature pedagogy Amy Ash's chapter will further describe) that they founded centering on criticism from a lead (renowned) author and the rest of the class members. Graduates of the Iowa program went on themselves to form writing programs at universities around the country, and thus the "workshop model" was born and then reborn everywhere.

Although it can work well for the kind of experienced writers that were recruited into Iowa and who are selected to pursue graduate study in creative writing today, the workshop method does not always work well for less-experienced writers who don't already know about different strategies for composing or understand that writing is a challenging, recursive process. In a word, it doesn't work as effectively or as efficiently for people who are not well along the path to being and considering themselves writers. It took a long time for people to figure this out, however, because of the inverted, trickle-down way creative writing grew in higher education—from more experienced, advanced learners in graduate school in the 1940s through the 1970s to those who were less so as undergraduate programs multiplied in the 1980s. In part, creative writers didn't pay much attention to creative writing theory and pedagogy—to how people actually learn to write—because they just didn't have to for a long time. They were already working with more fluent, experienced writers. During this time, creative writers also developed a defensive stance that was, to an extent, anti-theory and anti-pedagogy, clinging to the idea that examining how creative writing happened took away the magic and mystique of the work itself.

Fortunately, this stance started to change in the late 1980s and 1990s, with the pioneering work of Wendy Bishop, Joseph Moxley, Hans Ostrum, and Kate Haake, and continued to gain momentum in the aughts with a long list of scholars, including Tim Mayers, Anna Leahy, Kelly Ritter, Dianne Donnelly, Mary Ann Caine, and Patrick Bizarro; the list is quite long and ultimately includes editors of and contributors to this book. Many of these scholars came from the field of Rhetoric and Composition, where examining how writing is taught and learned had been deemed an acceptable research subject for a few decades already. Fast forward to the present day, and it is fair to say that reflection on the teaching of creative writing in the form of research is experiencing a renaissance, with lots of scholars, including those in this book and many others, finally reflecting on their teaching practice and on the theory of creative writing. It has its own organization, the Creative Writing Studies Organization, founded in 2015, with an annual conference and a website with loads of teaching resources, as well as a similarly rich journal, the *Journal of Creative Writing Studies* that is also open access and has published several articles on the teaching of creative writing in elementary and secondary schools by authors in this book and others. And they are always looking for more. That doesn't mean that there aren't still writer/teachers out there who proudly claim to be ignorant of research about how creative writing is taught, but their generation is slowly retiring and being replaced by people who know their teaching game—and the research that supports it—is important.

Myth Buster #1: Do You Love Writing?

Creative writing in academia is changing its attitude toward the teaching of writing and beginning to take an active role in dismantling the myths that accompany it. What, then, would a secondary ELA classroom that has overcome these myths look like? First, it would be a classroom where the teacher feels personally comfortable writing, where they feel they have a "right to write" as much as anyone and can pass that sense on to their students. I am reminded of the reading professor I know who is often approached by ELA teachers asking her, "How can I get my students to love reading?" "Do you love reading?" is the first question she asks. If the answer is "not really," she knows the teacher has some work to do.

Writing can be challenging; it can sometimes be hard to love. As a teacher, how do you show you love writing? One way is to write along whenever you ask your students to write. Just as the teacher is expected to be reading during a DEAR (drop everything and read) session, so is the teacher expected to write along with their students during a writing session. This communicates that writing is not just busywork the students are being asked to do while the teacher does something else. Instead, writing is an important part of expressing our creativity that belongs to everyone—from the teacher to the student. Moreover, when the teacher reads something aloud they have just written, they may also model that not everything we write is perfect on the first try. They may also model the joy of discovery that can come during a writing session.

Myth Buster #2: Everyone Here Is a Writer

In a classroom where everyone is a writer, it goes without saying that the goal is not to separate the wheat from the chaff and identify the best writer in the room, but instead to understand that as teachers, we teach them all. This requires honoring the process and looking for the strengths in every writer. I often ask my students to share their work aloud, and as they do so, I keep a pad in front of me so I can jot down at least one thing that struck me from each student's writing, even if it's something I observed or felt after I heard the piece, like, "Wow, Frank, I can see you know a lot about how thirsty someone can get playing soccer." I do the same when I critique a student's work on the page, always making sure I point out the strengths before I make suggestions. I'm careful, too, to meet students where they are and to note, in class and on the page, where each student is making personal strides rather than calling out one student as "the best writer" in the room.

Myth Buster #3: Good Writing Takes Time

I encourage students to share writing exercises we do on the spot in class because it's good for them to hear a range of voices and styles and to learn, over time, that our first efforts are just the beginning. Invariably, even as students gain the confidence to read out loud, they often qualify their work with "It's kind of rough." Even if I sound like a broken record after a while, I never miss a chance to say, "Of course, it is. It's a first draft." I don't think my students can ever hear this enough.

I also give my students lots of time and opportunities to write, explaining that creativity can often flourish best within the limits set by creative writing exercises and giving them many to choose from. This breaks down the myth that writers just sit down and pull a great poem or story out of their heads. Instead, they often use strategies to enhance their creativity and productivity. Just like the rest of us.

The Writer-Safe Classroom

There are scores of resources that can help you make your classroom safer for writing and enjoy the process more by flexing your own muscles as a writer. The National Writing Project focuses on "improving the teaching of writing and learning in schools and communities nationwide"[12] through summer institutes that empower teachers as writers and a website chock-full of resources. Working with them has been one of the best experiences of my professional life. And while I have focused on debunking myths that are barriers to optimizing creative writing teaching in the secondary ELA classroom, there are many writers and books out there on how to make yours a writer-safe space. Some of my favorites include works by Ralph Fletcher, Vickie Spandel, Katherine Bomer, and Penny Kittle—but that's just scratching the surface.

Most of all, I hope you come away from this chapter feeling that writing is just as available to you, as a way of expressing yourself and your creativity, as it is anyone else, and that if you haven't felt "like a writer" in the past, it may be the result of cultural forces beyond your control. I hope you claim the notion that you *are* a writer if you write and that once you do, you give that gift to your students to ensure that all of us, students and teachers, can experience the sense of empowerment that writing can bring as we meet the communication demands of the twenty-first century personally and professionally.

Notes

1. Patrick Blessinger, "Transforming Higher Education's Creative Capacity," accessed April 14, 2017, https://www.universityworldnews.com/post.php?story=20170410233217814.
2. Vicki Spandel, *The 9 Rights of Every Writer: A Guide for Teachers* (Portsmouth, NH: Heinemann, 2005), xi.
3. "Toni Morrison: In Her Own Words," *Zora*, August 7, 2019, https://zora.medium.com/toni-morrison-in-her-own-words-562b14e0effa.
4. Joshua Wolf Shenk, "The End of Genius," *The New York Times*, last modified July 19, 2014, https://www.nytimes.com/2014/07/20/opinion/sunday/the-end-of-genius.html.
5. Marjorie B. Garber, *Loaded Words* (New York: Fordham University, 2012), quoted in Shenk, "End of Genius."
6. Shenk, "End of Genius."
7. Ibid.
8. Ibid.
9. Wendy Bishop, *Released Into Language: Options for Teaching Creative Writing* (Urbana, IL: National Council of Teachers of English, 1991).
10. "A Vision: The Inspiration of the Poet (Elisha in the Chamber on the Wall)," *Tate*, accessed March 31, 2020, https://www.tate.org.uk/art/artworks/blake-a-vision-the-inspiration-of-the-poet-elisha-in-the-chamber-on-the-wall-t05716.
11. "Mihaly Csikszentmihalyi," *The Age of Ideas*, accessed March 31, 2020, https://theageofideas.com/mihaly-csikszentmihalyi/.
12. "National Writing Project," accessed March 25, 2020, www.nwp.org.

2

Creativity and "Common" Sense: The Standardization of Creative Writing in the Secondary Classroom

Chris Drew
Indiana State University

Secondary English Language Arts teachers who have read the material preceding this chapter can see that much exciting work has occurred in the field of postsecondary creative writing pedagogy over the past twenty years. However, it's fair to assume that these teachers may also be a bit skeptical about the applicability of these developments in their classrooms. After all, few college professors face anything quite as prescriptive as secondary teaching standards, whether Common Core or other state standards (which, in all probability, still look a lot like Common Core). Either way, these teachers may justifiably feel a bit overwhelmed at the thought of continuing to meet the ELA standards for their grade level(s) while also grafting substantial work in creative writing onto their existing curricula.

However, in my work training future secondary English teachers, teaching creative writing courses, and supervising my university's dual credit English program, I've found that the majority of Common Core and other similar ELA standards can be effectively addressed by current creative writing pedagogies and that when secondary teachers explore such alignments, they get excited to introduce them into their classrooms. Put simply, creative writing's perceived irrelevance in the secondary standards-based environment has been greatly exaggerated, due to both a lack of specific training in creative writing pedagogy and shortsighted readings of the standards themselves. Through an examination of thematic groupings,[1] this chapter will demonstrate that teaching creative writing can satisfy a majority of the current secondary ELA Common Core standards,[2] either independently or through synthesis with other English disciplines.

But First, Some Background

Any secondary teacher reading this chapter is familiar with Common Core or their state's equivalent standards. The history of these standards and the role (or lack) of creativity within them, however, may be a bit more opaque. Common Core itself proclaims that the purpose of the ELA standards is to "help ensure that all students are college and career ready in literacy no later than the end of high school."[3] The sorts of literacy the goals target, however, are a product of their origins. Common Core grew out of the National Governor's Association in the 1990s, as increased citizen mobility and federal testing standards convinced state governors and other officials that a shared set of educational standards would help ensure quality education throughout the United States. These stakeholders were particularly interested in shoring up American secondary education in science, technology, engineering, and math (STEM) to help produce a more highly trained workforce that could keep pace with growing international competition. Springing from the Cold War curricula preceding it, Common Core's primary ELA focus is the informational and expository literacy of STEM, college preparation, and career readiness.

Common Core also resulted from passage of the No Child Left Behind law in 2001, which mandated a rigorous schedule of standardized testing in targeted grade levels. Because a shared set of standards ensured these tests' interstate uniformity, a renewed push for Common Core resulted in the completion of standards in English Language Arts in 2010. Current ELA standards are divided into categories that include reading, writing, language, and speaking/listening. As the Common Core materials state, "[S]tudents who meet the Standards develop the skills in reading, writing, speaking, and listening that are the foundation for any creative and purposeful expression of language."[4] It's worth noting that, despite the perception that creative writing has been deemphasized in the ELA standards, the language used here values creativity enough to include it in the standards' statement of purpose. Still, due to the initial impetus of STEM and workforce preparation, as well as the difficulty of translating creative activity into standardized scores, creative writing in Common Core ELA standards remains largely excluded in favor of literary/informational analysis and expository writing.

Resistance to this perceived exclusion was voiced from the beginning of Common Core. As the standards rose to educational prominence, James Arnold, a Georgia public school superintendent, declared his opposition, arguing that "[s]tandards, by their very nature, insist that if anything at all must be excluded because of the constraints of time in class … it must not, at any cost, be the standards themselves. Creativity will no doubt be the first casualty."[5] While the scope of his concern included all primary and secondary instruction, it was more specifically focused on ELA in a 2014 issue of *English Journal* dealing with "The Standards Movement." In it, active secondary ELA teachers described the effect of Common Core on their classrooms, arguing that "the practice of common formative assessments has the potential to limit how freely we think, how creatively we operate"[6] and labeling the standards as "omnipresent and restrictive."[7] Many teachers noted Common Core's required shift from students reading and writing fiction and poetry to the careful study of "informational texts"[8] that emphasize process and argument over aesthetic concerns. As Robert J. Sternberg wrote, "[V]ery few implementers of the Common Core ... will teach the Common Core in a way that promotes creativity" because "very few standardized tests make any provision for, or even encourage in the slightest way, creative thinking."[9] An evaluation of "curriculum maps" based on the Common Core standards supports these concerns. *Common Core Curriculum Maps in English Language Arts, Grades 9–12*, one of many curricular tools available to educators nationwide, includes a Grade 9 map focusing on literary forms including the short story, poetry, and drama. The sample activities offered for the short story unit include the following: informative/explanatory writing (four discrete activities), class discussion, speech, seminar question and writing, research, grammar and usage, and mechanics.[10] In all, nine activities are provided, none of which include creative writing of any kind. In the yearlong map for studying genres of creative writing in the ninth grade, only four of *seventy* activities include a creative component. In the Grade 10 map, two "narrative" (the preferred Common Core term for creative writing) assignments are provided for the full year, while in the Grade 11 map, only one is provided. None are included in the Grade 12 map, which is focused almost entirely on informational and argumentative writing.[11] In the age of Common Core, available curricular materials suggest that, as Maria Shreve writes, "[N]arrative has become a four-letter word."[12]

However, teachers alarmed by this denigration of creative writing should take heart. Graeme Harper writes that "creativity and critical thought are reciprocally connected, more like each other than they are separate from each other,"[13] and if inroads are to be made by creative writing in the secondary classroom, this link will be at the heart of it. What follows is an attempt to weave the Common Core standards into current creative writing pedagogy using Harper's reciprocity, offering practical examples of classroom activities that allow secondary teachers to usefully engage creative writing and laying the groundwork for additional concepts explored later in this book.

The Explicit Creative Writing Standards

Despite the mistaken belief that creative writing has little currency in the Common Core standards, two standards within the larger assemblage explicitly address and require its presence in the classroom. The first is a catch-all that is applicable to any genre of creative writing, though probably most clearly to fiction and creative nonfiction:

- *Writing Standard 3: Write narratives to develop real or imagined experiences or events using effective technique, well-chosen details, and well-structured event sequences.*[14]

For teachers who like to assign "story writing," this is their justification, but a thoughtful teacher will see the value of specific craft lessons. In fact, the second half of this standard opens the door to the craft criteria I use in my own classes: point of view, detail, setting, stakes, voice, dialogue, and structure, among others. Secondary teachers with some creative writing experience will see this standard as an opportunity to teach these components through creative exercises and assignments, and many of the activities provided in Part Two of this book offer practical guidance on how to implement them.

It is notable that, as with many Common Core ELA standards, more specifics are provided for this standard within specific grade divisions (6, 7, 8, 9–10, and 11–12). In this case, the subpoints for the general standard at the middle school level include attention to dialogue, pacing, description, and narrator,[15] while the high school subpoints include stakes (though not identified by that name), tone, and suspense.[16] In order to maximize the value of creative writing in the classroom, teachers at these grade levels might consider moving past the "write a story" assignment to instead create targeted, formative lessons focused on these craft elements, how to create them, and what purposes they can serve in narrative writing. Again, several chapters later in this book offer specific examples and guidance.

The second standard directly related to creative writing is found in the language section of the standards:

- *Language Standard 5: Demonstrate understanding of figurative language, word relationships, and nuances in word meanings.*[17]

If the previous standard relates primarily to prose narratives, then this could be viewed as the corresponding poetry standard, though such a binary is dismissive of the value of such language considerations across genres. Teachers can design a variety of activities that prompt students to create examples of the components mentioned in the standards, and once again, the subpoints in the grade-specific standards provide further guidance, focusing on personification, connotation, allusion, irony, euphemisms, and hyperbole, among many others.[18] David Yost and I have previously written about a type of Mad Lib activity using Wilfred Owen's "Dulce et Decorum Est," in which specific words have been removed and replaced by fill-in-the-blanks, which are then completed by the students.[19] Originally an exercise used to explore concepts of authority in creative writing, it can also serve as a useful tool for engaging students in the nuance of specific and creative word choice. Similar activities that engage the finer points of wordplay can be found in Tim Staley's chapter.

Additional Standards Addressed by Creative Writing

While the previous section's standards are most closely related to creative writing, three more can also be addressed through a wide variety of creative assignments and activities, though these standards should not be viewed as exclusively creative writing-based. Connecting these standards to creative work, however, becomes particularly useful for teachers struggling to cover all of the standards in a meaningful way over the course of a school year. If teachers have already successfully built creative work into their curriculum, then the methods available for meeting these three goals have widened, removing limitations on where and when they can be met. Additionally, the inclusion of creative writing broadens students' understanding of how these targeted practices can be implemented.

The first standard is writing-based:

- *Writing Standard 4: Produce clear and coherent writing in which the development, organization, and style are appropriate to task, purpose, and audience.*[20]

While this language evokes the sort of process-based writing long championed in composition, a good deal of work has also been done in recent creative writing pedagogy to value process-based writing over the typical focus on finished products. A later section of this chapter will deal with a number of more specifically process-based standards, but it's generally important to note that creative writing-oriented applications of Writing Standard 4 should not be overlooked in favor of exclusively expository assignments. A closer analysis of the standards themselves supports this reading. While the generic standard reads exactly as cited above, in each grade-specific standard, the language is followed by a parenthetical: "Grade-specific expectations for writing types are defined in standards 1–3 above."[21] Writing Standards 1–3 focus on three types of writing: argumentative, informative/explanatory, and narrative.[22] So not only is creative writing a viable avenue for meeting this standard, but according to the standards themselves, it's a *necessary* requirement for doing so. What's more, it broadens students' understanding of the writing process. The specifics of the standard bear this out: appropriateness of style is a universal concern—one that is not adequately addressed by only developing the "academic" voice of typical secondary expository writing—and audience is an equal consideration between creative and other types of writing. (See Justin Longacre's chapter in this volume book for more specifics on audience). In fact, such consideration is often more nuanced in creative writing, given its usual lack of an explicit thesis.

The remaining two standards in this section are included in the language category:

- *Language Standard 1: Demonstrate command of the conventions of standard English grammar and usage when writing or speaking.*
- *Language Standard 2: Demonstrate command of the conventions of standard English capitalization, punctuation, and spelling when writing.*[23]

Many teachers address these standards as part of expository writing assignments, in-class writing, and worksheets. Realistically, though, any time students write, these language standards can be taught and assessed, as long as it's made clear to students that it is occurring. It's less common for secondary teachers to attach these standards to creative work, not only because they are more readily associated with traditional essays, but also because creative work is often considered to be less stringent about such requirements. However, this is a strength of creative writing in relation to these standards. Not only can teachers require correct use of conventions in a poem or narrative, but they can also create space for intentionally designed alternative conventions—slang in dialogue, for example, or unorthodox poetic punctuation—and this subtlety can broaden students' understanding of such concepts. Staley's chapter explores these opportunities in poetry, but they can be addressed in more unexpected ways, too, as Kelli Krieger argues in her chapter on the poetry of math and science.

As Tom C. Hunley and Sandra Giles write in the book *Creative Writing Pedagogies for the Twenty-First Century*, "It would be much more useful to design class activities and discussions around the rhetorical functions of grammatical choices than memorizing and naming the categories. This is applicable, we argue, not just for the creative writing class, but for composition and other writing and communication courses as well."[24] By embracing such activities through creative writing, the relevant language standards can often be met creatively and contextually, rather than through rote memorization, leading to better retention.

The Workshop Standards

The creative writing workshop, addressed more fully in this book's chapter by Amy Ash, has been the primary pedagogical tool of postsecondary creative writing instruction for decades. While recent scholarship suggests that this model has perhaps been overvalued in college classrooms, it has often been bypassed completely in secondary ones, where many teachers have neither been taught creative writing pedagogy nor participated in a creative writing workshop, since such activities are not usually part of their required training. It is important, then, to consider the workshop's specific benefits for secondary students who are often put into peer review groups and simply asked to respond to their classmates' writing in general terms. The workshop offers detailed procedures that can help them instead consider others' texts more usefully while meeting Common Core standards in the categories of writing, language, and speaking and listening.

The writing standard addressed in this category centers on one of the central workshop artifacts—the workshop letter:

- *Writing Standard 9: Draw evidence from literary or informational texts to support analysis, reflection, and research.*[25]

For beginning writers, the workshop letter, written by their classmates to evaluate their submitted texts, is treated primarily as a resource for improving their work. Standard 9 identifies the text under consideration as "literary or informational," which teachers often translate as published stories or essays, but student-written stories or poems are also literary and often more approachable than published texts. If students are carefully taught to write a workshop letter, including its necessary focus on specific textual evidence, it becomes a central tool for meeting this standard. Additionally, Janelle Adsit suggests that the student authors themselves could be asked to provide a "cover sheet" for their works, giving a reflective sense of their own writing processes and goals for their texts.[26] This approach adds an additional level of analysis for this standard, since both the readers *and* the author engage the text critically.

The next two workshop standards are found in the language category:

- *Language Standard 3: Apply knowledge of language to understand how language functions in different contexts, to make effective choices for meaning or style, and to comprehend more fully when reading or listening.*
- *Language Standard 6: Acquire and use accurately a range of general academic and domain-specific words and phrases sufficient for reading, writing, speaking, and listening at the college and career readiness level; demonstrate independence in gathering vocabulary knowledge when considering a word or phrase important to comprehension or expression.*[27]

Through both written feedback and the accompanying discussion, these goals are met by a well-structured workshop. Students can't talk about the language choices in a given story or poem without generally understanding them. The additional grade-specific language contained in the standards document affects the sophistication with which students can be expected to articulate such concerns, but even middle school students are capable of discussing the particular connotations of word choices or phrases, especially when a talented teacher actively draws attention to them. Seeing such criticism modeled by their classmates (another value of the workshop format) will reinforce this skill, and the disagreements that invariably arise regarding such choices will help demonstrate to students the contexts mentioned in the first standard.

Beyond the fact that creative writing itself is a different context from composition or published literature, the first standard can also be met by considering the different contexts contained within a single story or poem. For example, the way language choices function within dialogue and narration are often different, especially when they portray notably different voices. Similarly, language choices used to render scene are not always approached with the same considerations that affect choices within summarized passages.

The final two workshop standards come from a section of the ELA Common Core not yet considered in this chapter—the speaking and listening standards. Creative writing is uniquely suited to foster these specific skills, due not only to its often-overlooked performative nature, but also the critical role of effective speaking and listening in a successful workshop. Two specific speaking and listening standards are addressed in such an environment:

- *Speaking and Listening Standard 1: Prepare for and participate effectively in a range of conversations and collaborations with diverse partners, building on others' ideas and expressing their own clearly and persuasively.*
- *Speaking and Listening Standard 4: Present information, findings, and supporting evidence such that listeners can follow the line of reasoning and the organization, development, and style are appropriate to task, purpose, and audience.*[28]

Standard 1's emphasis on "conversations and collaborations" gets to the heart of what occurs in an effective workshop, and the "diverse partners" are not only the variety of students themselves, but also the unique backgrounds and voices those students bring to their writings. The necessity of "building on others' ideas and expressing their own clearly and persuasively" is practically a course objective for a workshop-based class and certainly would be addressed in a properly implemented secondary workshop environment. Similarly, a student successfully offering constructive feedback in a workshop will inherently address Standard 4's requirement to "present information" so that "listeners can follow the line of reasoning." Of course, such connections only scratch the surface of the workshop's value in the ELA classroom, so for a full exploration of its format, pedagogy, and limitations, see Ash's chapter.

Literature-Based Standards That Engage Creative Writing

Creative writing is an important component of literary study because examples can only teach so much. Just as medical students can only study anatomy for so long before engaging it, to fully understand any art or science, it must be practiced. In fact, the origins of the Iowa Writers' Workshop, the progenitor of most modern postsecondary creative writing programs, are tied closely to the study of literature. One of its creators, Norman Foerster, "believed that students studying literature should know something about how literature is made. He thus saw creative writing as an essential counterpart to interpretive criticism, and believed that students should have practice in both."[29] Unfortunately, this natural alliance between disciplines has often fallen into disuse at the secondary level.

The seven standards below can be applied solely to published texts, of course, but how much more valuable might they become if turned toward students' in-progress work? How might practicing these standards alter student understanding if applied as revision considerations to their own texts rather than simply analytical considerations of canonical writings? The word "author" appears over forty times in grade-specific ELA standards. What if students were encouraged to apply this term to themselves and their classmates, as well as Shakespeare, Wordsworth, Dickinson, and Poe?

For this section, it seems most useful to consider all seven relevant standards together:

- *Reading Standard 1: Read closely to determine what the text says explicitly and to make logical inferences from it; cite specific textual evidence when writing or speaking to support conclusions drawn from the text.*
- *Reading Standard 2: Determine central ideas or themes of a text and analyze their development; summarize the key supporting details and ideas.*
- *Reading Standard 3: Analyze how and why individuals, events, and ideas develop and interact over the course of a text.*
- *Reading Standard 4: Interpret words and phrases as they are used in a text, including determining technical, connotative, and figurative meanings, and analyze how specific word choices shape meaning or tone.*
- *Reading Standard 5: Analyze the structure of texts, including how specific sentences, paragraphs, and larger portions of the text (e.g., a section, chapter, scene, or stanza) relate to each other and the whole.*
- *Reading Standard 6: Assess how point of view or purpose shapes the content and style of a text.*
- *Reading Standard 9: Analyze how two or more texts address similar themes or topics in order to build knowledge or to compare the approaches the authors take.*[30]

While the nuances of these standards are too numerous to discuss in detail here, a cursory glance shows how closely aligned they are with central components and purposes of creative writing instruction, including close reading, textual evidence and development, theme, interpretation, structure, point of view, and intertextuality. What's more, as students become more adept at identifying the elements discussed in these standards through workshop and revision, a careful teacher can create assignments that ask students to transfer these understandings from their own works to the more complex ones found in published literary texts. It's common knowledge among creative writers that to be a good writer, you must also be a good reader, but this *bon mot* is more circular in practice, since being effective writers also equips students to be better readers.

Of course, it would be reductive and limiting to attempt to meet these standards exclusively through creative writing. Instead, teachers should recognize that literature is often best taught with a creative component to help students not only appreciate it, but also understand its construction on a craft level. As Mayers points out, "One of the most important things an undergraduate creative writing course can offer to students as part of a well-rounded literary or liberal arts education is a *way of looking* at fiction, poetry, and literature that differs from the way such things are often looked at in school settings."[31] This is no less true in secondary schools, but much less utilized as a pedagogical approach.

Hunley and Giles also echo this sentiment, drawing on more venerable practices: "The ancient art of stylistic imitation provides a mechanism for consciously learning aspects of craft from other writers. It makes our reading time more productive, enabling us to read as writers."[32] They follow this statement with a handful of sample activities that effectively blend the study of literature and creative writing, including a writing prompt that can only be completed after reading George Orwell's "Shooting an Elephant,"[33] and another that requires students to first read and consider Molière's *Tartuffe*.[34] In the book you're currently reading, similar explorations of the intersections between literature and creative writing are presented by Stacy Haynes-Moore, Erik Burgeson and Tom Strous, Amanda Clarke and Nan Cohen, and Heather J. Clark. In each case, the understanding of both literature *and* writing is improved by bringing them into contact with each other.

A Standard Addressed by Creative Nonfiction

Until now, this chapter has focused primarily on the genres of poetry and fiction for two reasons. First, the obvious creative writing standards in the Common Core relate most clearly to these two genres. Writers of creative nonfiction might disagree, but that informs the second reason: if few secondary teachers have training in how to teach the writing of poetry and fiction, that number decreases dramatically in relation to creative nonfiction. In fact, "creative nonfiction" as a term is not common in secondary textbooks or English teaching curricula. Of course, similar terms are used (essay, personal essay, memoir, literary journalism, narrative nonfiction, etc.), but whereas secondary teachers are amply familiar with poetry and fiction, creative nonfiction as a unified genre containing these subgenres keeps its home more fully in college English departments.

Though the term may be uncommon among secondary teachers, the components of creative nonfiction have been taught in one form or another in secondary classrooms for decades. Orwell's "Shooting an Elephant" makes frequent appearances, as do Elie Wiesel's *Night* and Dave Pelzer's *A Child Called "It."* The speeches of Martin Luther King, Jr., and Maya Angelou's *I Know Why the Caged Bird Sings* are included in many secondary curricula. Quality teachers will recognize the opportunity to create engaging writing assignments examining such readings, but these often take the form of expository essays. Familiarizing teachers with the craft-based aspects of creative nonfiction will allow for many of the standards-based approaches to creative writing to resonate more usefully in such assignments. Additionally, one Common Core standard is particularly suited to creative nonfiction:

- *Writing Standard 2: Write informative/explanatory texts to examine and convey complex ideas and information clearly and accurately through the effective selection, organization, and analysis of content.*[35]

The obvious approach to meeting this standard is to assign an expository essay, and certainly, that effectively addresses the "informative/explanatory" aspect of the standard. However, there are other equally useful approaches. No one would argue that Joan Didion's "At the Dam" or John Hersey's *Hiroshima* doesn't inform or explain, and the creative artistry they demonstrate is integral to conveying particularly complex ideas—those that go beyond simple research or opinion and reach for something less concrete. Secondary students won't often master such elements, but if they can see the full spectrum of "selection, organization, and analysis" present in these texts, their own writing will benefit from it. For further consideration of creative nonfiction's standards-based pedagogical value, see Sara C. Pendleton's chapter later in this book.

Creative Writing Process Standards

Too often, creative writing at the secondary level is treated as a short break from more substantial work, and because of accompanying time limitations, the creative writing activities teachers *do* embark on are necessarily product-oriented. "This week, we're going to write a short story" implicitly directs students toward a finished product five days later. However, longer and more pedagogically thoughtful creative writing activities can focus instead on process, meeting standards commonly associated with expository writing. As Harper notes, "Whereas linear creative writing pedagogics predominantly rely on notions of material completion, achievement defined by reaching a material end point, nonlinear pedagogics can produce a wider variety of results in the area of ... understanding and knowledge."[36] The value of the creative writing process in developing such "understanding and knowledge" can be found in a variety of pedagogy-based activities but is particularly clear in the workshop because its successful completion requires students to view their drafts as unfinished. As Priscila Uppal writes, "To benefit from the workshop environment, student writing has to be assessed in terms of *progress* rather than *product*."[37] The current explorations of process-based writing in creative writing pedagogy, whether via workshop or newer methodologies, will help secondary students look beyond product-based concepts like the finished story or poem and focus instead on the learning opportunities embedded in steady writing progress.

The first writing standard addressed by the creative writing process focuses on the generic components of nearly any writing method:

- *Writing Standard 5: Develop and strengthen writing as needed by planning, revising, editing, rewriting, or trying a new approach.*[38]

Because students are too often trained to consider literature as a finished product, preserved in their textbooks for generations of students, they can incorrectly assume a text sprang from the author's imagination more or less fully formed. By asking students to explore the writing process through creative work and its nonlinear nature, teachers can meet Standard 5 while also connecting their activities to the literature standards discussed earlier.

Similarly, the second process-based standard creates an opportunity to weave creative writing activities into established curricula:

- *Writing Standard 10: Write routinely over extended time frames (time for research, reflection, and revision) and shorter time frames (a single sitting or a day or two) for a range of tasks, purposes, and audiences.*[39]

This standard addresses the variety of creative writing activities that can be brought into the classroom, including not only full-scale works that explore the potential spectrum of the writing process, but also shorter, in-class activities that target individual aspects of creative writing. Many of the activities used to meet this standard grow out of familiar writing prompts and can again be tailored to fit units including a literature component. Asking students to write a paragraph from the point of view of a character with no narrative voice in a novel, for example, addresses this standard while also helping to enhance students' literary analysis skills. Teachers might also construct brief, tailored exercises to help students explore figurative language. As Hunley and Giles write about such prompts, "As with any creative writing exercises, these may or may not lead to polished, publishable literary works, but we would argue that the process is more important than the literary product."[40] If students can better understand metaphor by writing original examples, regardless of whether those metaphors are later reused, then Hunley and Giles's point is proven, and the writing has accomplished its purpose.

The Publication Standard

A sub-focus of Common Core standards is an emphasis on engaging technology, which is often an integral component of college and career preparation. One of the technology-oriented ELA standards can be met by exploring publication options for creative work:

- *Writing Standard 6: Use technology, including the Internet, to produce and publish writing and to interact and collaborate with others.*[41]

A good deal of this chapter has been spent championing process over product in secondary creative writing, but the discipline is malleable enough to support both approaches when appropriate, and the standard above creates space for some focus on product. If a teacher has spent time exploring the process-based opportunities of creative work, an eventual shift to product is reasonable, especially if it can be used to address a standard that is sometimes difficult to successfully engage. Students are often more adept at technology than their teachers, but they don't always see its educational value. Likewise, they enjoy creative writing but don't always understand its purpose beyond the classroom. In discussing Barriss Mills's thoughts on process pedagogy in the 1950s, Mayers considers the value of students knowing there's an end game for their work:

> Outside of classroom settings, Mills asserted, writers and readers are always guided by *purpose*; writers have specific reasons for writing, and these reasons guide virtually every choice they make, from the genres in which they write

to the topics they write about to the stylistic and mechanical conventions they follow .... In far too much school writing, however, this sense of purpose is missing.[42]

This sense of purpose can be a valuable motivator for students to take creative work seriously and also encourages them to consider the sorts of publication opportunities referenced in Writing Standard 6.

What might such collaborative, technology-based opportunities look like in practice? Current pedagogy offers numerous possibilities, but two seem particularly suitable for the secondary classroom. The first is creative use of presentation software. Anna Leahy and Douglas Dechow describe the use of the online software Prezi to create a shareable poetry portfolio. They write, "Most exciting ... was the variety among the portfolios when students moved off the 8 ½-by-11 format. Each portfolio had a different look, pace, and feel—worked differently with form, space, and time—and students recognized and took advantage of developing a distinct project."[43] Here, not only do students clearly meet Writing Standard 6, but they also construct and view their own work in new ways. Meeting the technology standard, too often the shallowest type of learning, in this case leads to deeper consideration and understanding. For more ideas about student publication and performance opportunities as teaching tools, see Justin Longacre's chapter in this book.

The Research Standard

Perhaps no Common Core standard seems more clearly tailored for a specific type of writing than this one:

- *Writing Standard 7: Conduct short as well as more sustained research projects based on focused questions, demonstrating understanding of the subject under investigation.*[44]

This standard is most clearly met by asking students to write a traditional research paper, but for teachers interested in creating research-based assignments that broaden students' understanding of what research can look like and how it can be used, current creative writing pedagogy offers intriguing possibilities that challenge not only typical readings of Common Core standards, but also established ideas regarding creative writing. It's a commonly held axiom in creative writing classrooms that students should write what they know, but as

Joseph Rein writes, sometimes it's important for students to write what they *don't* know.⁴⁵ More specifically, he says that

> instructors often overlook creative research as an important lesson, applauding it when it appears but never deliberately bringing it into the classroom. By making research an explicit goal in my course, however, I can equip my students with the skills to compose not only pseudo-personal poetry, prose, and drama, but also works that delve into unfamiliar worlds and promote discovery, investigation, and exploration.⁴⁶

If the goal of a lesson or unit is to teach formal research, replete with citations and references, the research paper functions better than the activities Rein mentions here. If, however, the purpose is a more general familiarity with avenues of research, including less formal ones, creative writing not only offers a broader palate of primary and secondary research, but also the added interest and motivation that can come with creative work. Alexandria Peary argues that the contextualization required to integrate research into imaginative writing leads to a deeper consideration of the information than in summary- or analysis-based writing, resulting in what she calls "the critical distance made possible by creative writing."⁴⁷ If teachers accept that formal research is only one possible avenue for meeting Writing Standard 7, a wider variety of learning opportunities becomes available.

Beyond secondary research, creative writing also offers opportunities for primary research. Stephanie Vanderslice and Carey E. Smitherman argue for authentic learning opportunities that can also be used as research for creative work—specifically, that students "will have the chance not only to read about the topics they are interested in, but … also be able to conduct primary research (i.e., observations, interviews, etc.), and, through these experiences … become experts in their own right and have their own ideas to share."⁴⁸ Such activities are similar to the familiar assignments asking students to interview a grandparent or community member and write a report about it, but again, Peary's "critical distance" and the accompanying contextualization help to create the expert students Vanderslice and Smitherman discuss.

Next Steps

The perceived shunting of creative work in middle and high school English classrooms by Common Core and similar standards creates a critical need for creative writing pedagogy to be further developed in secondary environments, and this chapter has offered initial suggestions for both implementing such pedagogies and defending their inclusion against prevailing STEM-centric perceptions of various standards systems. For these developments to continue, however, it is critical that secondary ELA teachers further refine and communicate how creative writing pedagogy and practice serve as powerful tools in reimagining and expanding the ways secondary English educators can help their students succeed. This can certainly be a daunting task, but it is my pleasure to inform readers that each chapter of this book successfully accomplishes a remarkable amount of this challenging work, offering thoughtful, pedagogically defensible approaches and activities that treat creative writing as a central standards-based classroom tool. I hope that any reader's "next step" is to explore these contributions to our increasingly robust discipline.

Notes

1 The organization, structure, and some of the content of this chapter are drawn from a previous iteration of the material, written specifically for the primarily postsecondary audience of the *Journal of the Creative Writing Studies*. That version of the material can be found in Volume 2, Issue 1 of that publication, under the title "Minding the Pedagogical Gap: Creative Writing Studies, Common Core Standards, and the Secondary Creative Writing Moment."
2 I've chosen Common Core for this chapter because it's the most, well, *common* set of standards in use today in the United States, and also because most non-Common Core states have aligned their standards closely enough with Common Core that the content of this chapter will still be relevant to teachers in those states.
3 National Governors Association Center for Best Practices, Council of Chief State School Officers, *Common Core State Standards for English Language Arts & Literacy in History/Social Studies, Science, and Technical Subjects* (Washington, DC: National Governors Association Center for Best Practices, Council of Chief State School, 2010), 3.
4 Ibid.
5 James Arnold, "Rotten to the (Common) Core," Journal of Language and Literacy Education, University of Georgia, November 1, 2012, http://jolle.coe.uga.edu/aims-and-scope/.
6 Stephen Heller, "The End of Innovation," *English Journal* 104, no. 2 (2014): 24.
7 Chris Gilbert, "A Call for Subterfuge: Shielding the ELA Classroom from the Restrictive Sway of Common Core," *English Journal* 104, no. 2 (2014): 27.

8   Marci Glaus, "Teacher Perspectives and Classroom Changes during the Standards Movement," *English Journal* 104, no. 2 (2014): 49.
9   Robert J. Sternberg, foreword to *Teaching for Creativity in the Common Core Classroom*, by Ronald A. Beghetto, James C. Kaufman, and John Baer (New York: Teachers College Press, 2015), xi.
10 *Common Core Curriculum Maps in English Language Arts, Grades 9-12* (San Francisco: Josey-Bass, 2012), 5–7.
11 Ibid., 67–254.
12 Maria Shreve, "Common Core and Fostering Creativity," *California English* 20, no. 1 (2014): 19.
13 Graeme Harper, "Creative Writing in the Age of Synapses," in *Creative Writing in the Digital Age: Theory, Practice, and Pedagogy*, ed. Michael Dean Clark, Trent Hergenrader, and Joseph Rein (New York: Bloomsbury, 2015), 10.
14 National Governors Association, *Core State Standards for English Language Arts*, 41.
15 Ibid., 43.
16 Ibid., 46.
17 Ibid., 51.
18 Ibid., 53, 55.
19 Chris Drew and David Yost, "Composing Creatively: Further Crossing Composition/Creative Writing Boundaries," in *Dispatches from the Classroom: Graduate Students on Creative Writing Pedagogy*, ed. Chris Drew, Joseph Rein and David Yost (New York: Continuum, 2012), 204–5.
20 National Governors Association, *Core State Standards for English Language Arts*, 43.
21 Ibid., 43, 46.
22 Ibid., 41.
23 Ibid., 51.
24 Tom C. Hunley and Sandra Giles, "Rhetorical Pedagogy," in *Creative Writing Pedagogies for the Twenty-First Century*, ed. Alexandria Peary and Tom C. Hunley (Carbondale, IL: Southern Illinois University, 2015), 20–1.
25 National Governors Association, *Core State Standards for English Language Arts*, 41.
26 Janelle Adsit, "Adapting Writing Center Pedagogy for the Undergraduate Workshop," in *Dispatches from the Classroom* (see note 18), 178.
27 National Governors Association, *Core State Standards for English Language Arts*, 51.
28 Ibid., 48.
29 Tim Mayers, "Creative Writing and Process Pedagogy," in *Creative Writing Pedagogies* (see note 23), 38.
30 National Governors Association, *Core State Standards for English Language Arts*, 35.
31 Mayers, "Creative Writing and Process Pedagogy," 48.
32 Hunley and Giles, "Rhetorical Pedagogy," 18.
33 Ibid., 25.

34 Ibid., 26.
35 National Governors Association, *Core State Standards for English Language Arts*, 41.
36 Harper, "Creative Writing in the Age of Synapses," 9.
37 Priscila Uppal, "Both Sides of the Desk: Experiencing Creative Writing Lore as a Student and as a Professor," in *Can It Really Be Taught?: Resisting Lore in Creative Writing Pedagogy*, ed. Kelly Ritter and Stephanie Vanderslice (Portsmouth, NH: Heinemann, 2007), 54.
38 National Governors Association, *Core State Standards for English Language Arts*, 41.
39 Ibid.
40 Hunley and Giles, "Rhetorical Pedagogy," 17.
41 National Governors Association, *Core State Standards for English Language Arts*, 41.
42 Mayers, "Creative Writing and Process Pedagogy," 33.
43 Anna Leahy and Douglas Dechow, "Concentration, Form, and Ways of (Digitally) Seeing," in *Creative Writing in the Digital Age* (see note 12), 37.
44 National Governors Association, *Core State Standards for English Language Arts*, 41.
45 Joseph Rein, "Write What You *Don't* Know: Teaching Creative Research," in *Dispatches from the Classroom* (see note 18), 111.
46 Ibid., 112.
47 Alexandria Peary, "Spectators at Their Own Future: Creative Writing Assignments in the Disciplines and the Fostering of Critical Thinking," *The WAC Journal* 23 (2012): 67.
48 Stephanie Vanderslice and Carey E. Smitherman, "Service Learning, Literary Citizenship, and the Creative Writing Classroom," in *Creative Writing Pedagogies* (see note 23), 155.

3

The Creative Writing Process: A View from the Classroom

Alexa Garvoille
Virginia Polytechnic Institute and State University

When I first taught a high school creative writing elective, I felt unprepared, to say the least, and though I'd never taken a creative writing course, I was assured the staff filing cabinet held many drawers of useful Xeroxes. Despite my initial fear, I soon realized my training as an ELA teacher had actually prepared me to teach creative writing. Now, after teaching ninth-grade ELA and creative writing classes, directing a secondary creative writing program, pursuing an MFA, and engaging in Creative Writing Studies scholarship, I am even more aware of how the teaching techniques I used in ELA are central to my creative writing pedagogy.

Granted, there are limitations to applying education research to creative writing—short stories and timed essays are wildly different beasts—but given the common ancestry of the two fields,[1] each discipline can learn plenty from the other. This chapter is a view from the bridge between ELA best practices pedagogy and Creative Writing Studies. I'll situate within my own classroom experience both Chris Drew's argument about the relevance of creative writing to ELA standards and the explanation of Creative Writing Studies that Stephanie Vanderslice includes in her broader justification for students (and teachers) to view themselves as writers. As her chapter explains, Creative Writing Studies challenges pedagogical lore and the "untested methods of instruction"[2] passed among teachers, instead favoring approaches grounded in research and theory. One troubling piece of lore is the supposition that creative writing can't be taught, which is problematic for educators because "it also suggests that [creative writing] cannot be learned."[3] Considering the rich collection of writing research driven by public interest in K–12 schools, the field of English education is well positioned to lend its methods to students learning creative writing. Moreover, creative writing fits into the classroom processes secondary writing teachers are already using, processes that can subtly shift to accommodate creativity.[4]

The writing process—prewriting, drafting, revision, and publication—has been used from elementary school to the MFA. The series of steps, designed to mirror the work of real writers, was articulated by Janet Emig in the process movement,[5] continued by Donald Murray[6] and then Donald Graves,[7] and popularized for K–8 classrooms by Lucy Calkins,[8] among others. A structure so familiar it's nearly invisible, this process is a useful framework for bridging creative work in secondary and higher ed classrooms. Below, I'll address building a creative writing-friendly culture and then, for each step of the writing process, provide an overview of ELA practices applied to creative writing with examples from my own classroom.

Creating a Culture of Risk-Taking

The steps of the writing process are illustrated on classroom walls and college textbooks as a series of arrows, starting with prewriting and ending with publication, but classroom culture is the background that allows each of these steps to occur. Before beginning the writing process, teachers at all levels must create environments that support student writers appropriate for secondary settings.

For teenagers, criticizing others can be a method of self-preservation that can make workshop and sharing difficult to facilitate. In my room, for instance, the class clown asked inappropriate questions after hearing others' poems and another student gained a reputation for tearing writing to shreds. The social compression of middle and high school means students see each other every single day for multiple hours for years on end, raising the stakes of even small moments of embarrassment. Since young people often use creative writing to express themselves, explore identity, and reveal life problems—issues they may even not feel comfortable speaking about[9]—building classroom trust is essential. When teachers suggest students can just not write about such personal topics, Calkins responds, "[A]dolescents very much need to write about the poignant, turbulent events of their lives."[10] So how can teachers create an environment where students feel comfortable taking social and aesthetic risks?

Norms and Procedures

Devising and enforcing clear norms and procedures can help establish a productive writing environment of "routine and predictability"[11] that ultimately increases learning.¹² Class norms (also known as rules) are often developed collaboratively with students to create buy-in. I generally develop norms on the first days of school, but revisiting them or making new ones just before a creative writing unit can reinforce an atmosphere of respect. With younger students, I spread pieces of craft paper out on the floor or the wall, attaching to each a different question about class culture: *What does a successful creative writing class look like?*, *What does it not look like?*, and so on. Students answer on the paper with markers, and then the teacher or student leader facilitates a discussion, which leads to a list of norms everyone agrees to. For older students, I facilitate a conversation about past creative writing horror stories, ending on a group pact to avoid repeating the experience. When we start sharing work, students use the same process to create workshop norms. In the past, their rules have included "What happens in Creative Writing stays in Creative Writing," "Give content warnings," and "Don't be mean." Janelle Adsit describes a similar method of eliciting norms in her college creative writing classes.¹³

Students also discuss appropriate consequences for violating norms, like leaving the classroom or changing groups. Restorative justice practices, which posit that individuals can restore group cohesion by acknowledging their wrongdoing, may be especially helpful in thinking through norm violations.¹⁴

When it comes to sharing and workshop, I explicitly teach procedures, posting a step-by-step list and reinforcing it with feedback. A set procedure can prevent unrelegated criticism and provide students with reassuring structure. If a student isn't following the procedure (i.e., not clapping after a share), I gently correct with a visual cue or quiet verbal reminder. When introducing students to a complex procedure like peer workshopping (see Appendix 3.1), I take time to explain the rationale and then conduct a practice round of feedback on non-student work. This allows me to give procedural feedback in a low-stakes setting. As the teacher, I need to actively enforce norms and procedures or I risk losing any trust I've earned.

Promoting Creativity

The shift from teaching expository writing to creative writing requires an intentional fostering of creativity. Beyond mitigating social problems, a fear-free classroom also promotes creativity, whereas an unsafe or unpredictable environment can impede it.¹⁵ Teaching creativity within the context of a tested course can be challenging, however, because students know "conventional assessments penalize [creativity]."¹⁶ Therefore, students who are learning to write creatively need to know they will be rewarded rather than punished for out-of-the-box thinking.[17]

One method of encouraging creativity comes from psychologist Carol Dweck's growth mindset, which creative writing, ELA, and visual arts educators have adapted for the classroom.[18] In applying this framework, teachers normalize error by publicly praising risk-taking even if it results in failure, actively announcing the learnability of skills, and reminding students of the connection between failure and learning. For more on this, Michael Dean Clark also addresses the need to support productive failure in his later chapter.

Modeling

Teachers can also normalize creative risks by participating in the writing process themselves. Modeling, or demonstrating a skill in front of students while talking through it, is more than just a teaching technique. When a teacher publicly models a task's difficulties, she normalizes error,[19] showing that struggling is part of the process.

Teacher participation in ELA class freewrites is a widespread, recommended practice.[20] High school teacher Penny Kittle explains that she does so "to stay in touch with what I'm asking of my students and to practice my craft as their writing teacher."[21] As students write, teachers can project their own work from a computer screen or document camera; they can then use this writing to model mini-lessons, from brainstorming to revision.

Certainly, modeling creative writing is more nerve-wracking than modeling a persuasive essay. Art has higher stakes, and regardless of genre, there's an intensely personal quality to creative writing. Moreover, ELA teachers are often not trained in creative writing, a lack of experience that has led some teachers to shy away from creative genres.[22] In response to teachers' "but I'm not a writer" doubts, Kittle reminds herself, "I wasn't supposed to *be a writer*—just someone trying to write—like them .... I was a better model because my hesitations and insecurities were just like theirs."[23]

Like reading, writing improves the more you do it, whether inside the classroom or out. To Tom Romano and others, the dictum for writing teachers is simple: "Please Write."[24] Teachers' willingness to participate can also strengthen relationships with students[25] and increase trust. If sharing personal details with teenagers seems too complicated, I recommend creating constraints around what you share. For instance, I sometimes use only life material from when I was my students' age and younger.

Modeling is a powerful teaching tool, even though it can feel like public humiliation. Kelly Gallagher reminds teachers that it's not enough to simply show students a teacher-created final product because "the most valuable part [of the writing process is] the steps, often torturous, I took to get to the polished product."[26] These steps should not be hidden from students. Modeling's show-all approach stands in contrast to the lore-based "expert practitioner" model of some creative writing programs.[27] If the work of the expert practitioner is only known to young writers in its final, published form, or if the teacher isn't showing their own lousy drafts, learners lose out.

Mentor Texts

Some students may think creative writing isn't for them because they've never seen a writer that looks, lives, or loves like them. The sense of alienation students with marginalized identities experience in school systems as a result of centuries of systemic oppression is only compounded when teachers present mentor texts that illustrate one kind of story, hero, or style. Since students' exposure to writing may be limited to the "canonical" works of mostly male, mostly white writers anthologized in textbooks, selecting a wide variety of mentor texts for use before and during writing can serve to affirm student identities and writing styles.

Selecting diverse texts, providing pictures of authors, and giving relevant biographical information about authors can help more students feel their voice matters. For instance, I make sure to tell students that James Baldwin was gay and black or that Mary Oliver, whose work is frequently read in secondary classrooms, was a lesbian. Teachers should provide mentor texts that are both windows and mirrors, texts that allow students to see into other worlds *and* see reflections of their own lives.[28] Limiting mentor texts limits student writing, which I have seen in adjudicating school literary magazines. Students across the country still write poems with inverted syntax on Romantic topics, suggesting a lack of exposure to contemporary, non-white, or international poetry.

Teachers have access to rich conversations around diversifying reading on Twitter, where educational leaders have organized chats and resource lists. For instance, #TeachLivingPoets encourages the use of contemporary poetry in ELA and advocates for author visits.[29] #DisruptTexts is a crowdsourced interrogation of the canon, alternately suggesting more inclusive titles and reframing texts through anti-bias frameworks.[30] Teachers can also look to the local community to find real-life mentors from a variety of backgrounds—local writers and teaching artists—to visit the classroom. Such resources extend students' definition of good writing beyond a Eurocentric canon.

In selecting diverse mentor texts, teachers need to interrogate assumptions about aesthetics. Adsit suggests complicating our understanding of what makes "good writing," by simply putting "a diverse range of texts into conversation and ask[ing students] what is possible,"[31] rather than declaring one text the exemplar. Because students' writing styles, their characters, and even their plotlines reflect individual cultures, student aesthetics may not match teacher sensibilities. Learning how to embrace students' writing without imposing assumptions about art is key to earning trust and helping writers take greater risks.

The (Creative) Writing Process

Assignment Design or Writers Workshop?

In implementing the writing process, teachers should consider how their unique classroom context will lend itself to either assigning specific creative writing projects or allowing students full choice of what they write, as in a workshop-style classroom.

The word "workshop," it should be noted, signals two completely different activities to different communities. Until now, I've used "workshop" in reference to creative writing workshop, a postsecondary creative writing course (usually) that relies on the pedagogy of "workshopping," bringing a piece of writing to peers, who then discuss it in detail with an eye toward revision. (For more on this approach, see Amy Ash's chapter.) In K–12 schools, however, "a writing/writers' workshop" is a widely used method of structuring open class time. This model allows young writers to choose their topic and genre and then move through the writing process based on their own needs and timing. Mini-lessons, peer feedback, a writer's notebook, and conferring are all central elements of writers' workshop. Whereas the creative writing workshop grew out of Iowa's MFA program,[32] the writing workshop evolved from the process movement applied to school children.[33] The individualized nature of process writing worked against standardization in education, and the writing workshop was refined and popularized for elementary[34] and middle school[35] classrooms.

In its purest form, the writing workshop does not consist of whole-class exercises, prompts, or assignments in which all students "[move] in unison through a series of prescribed, teacher-assigned steps,"[36] but this presents a difficulty, as most secondary writing projects do follow a series of scaffolded steps—my own included. Considering the reality of grades and curricular requirements, many ELA teachers feel compelled to use assignments and projects, the design of which I discuss below, rather than a pure workshop approach. From the workshop model, though, secondary teachers can learn how to set up a flexible structure that meets a variety of student needs during long-term projects. Workdays in my classroom certainly resemble a workshop: kids sprawled around the room, some writing in notebooks, some sitting in the hall with laptops giving each other feedback. This orchestrated chaos, key to the writing workshop, is terrifying but effective.

Given, then, that designing specific assignments is necessary in most classrooms, creative assignments can share much with analytical ones. When designing creative projects, I focus first on the skills I'll teach and assess, just like with any other academic assignment. This skill-based teaching and assessment approach is widely used in arts education at the primary and secondary levels, so it makes sense to use it in creative writing as well.[37] Determining which skills a creative assignment will strengthen also helps clarify its rationale to teacher and students alike.

Since mainstream ELA teachers use creative writing to teach ELA skills, it only makes sense to identify these skills before planning a creative writing assignment.[38] Such assignments can even be crafted to address gaps in the curriculum or reinforce topics students struggle with. When my ninth-grade team realized we hadn't been teaching text structure (CCSS.RL.5),[39] playwriting provided an opportunity to reinforce sequencing and teach the three-act plot. Knowing exactly which craft techniques and structural content I would focus on helped me plan mini-lessons, give feedback, design workshops, and assess final products.[40] In another unit, I designed a flash fiction assignment in response to students struggling to understand syntactical choice. (See Appendix 3.2.) Here, the focus skills were sentence variety, plot structure, and vivid descriptions, so those skills appeared in my lesson plans, handouts, and assessments. Focusing on only a few concrete skills makes planning and grading much easier throughout the writing process.[41]

Prewriting

Prewriting goes by many names: rehearsal, brainstorming, freewriting, noticing, and planning. To push against the myth of the linear writing process, some have noted that prewriting activities happen all the time throughout the process, not just before drafting occurs, as its name would suggest.[42] The prewriting stages of creative and analytical writing may mirror each other perfectly or vary greatly, depending on your perspective (and your students). For instance, in both genres, prewriting might involve research. Likewise, ELA strategies like "Talking the Paper Out"[43] and using graphic organizers help students explore concepts and flesh out characters, plotlines, and image systems—even if those change once drafting begins. Nancie Atwell recommends starting students with "Writing Territories,"[44] a giant list of personalized, student-generated writing topics. In creative writing, students can make a similar list of ideas, noticings, and images that could find their way into drafts. Lynda Barry describes a similar creative-friendly "daily diary" of noticing in her book *Syllabus*.[45]

One challenge of prewriting in a creative context is responding to different students' processes. For instance, while some fiction writers swear by letting the sentences guide the plot, others plan it from beginning to end, fleshing out scenes only after they all have a place in the larger whole. Some students will see the story flash in their mind with round characters ready to roll, whereas others may need to spend more time developing characters or worldbuilding. I balance the gap of styles by providing prewriting support for everyone, requiring all students to engage in some planning, and then releasing them to either continue prewriting or begin drafting.

Drafting

The drafting phase includes everything from false starts to a full piece ready for feedback. Like prewriting, drafting can work in different ways for different writers. An example: instead of drafting a piece and revising it three times, a writer may simply draft the selection from beginning to end four different times without looking back.[46]

For a traditional analytical assignment, drafting serves as a means to an end, but drafting in creative writing often leads to an entirely different end. The first draft, or "discovery draft,"[47] allows students to discover new ideas, a belief widely embraced by creative writers.[48] Robert Frost's adage comes to mind: "No surprise for the writer, no surprise for the reader." If an entire story is planned out in prewriting, there may be no opportunity for surprise during drafting. "Discovery" can be difficult to account for in the structure of a classroom, so I've found it helpful to model my own drafting discoveries, discuss with students how their work changed from prewriting to drafting, and praise them for jumping ship to follow exciting tangents.

Revising

Revision and editing can be a challenging step for young writers because for some it is more difficult and less exciting than drafting. For analytical assignments, revising and editing are often geared toward making a piece conform to genre conventions and increasing clarity; for creative assignments, revision often includes completely changing topics or forms.

I'll set aside peer workshop as a revision process and focus instead on a teacher's approach to feedback, which can have high stakes when applied to creative pieces. Even correcting grammar errors can have a net negative impact on students' approaches to analytical writing,[49] so intentional feedback is even more significant to young creative writers. First, as mentioned above, students sometimes share extremely personal content, so feedback needs to affirm rather than question or shame identity development. Second, because markers of aesthetic success are culturally constructed, the comparison to models that often work when assessing analytical essays (i.e., "This does/does not look like the A papers I've seen in the past") does not always translate to creative pieces.

Providing effective feedback was the most difficult new skill I had to acquire to teach creative writing. Though many of the feedback practices of ELA pedagogy apply to creative writing—shortening the feedback loop, responding as a reader, using minimalist approaches to editing, empowering the writer—I'll share some practices I've learned from teachers working with higher education students.

The use of descriptive rather than prescriptive feedback is sometimes used in ELA classrooms, but it is far more prevalent in upper-level creative writing workshops. Instead of providing edits, teachers give a close reading of the piece, commenting on what they notice about the elements of craft, like stanza length or pacing, and how those elements impact the reader. Student writers can then revise based on how the provided interpretation, often written as end comments, aligns with their goals.

Bringing in mentor texts for a specific student or a craft issue also assists with creative revisions. If creative writing teachers can develop the ability to match young writers with "the right [poem/story/novel/essay] at the right time,"[50] that mentor text may help the student solve problems in their revision. Just as teachers who have implemented independent reading can only recommend books to teens after immersing themselves in reading, those teaching creative writing can familiarize themselves with contemporary poetry, fiction, or essays to help guide students in their next draft.

Sharing

Also referred to as publishing, sharing acknowledges that writers write for an audience. Even though sometimes the extent of publishing is simply printing off a document and giving it to the teacher, students are motivated by authentic writing opportunities,[51] whether facilitated through publishing online, in a zine, or just sharing out in class. There are many ELA sharing methods that can be used with creative pieces. The National Writing Project has popularized the use of the "author's chair," in which a willing student takes a seat in front of the class and reads aloud. My ninth-grade students have self-published memoir anthologies and hosted blog pages. And my colleague Teresa Del Dotto distributes whole-class "Kudos Sheets" at the end of each unit, containing a great line from every student essay.

Creative writing provides a special opportunity to share work with audiences beyond the classroom. Some teachers self-publish novels collaboratively written within their ELA classes.[52] Others ask students to submit to school literary magazines. Still others hold in-class readings and spoken word poetry events, made more exciting with a microphone and amp borrowed from the media center. Students may also organize readings outside of class, participate in community writing contests, make zines to distribute around school, or design and self-publish single-author books. Collaborating with other departments can also provide publication opportunities. My students combined with an art class to put together a gallery show, worked with guitar players to make a spoken word album, and collaborated with the theater program, whose young directors staged student-written plays. The possibilities for sharing creative work are endless, and are further addressed in Justin Longacre's chapter.

Creative Writing Works

Using creative writing assignments in ELA classes makes my job more fun and increases student investment. When I assign a poetry response in addition to an essay, or a piece of flash fiction instead of a worksheet, students appreciate it. My colleagues and administrators support this work because it brings excitement and often ends with a tangible product, like a book or magazine that looks good sitting in the front office. More seriously, students have told me years later that the flash fiction story they wrote as freshmen were their favorite pieces to date or that they reread our memoir collection and were surprised their writing was so good.

For educators, a key benefit of creative writing is that every assignment lends itself to differentiation. Differentiating content, process, and product helps students learn more by engaging them at their proximal level of interest and readiness as well as within their specific learning styles.[53] Creative assignments allow for personalized content and encourage an individualized approach to process. These assignments can also be simplified or made more complex depending on the readiness of the student. And depending on assignment goals, the product—here, the genre—may be differentiated as well. Instead of creating an elaborate menu of choices for students, teachers can simply assign creative writing tasks thanks to the flexible nature of creative writing itself.

Moreover, creative writing can have an incredible personal impact on adolescents. While admittedly teachers are not therapists, writing does have therapeutic benefits,[54] helping reduce feelings of alienation in young people and aiding self-expression.[55] Of course, none of this is surprising. Teachers know from experience how poetry assignments open up the most withdrawn student. Teachers also know teens fall in the psychosocial stage of Identity Formation,[56] meaning that exploring identity through creative writing serves their growth into adulthood.

The presence of creative writing in the general curriculum now may be more important than ever. Imagining other lives builds empathy in young writers during a time of increasing division.[57] As ELA teachers we try to engage students with our material—the thoughts, feelings, and arguments of being human—in as many different ways as possible. ELA classes are already dynamic places where young people make podcasts, produce plays, and even paint. Given the familiarity of the writing process and creative writing's ability to address the goals of existing curricular units, the addition of creative assignments to writing classrooms only makes sense, both academically and developmentally, as the young human beings in our classes learn how to better exist in the world.

Notes

1 D. G. Myers, *The Elephants Teach: Creative Writing since 1880* (Englewood Cliffs, NJ: Prentice Hall, 1996), 101.

2 Patrick Bizzaro, *Responding to Student Poems: Applications of Critical Theory* (Urbana, IL: National Council of Teachers of English, 1993), xi.

3 Greg Light, "Investigating Creative Writing: Challenging Obstacles to Empirical Research," in *Can Creative Writing Really Be Taught: Resisting Lore in Creative*

       Writing Pedagogy, ed. Stephanie Vanderslice and Rebecca Manery (New York: Bloomsbury, 2017), 198.
4 In this chapter, I'll focus on teaching creative writing within the ELA classroom.
5 Janet Emig, *The Composing Processes of Twelfth Graders* (Urbana, IL: NCTE, 1971).
6 Donald Murray, *A Writer Teaches Writing* (Boston: Houghton Mifflin, 1985).
7 Donald Graves, *Writing: Teachers and Children at Work* (Portsmouth, NH: Heinemann, 1983).
8 Lucy Calkins, *The Art of Teaching Writing*, 2nd edn. (Portsmouth, NH: Heinemann, 1994).
9 Bruce Roscoe, Karen Krug, and Jane Schmidt, "Written Forms of Self-Expression Utilized by Adolescents," *Adolescence* 20, no. 80 (1985): 841–4.
10 Calkins, *The Art of Teaching Writing*, 174.
11 Ibid., 183.
12 Robert Marzano, *The Art and Science of Teaching: A Comprehensive Framework for Effective Instruction* (Alexandria, VA: ASCD, 2007), 118–21.
13 Janelle Adsit, *Toward an Inclusive Creative Writing: Threshold Concepts to Guide the Literary Curriculum* (New York: Bloomsbury, 2017), 119.
14 Jill Davidson, "Restoring Justice," *Teaching Tolerance Magazine* 47 (2014).
15 Donna Miller, "Cultivating Creativity," *English Journal* 104, no. 6 (2015): 27.
16 Yigal Rosen and Maryam Mosharraf, "Online Performance Assessment of Creativity Skills: Findings from International Pilot Study," *International Association for Educational Assessment Conference* (2014), 2.
17 Linda A. O'Hara and Robert J. Sternberg, "It Doesn't Hurt to Ask: Effects of Instructions to Be Creative, Practical, or Analytical on Essay—Writing Performance and Their Interaction with Students' Thinking Styles," *Creativity Research Journal* 13, no. 2 (2001).
18 Anna Leahy, "'It's Such a Good Feeling': Self-Esteem, the Growth Mindset, and Creative Writing," in *Can Creative Writing Really Be Taught* (see note 3); Miller, "Cultivating Creativity"; Heather Michele Seibel, "Growth Mindset and Fluency in the Art Classroom" (MA diss., University of Iowa, Iowa City, 2016).
19 Doug Lemov, *Teach Like a Champion: 49 Techniques That Put Students on the Path to College* (San Francisco: Jossey-Bass, 2010).
20 Murray, *A Writer Teaches Writing*; Tom Romano, *Clearing the Way: Working with Teenage Writers* (Portsmouth, NH: Heinemann, 1987); Kelly Gallagher, *Teaching Adolescent Writers* (Portland, ME: Stenhouse, 2006).
21 Penny Kittle, *Write Beside Them: Risk, Voice, and Clarity in High School Writing* (Portsmouth, NH: Heinemann, 2008), 33.
22 Tanya J. Hannaford, "Behind the Curtain: A Teacher's Quest to Better Understand, Write, and Model Poetry," *English Journal* 104, no. 4 (2015): 37–8.
23 Kittle, *Write Beside Them*, 9.

24 Romano, *Clearing the Way*, 37.
25 Geraldine Lee Susi, "The Teacher/Writer: Model, Learner, Human Being," *Language Arts* 61, no. 7 (1984): 715.
26 Gallagher, *Teaching Adolescent Writers*, 52.
27 Rebecca Manery, "Myths, Mirrors, and Metaphors: The Education of the Creative Writing Teacher," in *Can Creative Writing Really Be Taught* (see note 3), 228.
28 Rudine Sims Bishop, "Windows and Mirrors: Children's Books and Parallel Cultures," *Proceedings of the 14th Annual Reading Conference: Celebrating Literacy* (1990).
29 Melissa Smith, "#TeachLivingPoets: Complicating the Canon and Empowering Students Through Poetry," teachlivingpoets.com.
30 Tricia Ebarvia, Lorena Germán, Kimberly N. Parker, and Julie E. Torres, "#DisruptTexts," disrupttexts.org.
31 Janelle Adsit, "Polemics against Polemics: Reconsidering Didacticism in Creative Writing," in *Can Creative Writing Really Be Taught* (see note 3), 169.
32 Myers, *The Elephants Teach*, 146.
33 Graves, *Writing*.
34 Calkins, *The Art of Teaching Writing*.
35 Nancie Atwell, *In the Middle*, 2nd edn. (Portsmouth, NH: Heinemann, 1998).
36 Calkins, *The Art of Teaching Writing*, 166.
37 National Coalition for Core Arts Standards, "National Core Arts Standards," State Education Agency Directors of Arts Education (2014), www.nationalartsstandards.org.
38 See Chris Drew's close reading of the Common Core Writing Standards to explore how creative writing is already well within the curriculum: "Minding the Pedagogical Gap: Creative Writing Studies, Common Core Standards, and the Secondary Creative Writing Moment," *Journal of Creative Writing Studies* 2, no. 1 (2016).
39 Common Core State Standards.
40 This assignment also included a research component. See also Mary Frances Buckley-Marudas and Joshua Block, "Putting Research on Stage: Playwriting in the English Classroom," *English Journal* 105, no. 2 (2015).
41 Selecting which skills to teach and evaluate necessarily engages with aesthetic bias, but I have found being transparent about such bias and offering students an opportunity to explain their choices can mitigate problems.
42 Murray, *A Writer Teaches Writing*, 13.
43 Gallagher, *Teaching Adolescent Writers*, 54.
44 Atwell, *In the Middle*, 123.
45 Lynda Barry, *Syllabus: Notes from an Accidental Professor* (Montreal: Drawn & Quarterly, 2014), 62–3.

46 Peter Elbow, *Writing without Teachers*, 2nd edn. (New York: Oxford, 1998), 18–22.
47 Murray, *A Writer Teaches Writing*, 51.
48 Richard Hugo, *The Triggering Town: Lectures and Essays on Poetry and Writing* (New York: W. W. Norton, 1979).
49 John Truscott, "The Effect of Error Correction on Learners' Ability to Write Accurately," *Journal of Second Language Writing* 16, no. 4 (2007).
50 Donalyn Miller, *The Book Whisperer: Awakening the Inner Reader in Every Child* (San Francisco: Jossey-Bass, 2009).
51 Kathy Brashears and Virginia White, "Strategies and Ideas for Teaching Writing in the Middle Years," *Literacy Learning: The Middle Years* 14, no. 2 (2006).
52 See Claudia Felske's work with high school students' collaborative novels *First Draft*, *Epoch*, and others (2017, 2018) and mine with the middle schoolers who wrote *Running for Hope* (2014). All were published through CreateSpace via print-on-demand services.
53 Carol Ann Tomlinson, *How to Differentiate Instruction in Mixed-Ability Classrooms*, 2nd edn. (Alexandria, VA: ASCD, 2001).
54 Nicholas Mazza, "The Use of Poetry in Treating the Troubled Adolescent," *Adolescence* 16, no. 62 (1981).
55 Morris R. Morrison, "Poetry and Therapy," in *Poetry as Therapy*, ed. Morris R. Morrison (New York: Human Sciences Press, 1987).
56 Erik Erikson, *Identity: Youth and Crisis* (New York: W. W. Norton, 1968).
57 Bree Kitt, "Creating Connections between Senior and Middle Years: Perceptions on Teaching the Art of Creative Writing," *Literacy Learning: The Middle Years* 27, no. 1 (2019): 52.

4

"Workshop" as Verb and Environment: Imagining New Possibilities and Approaches

Amy Ash
Indiana State University

"Workshop" Defined

"Workshop" is a tricky word in the context of creative writing. Though the workshop is often considered the defining pedagogy of the field, existing since the advent of creative writing in academia, its definition is sometimes taken for granted. And yet it can mean and look like so many different things. In secondary classrooms, as Alexa Garvoille notes in the previous chapter, the term often highlights the *work* of writing, allowing students class time to navigate the writing process at their own pace in a semi-structured environment. In college classrooms, the term suggests something entirely different. At first glance, it might seem to resemble a large-scale version of a peer review activity in a composition class, but as Anna Leahy argues, the creative writing workshop is more than a "discreet task." It is "a principled, focused, inclusive methodology"[1] that invites students to explore and understand craft and process through their communal discoveries. Though it is often used as a noun, many have noted the workshop is "not a *thing*"[2] (author's emphasis) but rather, an experience, a human event or exchange.

The creative writing workshop as a concept, pedagogical strategy, and environment is often unfamiliar and intimidating to teachers without explicit experience and training in creative writing; however, the workshop remains a foundational approach in creative writing instruction that, when incorporated in pedagogically useful ways, may benefit secondary ELA teachers and their students. At its best, the workshop offers opportunities for community, communication, experimentation, and growth. Handled less effectively, it risks silencing, stifling, and even excluding writers—especially writers from already marginalized groups. Given its problems, possibilities, and ubiquity, the workshop is a necessary starting point for any larger conversations about the teaching of creative writing. This chapter outlines the history and evolution of the creative writing workshop, addresses some of the potential issues that surround its implementation, and presents various strategies for inclusive, pedagogically grounded approaches to the workshop in both postsecondary and secondary environments.

Ideally, the creative writing workshop creates a unique space for discussion, collaboration, exploration, and discovery, offering writers an opportunity to get honest feedback from careful, attentive readers engaging in knowledgeable discussion of writing that highlights a poem, story, essay, or hybrid piece's possibilities, challenges, and potential successes. After an effective workshop, the writer should be able to return to the work with new perspectives and ideas, focusing on the forward progress of their piece and their work in general. Ultimately, writers contributing work for discussion should walk away with a sense of new possibilities for their writing, and all workshop participants should be challenged and inspired by what writing can do. Indeed, one of the benefits of workshop is that *all* workshop participants can learn from reading and discussing the work of their peers.

In the most common iteration of the creative writing workshop, derived from a model developed in the late 1930s at the University of Iowa, the whole class is organized into a large circle and the writing of one student is discussed by their classmates, who have all read the piece ahead of time and have prepared written comments that will drive the conversation. While the discussion occurs, the author of the piece silently observes, listens, and takes notes. Due to the diverse and sometimes divergent interests and perspectives of workshop participants, the responses can vary from clarifying to conflicting. The teacher mediates and facilitates this "workshopping" of the text, aimed at elucidating the workshop draft-in-progress, giving the writer a sense of how it has been received by an audience and introducing possible directions and considerations for revision.

Though it may sound straightforward enough—an authentic example of student-centered, engaged learning—there is much to unpack and consider before it can be most effectively and thoughtfully utilized.

History

Many scholars of creative writing, including Wendy Bishop, D. G. Myers, and Joseph Moxley, have historicized and contextualized the field of creative writing pedagogy and the role of the creative writing workshop in some of the foundational texts of Creative Writing Studies (*Released into Language*, *The Elephants Teach*, and *Creative Writing in America*). While the roots of creative writing in formalized education trace back to 1880, studies by these scholars highlight a distinct shift in creative writing in the academy in the 1930s and 1940s.

In her discussion of the origination of the traditional workshop format, Bishop points to the graduate program developed at the University of Iowa by Norman Foerster, where the first MFA degree was awarded in 1941, marking the "movement away from the scientific, philological roots of English studies toward a more scholarly professional view of the discipline."[3] This move brought with it the inclusion of contemporary, living authors into the canon and solidified the workshop approach of a mentor writer who leads students' discussion of and response to each other's work. Foerster's conceptualization of the workshop, Bishop explains, "reflects an essentially romantic, subjective view of literary creation and writing instruction" based on nurturing talent rather than teaching writing.[4] The most problematic element of this philosophy—one still pervasive in creative writing programs today—is that, since the "most important requirement is that the 'master' be a wise man [sic] who has been or is a practicing artist and has learned to read with an artist's eye,"[5] a theoretically grounded, research-driven approach to creative writing pedagogy had, for quite some time, been largely neglected in favor of lore, bolstered by a reliance on the unfounded belief that good writers necessarily make effective teachers.

Creative writing programs in universities thrived in the mid-twentieth century, fueled in part by the influx of students entering colleges with support from the GI Bill in the 1950s, marking the 1950s and 1960s as a tumultuous and revolutionary period in creative writing. Around this time, many universities began offering undergraduate programs in creative writing in addition to their graduate programs, which helped secure positions in the university for many writers with MFA degrees, but which also complicated traditional conceptions of the workshop. Because the traditional workshop format was designed to serve writing aspirants with background knowledge in creative writing and with goals of professional publication and university teaching posts, it did not adequately meet the needs of "more varied students drawn from a broader set of open-admissions applicants."[6] These students were not necessarily aspiring professional writers, and the background knowledge they brought to the creative writing workshop as well as the goals they had for their own writing were simply not as focused or homogeneous as they were once presumed to be.

In his 1989 study, Moxley also laments the lack of evolution in pedagogical approaches and theories in the field of creative writing in the twentieth century, noting that "most creative writing teachers at undergraduate and graduate levels follow the same studio method established at Oregon and Iowa over ninety years ago."[7] He contends that while creative writing programs in America have expanded and developed at a rapid pace in the twentieth century, the progress of creative writing pedagogy moved more sluggishly forward, in part due to a lack of self-reflection and an uncritical embrace of the traditional, normative workshop. While creative writing has grown as a field of study since the first academic program in Iowa, and while there have been many changes and advances, the Iowa program and approach maintain a lasting impact. All these years later, the workshop remains the defining pedagogy of the field. But as we can see, even as the creative writing "workshop" has almost become synonymous with the creative writing class, the term is fraught. As teachers, we need to be aware of the various implications of the term, as well as the problems and possibilities each definition or approach offers.

Over the past few decades, Creative Writing Studies and its accompanying pedagogies have come a long way. Building on the work of Bishop, numerous scholars, including Stephanie Vanderslice, Anna Leahy, and Janelle Adsit, have done important work to question, challenge, and reconceptualize traditional approaches to creative writing. Much of this reflection and change centers on a critique of the traditional/normative workshop model.

Problems

Vanderslice's book, *Rethinking Creative Writing*, provides a thorough investigation and critique of the outdated workshop model in its chapter titled "Workshopping the Workshop." Vanderslice synthesizes and presents common complaints and shortcomings of the workshop—from the overwhelming and often conflicting advice and feedback offered by classmates, to the avoidance of risk in favor of conformity in workshop submissions, to the focus on product over process.[8] Additional problems with the traditional workshop, explored by various scholars in the field of Creative Writing Studies, entail issues of authority and apprenticeship, potential problems with group discussion and response, and the need for a clearer focus in creative writing courses on reading literature. The scholars included in Leahy's *Authority Project: Power and Identity in the Creative Writing Classroom* address, among other concerns, the role of the teacher in the creative writing classroom and investigate the dubious and complicated authority of the artist/mentor in the traditional workshop setting, envisioning new, more democratic approaches to workshop structures, conventions, and procedures.

In many ways building on and from concerns explored in Leahy's study, Adsit argues that the creative writing workshop, approached unreflexively and without adequate guidance and critical preparation, can devolve into uninformed arguments based on taste, unveiling biases, reinforcing damaging power dynamics and hierarchies, and contributing to micro-aggressions and other forms of marginalization and exclusion in the creative writing classroom.[9] Adsit elucidates the need for inclusive approaches to the teaching of creative writing, working against "a discipline that serves to exclude and police literary expression"[10] and moving toward more open conceptions of craft and artistic value that acknowledge and honor the diversity within contemporary writing. An important part of Adsit's conceptualization of an inclusive creative writing classroom involves inviting students to co-create the parameters and practices of the workshop, establishing an environment of mutual respect, envisioning a workshop that best meets the needs of all students, and reinforcing an emphasis on collaboration. Additionally, she emphasizes diverse, wide-ranging, and inclusive conceptualizations of craft and aesthetics through the assigned readings of the course. Adsit and others also challenge some of the deeply ingrained elements of the traditional workshop model, including both its deficit model and its silencing of the author, noting that "the silent writer is forced into the position of passive student who cannot be trusted to speak, and the workshop becomes more hierarchal than collaborative."[11] This becomes especially damaging when the voices silenced or overwritten in these contexts—the voices of women writers, writers of color, and writers who identify with other marginalized groups—are those whose perspectives and aesthetics might not be immediately recognized, valued, or upheld if they are perceived to go against ingrained, often unspoken norms.

A reenvisioning of the workshop as a more inclusive pedagogy involves tackling issues of authority in the workshop, considering how to prepare students for (and mediate) discussion and response, positioning the author as an active participant rather than a passive observer, and shifting workshop discussions from fault-finding excursions into particular workshop pieces to more open-ended explorations of craft—challenging how "good" writing is defined and who controls those definitions. It involves the inclusion of a diverse range of contemporary literature in the creative writing classroom, increased attention to invention and process, and more awareness of the needs and goals of our particular students.

Approaches to Workshop

The workshop approach is so entrenched in creative writing pedagogy at the postsecondary level that many creative writing courses have the word "workshop" in their course titles. But as we can see, much important work has been done to broaden our conceptions of and approaches to the creative writing workshop, reforming and reinvigorating this once monolithic pedagogy. Karen Craigo's "A Case for Workshop Alternatives" outlines a variety of approaches to the workshop that her students can choose from, granting them the power and agency to determine how their work is discussed. The options begin with what she calls "Old Faithful," an approach that most closely resembles the traditional workshop format, though she encourages students to make it new by moving beyond simply offering a few words of praise followed by negative critiques and prescriptive statements. Other options include writer-driven discussions in which the writer of the piece up for workshop offers questions they have about their work to the class, workshop-generated discussions in which the class directs questions to the writer, and generative methods in which workshop members write creatively in response to the workshopped piece and then share and discuss what they've come up with.[12] Approaches such as these not only allow students to shape and focus the discussion of their work, but also introduce important discussions about the effects of different types of feedback and response.

Another approach that has enlivened and enhanced the traditional workshop, affording agency to writers, is Liz Lerman's "Critical Response Process." With its focus on communication and collaborative interaction, this workshop design has been adapted successfully to various contexts, fields, and interactions from visual art to dance to laboratory science and can be particularly useful in the creative writing classroom. The process involves workshop members inhabiting one of three roles: artist/maker, responder, or facilitator. The conversation begins with responders offering objective comments and observations about the piece offered for workshop. Next, the artist/maker directs the conversation, asking questions of the responders. The key element of this approach comes next: responders offer "neutral questions" not based on judgment or subjective opinion. Finally, the responders may offer opinions, but only with the permission of the artist, who maintains control over the conversation.[13]

In my own creative writing courses, I strive to include a variety of these approaches, giving students opportunities for various kinds of feedback and interaction in whole class, small group, anonymous, and digital interactions, continually reinforcing student-generated goals and concerns as well as course learning objectives, and reflecting on the benefits and limitations of different workshop formats. Indeed, there are many ways a workshop can be useful. The creative writing workshop offers exposure, revealing to students various styles, voices, methods, and concerns through the work of their peers that they may not have otherwise considered. Workshop discussions can uncover, affirm, and celebrate strengths as well as offer new possibilities and directions that capitalize on these moments. The workshop offers practice in close reading as well as public speaking, challenging students to articulate their thoughts and ideas aloud—a skill that will serve them well in education, in future careers, and beyond. Perhaps most importantly, with critical foundations and considerations in place, the workshop can become a supportive, collaborative environment that effectively addresses numerous secondary ELA standards involving language comprehension, analysis, reflection, listening, and speaking, as explored more thoroughly in other chapters of this book.

Preparation for Workshop

No matter which version or variation of the workshop is utilized, for a workshop to be successful, all participants must begin with respect for one another and their writing. Often, that means coming to the workshop prepared—having thoroughly read and annotated the pieces scheduled for discussion and talking about the work on its own terms, with civility and consideration. The prepared workshop comments can take several forms: the formal workshop letter (as Chris Drew describes in his chapter), a combination of in-text and summary notes and comments, or even a list of questions. However, workshops can also be successful, particularly in introductory courses, with less preparation beforehand on the part of the readers. In this circumstance, the emphasis may shift from discussions of craft and critique to an emphasis on audience and sharing.

In my own poetry writing workshops, there are times when the emphasis is on sharing and celebrating work, often immediately after a generative writing exercise. When we engage in a variation of the traditional workshop method, I require more preparation, instructing my students to read and comment on all poems scheduled for workshop discussion before coming to class. I ask them to begin by providing at least ten observations about the poem in the margins (e.g., "the poem is written in four stanzas of equal length," "the poem incorporates a lot of natural imagery," "the poem is an extended metaphor"). Then, I have students circle, underline, and comment on words, phrases, images, elements of syntax, etc., that stand out to them. In addition to writing comments on the poem itself and in the margins, they are to include a short (3–5 sentence) summary response for the writer, written on the bottom or the back of the page. I specify that their comments should consist mostly of observations and questions, rather than direct suggestions for revision, noting that we are not here to make the poems our own, but to provide valuable reader-response feedback. For their written responses to the work of their peers, I provide the following questions/prompts:

- *Describe* the poem: What type of poem is it, and what do you notice about its form, style, language, and/or content?
- What are some of the poetic devices and strategies used in the poem? Describe their effect on you as a reader.
- What questions do you have about the poem, and what are some possible responses to those questions?
- Are there any aesthetic/stylistic/language choices that seem to work against the goals of the poem?
- How does the poem address the assignment and/or relate to the other poems we have read?

These questions are meant to invite connections between our course readings and student-generated texts, reinforce course concepts involving craft elements, guide conversations toward description and analysis rather than subjective opinion or prescriptive statements, and give writers a sense of a reader's response to their work. *Workshop* doesn't have to mean *critique*, and if it does, we should be wary of what is being critiqued and how, and what our role is in facilitating those conversations. Opportunities for students to share their work and think about the various issues that come into play with craft need not be evaluative but rather exploratory.

Often, what students may encounter in the future as the *only* way to workshop writing is in reality the most limited and problematic way, and we (and they) should be aware of this. In some creative writing classrooms at the postsecondary level, the workshop dominates class time, with little emphasis given to reading and discussing texts from a wide variety of published authors, reading about craft and critically analyzing assumptions and biases related to aesthetics and values, or even generating writing. Thus, the focus is disproportionately on product over process.

Whatever your creative writing classroom looks like, whether the emphasis is on generating writing together, engaging in the ritual of sharing and responding to one another's work, or some combination of the two, it is important to know the history and lasting impact of the creative writing workshop and to be purposeful in how this pedagogy is employed, especially knowing that students are likely to encounter the workshop in the future if they continue on in creative writing in their academic careers. As long as "workshop" continues to function as both a noun and a verb, and as long as the term appears as part of many official creative writing course titles, we as teachers need to be aware of the traditional workshop environment. More importantly, we need to question and challenge this approach, considering alternatives and articulating the reasons behind alternate approaches that push against the workshop's tendencies toward problematic aesthetic consensus or silencing already marginalized voices. If we are to employ a variation of the workshop method, we need to put in the effort to ensure that it *works* for our students.

Notes

1. Anna Leahy, "Teaching as a Creative Act: Why the Workshop Works in Creative Writing," in *Does the Writing Workshop Still Work*, ed. Dianne Donnelly (Bristol: Multilingual Matters, 2010), 75–6.
2. Philip Gross, "Small Worlds: What Works in Workshops If and When They Do?" in *Does the Writing Workshop Still Work*, ed. Dianne Donnelly (Bristol: Multilingual Matters, 2010), 54.
3. Wendy Bishop, *Released into Language: Options for Teaching Creative Writing* (Urbana, IL: National Council of Teachers of English, 1990), ix–x.
4. Ibid., xii.
5. Ibid., xiii.
6. Ibid., xii.
7. Joseph M. Moxley, *Creative Writing in America: Theory and Pedagogy* (Urbana, IL: National Council of Teachers of English, 1989), xiii.
8. Stephanie Vanderslice, "Workshopping the Workshop," in *Rethinking Creative Writing* (Cambridge, UK: Professional and Higher Partnership, 2011), 86–97.
9. Janelle Adsit, *Toward an Inclusive Creative Writing: Threshold Concepts to Guide the Literary Curriculum* (New York: Bloomsbury Academic, 2017), 1.
10. Ibid., 7.
11. Ibid., 129.
12. Karen Craigo, "A Case for Workshop Alternatives," *Whale Road Review: A Journal of Poetry and Short Prose*, https://whaleroadreview.com/a-case-for-worskhop-alternatives/.
13. Liz Lerman, "Critical Response Process," https://lizlerman.com/critical-response-process/.

5

Collaborative Worldbuilding: Bridging Critical Thinking and Creative Production

Trent Hergenrader
Rochester Institute of Technology

Composition studies has long grappled with students' self-imposed "political correctness" that prevents them from offering their genuine attitudes and opinions, instead opting for inoffensive platitudes they themselves may not fully believe.[1] In my experience in class discussions, especially in those dealing with questions of race and gender, students often gravitate toward quickly finding a consensus, or a "right" answer, that recognizes social inequality at face value but does little to dig deeper into more difficult questions, such as how bias manifests itself in daily life or how it became interwoven within our social and institutional structures in the first place. For students to find a correct answer to these complex questions in a single assignment, class, or even a semester is not the end goal; instead, we want to encourage new ways of seeing the world and, hopefully, wanting to change it for the better.

This is, in short, an effort to teach students *critical thinking*. Critical thinking is the opposite of rote memorization and regurgitation of facts that can be safely forgotten a moment after the exam ends; rather, critical thinking is an ongoing process of analysis, debate, and reflection. Professors Michael Scriven and Richard Paul define critical thinking as

> the intellectually disciplined process of actively and skillfully conceptualizing, applying, analyzing, synthesizing, and/or evaluating information gathered from, or generated by, observation, experience, reflection, reasoning, or communication, as a guide to belief and action.[2]

They further note that critical thinking has two components: (1) a set of information and belief generating and processing skills, and (2) the habit, based on intellectual commitment, of using those skills to guide behavior.[3] In short, when we say we want students to be good critical thinkers, we mean to develop their thinking skills so they can look at questions, problems, or situations from numerous different angles and use their reason to both draw a logical conclusion and, importantly, take action. Actions need not be as extreme as marching in demonstrations, though this is a possible outcome, but could be something as simple as challenging a racist or sexist remark or reaching an honest self-assessment of their own societal privileges.

Conscientious instructors have no desire to indoctrinate students with their own values but rather wish to help students come to well-reasoned ethical conclusions for themselves. How do we do this without coming across as having an overt political agenda or inadvertently driving students to retreat behind trite stock responses? Compositionists Karen Kopelson and Kevin Porter suggest approaches that decenter the classroom, removing the focus from the instructor as a source of indisputable wisdom and instead recognizing students themselves as producers and sharers of valuable knowledge. Most importantly, open and honest discussion reveals that students naturally possess different types of knowledge based on their own identities and experiences. To keep the class talking, Kopelson encourages instructors to adopt a position of self-imposed "neutrality" in the classroom despite their own political convictions. Rather than challenging students' presumptive statements, the instructor instead adopts a Socratic approach by asking probing, open-ended questions that challenge simplistic statements in a non-confrontational manner.[4]

Porter observes that our classrooms will always "be populated with people who possess different conceptions of reality—people who inhabit different worlds," yet we all must inhabit a similar "shared reality" because we are able to communicate with each other;[5] in order to communicate, we assume other people "are rational beings with mostly true and coherent beliefs."[6] This notion that people are both rational and have mostly true and coherent beliefs provides the basis of his *pedagogy of charity*, in which beliefs can be tried and tested by others who don't necessarily need to accept those beliefs themselves. In fact, Porter argues, none of us can fully know which of our beliefs are fully true, so class discussion becomes a process of arbitration and navigation of different beliefs as expressed in language.[7]

Kopelson and Porter's strategies place the instructor at the margin of the classroom and allow discussion between students to take center stage as they negotiate difficult questions surrounding hot button topics that so often close down conversation. The teacher still plays a vital role in asking students to probe deeper, to refuse pat answers, to disrupt the urge toward quick consensus, and to press speakers to provide concrete examples that support their beliefs. The exercise reveals that, while we all agree we share a common reality, individuals view the world in very different ways based on their experiences, and those experiences are based in large part in their identity: the color of their skin, their sexual orientation, their religious or spiritual beliefs, their socioeconomic class, their gender, and so on.

Scholars like Williams, Kopelson, and Porter offer strategies with *composition* classrooms in mind, but these approaches can be easily modified and applied in a wide range of humanities disciplines that require students to exhibit critical thinking and writing skills when grappling with tough questions that lack clear-cut answers. Nearly all courses in the humanities—such as those in anthropology, English literature, history, philosophy, and others—require *analytical* writing that demonstrates a student's mastery of the material, most often in the form of tests and papers. However, my position is that teachers can prompt students to *think critically* yet express it through *creative production*. I argue this can be accomplished through a methodology I developed called *collaborative worldbuilding*.[8]

Principles of Collaborative Worldbuilding

As the name implies, this approach jettisons the traditional fiction workshop format (see Amy Ash's previous chapter in this book) that focuses on literary forms (e.g., short story, novel, play) and minimizes attention on the lone writer in favor of group projects that require collective imaginative thinking and fiction writing. Collaborative worldbuilding evolved from college-level classroom projects over the better part of a decade and is heavily influenced by the academic field of *game-based learning* for using games and game-like approaches to leverage deeper learning, along with the educational theory that holds people shape their understanding of the world by building mental models of how we believe the world works, called *constructionism*. These mental models are built from personal experiences, and learning is the process of adding to and adjusting these models that grow in size and complexity as we age and mature. Another important piece of constructionism is that we learn the most when we are actively making things.[9] This is the rationale for doing class projects that allow students to experience class material rather than merely reading textbooks and taking standardized tests.

Collaborative worldbuilding grew out of the following observations in my writing classrooms:

- Students improve their writing through continual practice. Providing feedback on short writing exercises and vignettes or single scenes helps concentrate their attention on specific aspects of craft, such as careful word choice, use of vibrant imagery, and employing active verbs. These finer craft points often get lost in longer, story-length works as students tend to focus on plot to the near exclusion of all else.
- For many students, writing fiction feels more inviting than other analytical forms, which they tend to think of as formulaic and rigid. Fiction allows them more freedom to explore ideas that interest them. (As an educator, I don't accept these generalizations about different types of writing as true, but this attitude continues to be prevalent among students.)
- The wells of our imaginations are filled from our unique experiences and from the types of stories we've enjoyed previously. This includes film, television, comic books, theater, games, and of course print fiction, and our creative work consciously and subconsciously draws from this storytelling reservoir.[10] Even the deepest individual imaginations are limited to that person's own set of unique experiences. Since no two people have identical experiences, it follows that people sharing ideas with others increases the amount of potential story-making material and that no individual would have been able to come up with it alone.
- We live our daily lives operating within a "consensus reality" that collectively understands features of the world as true and real. No sane person doubts the force of gravity or the disastrous consequences of stepping in front of a speeding car. However, our consensus reality does not extend across our experiences as uniformly as people might assume. Studies have shown that race, class, gender, religion, sexual orientation, and other factors have significant influence in the ways people are treated in schools, in their professions, when applying for loans or buying homes, and more. Our lived experiences can be quite different based on various social forces at play in a given society.
- Good writers strive to create fictional worlds that feel realistic and operate in a natural and logical manner, even if those worlds contain speculative elements such as futuristic technology or magic and monsters. In collaborative writing projects, writers combine their imaginations to come up with unique elements they wouldn't have been able to create on their own. In order for their fictional world to feel realistic, these writers must agree on the broad strokes that describe how that world "works." In a classroom setting, the instructor can help refine their understanding of how

their world "works" by asking them to see it through many different types of characters living there: the man and the woman, the dominant and minority races, the wealthy and the poor, and all the gradients in between. And these are only a few demographic categories that may shape how an individual experiences the world.

To piece this all together, collaborative worldbuilding projects are an approach that bridges *critical thinking* with *creative production* in a discussion-centered classroom where students draw from their lived experiences to share their mental models of how they believe the world works. The teacher observes from the periphery, waiting for moments to direct conversation down more complicated paths or to probe students for more nuanced answers to challenging questions. While researchers state this has worked well in leading students to more thoughtful *analytical* writing, my position is that a similar approach can be taken with *creative* projects that students often approach with much greater enthusiasm than term papers.

Collaborative Worldbuilding Methodology

The collaborative worldbuilding methodology remains consistent regardless of whether the project is a one-time session, a unit of several weeks, or a semester-long undertaking. The work unfolds over a set of chronological stages from building a *foundation*, to establishing a *framework*, to developing the *social structures*. What follows are quick summaries of ideas explored more fully in my book on collaborative worldbuilding, which goes into greater depth as to the theories and terminology of worldbuilding and also provides a structured approach to building a fictional world with a group of people.

The first step is building the world's *foundation*, which helps ensure all writers have a common understanding of the project's parameters and goals. The foundation addresses questions from outside the fictional world. This includes questions of the *audience*, or who (if anyone) outside the class will see the world, as well as the specifics of the *genre* of fiction for the world (e.g., science fiction or fantasy) or whether the world will be realistic in nature, perhaps serving as a historically accurate depiction of an actual place in time. If it's a fantasy or science fiction world, having writers refer to familiar works of popular culture can help immensely to cement their collective understanding. For example, the creators of a dystopian future world might refer to aspects of Suzanne Collins's

Hunger Games series or Margaret Atwood's *Handmaid's Tale* to clarify what they mean. This discussion also allows writers to voice the kinds of worlds they're most interested in creating—or those they wish to avoid—and decide what speculative elements, like magic or advanced technology, exist in their world.

With the foundation sketched out, the next step is establishing the *framework*, which consists of another broad set of considerations, this time within the realm of the fictional world. These are regularly revised and refined as the project matures, but establishing some basics early on helps avoid misunderstandings down the road. The framework consists of the world's *scope, sequence,* and the *perspective* from which an audience learns about it.

- The *scope* can be thought of as the physical size of the fictional world being built. Is this place a planet or something smaller, like a single continent or nation? Or is the scope even tighter, dealing with regions or even districts within a single large city?
- The *sequence* has to do with the timeline of the world. What events in the past—which could include anything from ancient events to things that happened in the recent past—helped shape its current condition?
- The *perspective* has to do with what knowledge exists both inside and external to the fictional world. For example, imagine a fictional world depicting an alien invasion and occupation of a major US city. The writers of the project might know the aliens' ultimate goal for the occupation, but the human characters in the world might not. Or it could be that the writers want to leave the aliens' plans undecided, even among themselves. Perspective then deals with where the knowledge about the world originates, either from characters with limited perspective or from the more god-like position of the writers outside the world.

The bulk of the critical thinking comes in this next step of developing the *structures* and *substructures* of the world. The four broad structures are *governance, economics, social relations,* and *cultural influences*; within these four structures are fourteen *substructures* that describe social forces at play with more granularity.

- The governance substructures include *government presence, rule of law,* and *social services.*
- The economic substructures are *economic strength, wealth distribution,* and *agriculture and trade.*

- The social relations describe the levels of equality along the lines of *race, class, gender,* and *sexual orientation.*
- Finally, the cultural influences are *military, religion, technology,* and *arts and culture.*

The group needs to decide the relative strength and weakness of each of these fourteen substructures and discuss how the tensions between them produce friction within that society. I use a system that asks students to rate these structures in terms of their prevalence on a scale of 1 to 5, where a 1 is a weak or near nonexistent influence and a 5 is a ubiquitous, overwhelming part of the society. This same system can be used to think about times and places from literature or history too—for example, to build a model of the world of the Mississippi River seen in *Huckleberry Finn* or create an accurate depiction of Ancient Egypt based on primary sources.

Wikipedia as a Metanarrative Model

The framework and structures combine to provide material to write a *metanarrative* or the story about the world. As an example of this, I have students look up the Wikipedia entries for their hometowns and home states to see how the pages talk about a place with which they are very familiar. Wikipedia pages begin with few hundred words that describe the most prominent features of the place, called the *metanarrative lead,* followed down the page by separate sections on the area's history, geographic features, demographic data, significant people, and more, all in greater detail. A hallmark of Wikipedia pages is the number of outbound links to other Wikipedia entries, which underscores the idea that every entry for a person, place, or thing, real or imagined, is part of a sprawling network of connections. If a location is home to significant historical events, there will often be a brief description in the text with a link to another page providing much more specific information. For example, the page for Gettysburg, Pennsylvania,[11] describes the history of the borough itself, with an outbound link to an entry on its significance to the Civil War. This helps keep pages both condensed and focused on the topic at hand.

Wikipedia has grown to become the default research tool for all manner of topics, and it will be a familiar online resource to almost all twenty-first-century students. As such, Wikipedia serves as a concrete example of how people today use technology to collaboratively construct knowledge. Wikipedia is not a static resource delivering objective truth from the heavens but rather a collectively managed and endlessly updated database. One of the cornerstones of the site is its commitment to a neutral point of view (NPOV), defined as "representing fairly, proportionately, and, as far as possible, without editorial bias, all of the significant views that have been published by reliable sources on a topic."[12] Thus every Wikipedia page incorporates many different viewpoints that are vetted by a committee of editors. The result is that entries strive to present information in a manner that most reasonable people would agree with—an uncontroversial description of our consensus reality—while still acknowledging less popular opinions and beliefs exist, often presenting their merits and shortcomings. There is also a high degree of transparency, as discussion pages allow readers to review the debates held by contributing editors. However, data show that this editorial pool is overwhelmingly male[13] and that 77 percent of articles are written by just 1 percent of all total editors[14]—facts that throw open the question of whether Wikipedia's alleged NPOV may include a greater degree of unconscious bias than we would have guessed. This merely underscores the idea that our knowledge about the world is not fixed but is instead constantly changing as new information becomes available.

The other highly instructive aspect of using Wikipedia as a model for discussing worldbuilding deals with generalizations and how to avoid overgeneralizing in our descriptions of people and places. For example, everyone accepts that the United States is large and diverse in terms of geography and climate; we know that population demographics vary greatly between urban and rural locations and across the nation's different regions. With little trouble, we can point to aspects of the United States that differentiate it from Mexico, Canada, Central America, and Caribbean nations. We have differences in climate, political organization, economies, religious faith, racial demographics, and many other factors.

Yet if we zoom out a bit more, we can also find greater similarities between the nations of North America when we compare them to Asia, Africa, Europe, South America, and Australia. We can also zoom in and examine differences within our nation's borders, looking at how the states in the Northeast are different in climate and culture from those in the Southwest and other regions; we can zoom down further and talk about the similarities and differences between the Northeast states of New York State and Maine, or drill down further yet and talk about the similarities and differences between Buffalo and New York City, or go further to talk about the differences between the five boroughs of New York City, and we're still not done, as again we can still find significant differences between the neighborhoods of Harlem and the Lower East Side of Manhattan.

Each of these examples, from the level of continents down to neighborhoods, has its own Wikipedia page. When it comes to the short metanarrative lead that briefly describes each entry, the farther out the lens, the more general the statements must be. The metanarrative lead describes the continent's geographic position on the globe, its size, and the number of nations within it and the impact of European colonialism on North American culture. The lens is too distant to provide more meaningful information about people or cultures because they're too diverse. Even zooming in one level to an entry on the United States shows the nation is still too large and diverse to make many useful characterizations about the people, even noting this nation is only one of seventeen "megadiverse" countries.[15]

Reviewing Wikipedia pages at various levels of scope helps writers understand what types of useful generalizations can be made at each level and safeguard against lazy overgeneralizations. A strong tendency for novice writers of science fiction and fantasy is to err on the side of the sweeping generalization—for example, that a population of a certain fictional world adheres to a specific religion. While it might be convenient to depict every character from this region as a religious zealot from the exact same mold, we know that rarely do such totalizing statements hold up to scrutiny in our actual world. Each new level of detail should reveal new levels of complexity and diversity as well. While 90 percent of a population may adhere to a certain religion, what about the other 10 percent? Of the 90 percent, how many are devout believers versus more casual adherents to their faith? Teasing out these questions helps prevent stereotyping and can actually produce the most interesting characters and stories.

Worldbuilding Projects in the Classroom

The worldbuilding methodology is intended to be flexible enough to accommodate different purposes and age groups and has been used for everything from middle schoolers learning Roman history to graduate students in educational design courses. Obviously, it works for creative writing groups of all shapes and sizes, both in and outside classrooms. Instructors can adjust the level of complexity for their student audience and their specific learning outcomes. This chapter and some free resources on collaborativeworldbuilding.com offer you some tools you can experiment with right away.

One good approach is to choose a work of fiction and provide students a copy of the worldbuilding worksheet on collaborativeworldbuilding.com. As students read, have them rank the fourteen substructures mentioned earlier from 1 to 5, where a 1 represents a weak or limited influence in the world and a 5 indicates that it's an ever-present, overwhelming force. Have students fill out the worksheet and bring it to the next class period. To complete this assignment, students must concentrate on moments when social forces become relevant to the story. Before class discussion begins, emphasize that there are no correct answers and students may have felt that they had insufficient information for some categories or that an additional category would have been useful. Students sometimes criticize this exercise as being too simplistic for categorizing a complex world. This too is fine as it becomes fodder for discussion.

One key to running the discussion successfully is to always press students to ground their statements about the world in textual evidence. Not only does this help hone students' close reading skills, but it also shows how social forces can emerge in subtle ways. Of course, through discussion students are often surprised to find less consensus on the values than they expected and that their classmates interpreted moments in the text differently. While they usually reach a consensus about the text's major features—for example, post-apocalyptic works typically feature scarce resources and poor wealth distribution—they also find that things might not have been as clear cut as they thought. Imagine our hypothetical post-apocalyptic story is set in a world where society has collapsed and only small scavenging tribes remain. Is *government presence* low or high? On the one hand, the lack of a functioning government as we know it might suggest a value of a 1, but on the other hand, if you consider that the new tribal leadership regulates all aspects of daily life, is it more like a 4 or even a 5? Both interpretations could be valid, but the real value is directing the class discussion to the question of what it means to govern and how that is experienced by characters in the text.

I also encourage teachers to try the creative route of using the system to generate random worlds. To do this, randomly assign numbers 1 to 5 to each of the substructural categories and then have students work in small groups to write a metanarrative that describes how their randomly generated world "works" on a daily basis. One of the most effective parts of this approach is the way high and low values create points of tension within the society. It's logical these forces will create advantages for some groups of people while other segments of society will be disadvantaged and that individuals will find themselves at different places within this complex web of social forces. This provides a non-pedantic, non-confrontational way to illustrate that some people in the world are underprivileged simply for being who they are. Also stress that the numbers aren't (necessarily) value judgments, for example, that a 1 is undesirable and a

5 is superior. For example, a 5 in *government presence* simply means that the government, however you define it, is very involved in the daily lives of its citizens. It could mean it's a tyrannical dystopia or a beneficent commune; a 5 in *social services* could mean strong public education and healthcare for all, or it could mean "education" is just state propaganda combined with a strictly enforced diet and exercise system.

It's worth cautioning that collaborative worldbuilding methodology isn't magic and its purpose is not to convert students to progressive beliefs but rather to share perspectives and, hopefully, learn from one another. As Porter noted, the worlds of our *classroom* will always be populated with students who bring different experiences, and an engaged instructor can leverage those differences into meaningful discussions that encourage people to think through multiple viewpoints. That alone is a valuable outcome and can also bear fruit later in students' lives. Projects that tap into students' creativity and position them as active makers of their own knowledge are more likely to produce memorable learning experiences than rote drills, where much of the memorized content evaporates after students take the test.

If you recall, our definition of critical thinking includes *action*, or that critical thinkers must also act on what they've learned. A collaborative worldbuilding project should reveal that worlds are neither understood objectively, nor are they monolithic. Our personal understanding of the world is rooted in our experiences, which are in turn rooted into the places and times in which we live, and history teaches that the social forces at play differ between societies and change over time. We should take time to stop and examine the social forces at play in *our* world—or rather learn to appreciate the many overlapping experiences of a world we all inhabit—and ask ourselves whether we are satisfied with what we see. If we aren't, if we see parts of our world we believe need changing, it's a short step to a call to action, to that pressing question we all should be asking: *what can I do about it?*

Notes

1 Bronwyn T. Williams, "The Truth in the Tale: Race and 'Counterstorytelling' in the Classroom," *Journal of Adolescent & Adult Literacy; Hoboken* 48, no. 2 (October 2004): 164–9.

2 "Defining Critical Thinking," accessed June 21, 2019, http://www.criticalthinking.org/pages/defining-critical-thinking/766.

3   Ibid.
4   Karen Kopelson, "Rhetoric on the Edge of Cunning; Or, the Performance of Neutrality (Re)Considered as a Composition Pedagogy for Student Resistance," *College Composition and Communication* 55, no. 1 (2003): 115–46.
5   Kevin J. Porter, "A Pedagogy of Charity: Donald Davidson and the Student-Negotiated Composition Classroom," *College Composition and Communication* 52, no. 4 (2001): 589.
6   Ibid.
7   Ibid., 588.
8   Trent Hergenrader, *Collaborative Worldbuilding for Writers and Gamers*, 1st edn. (New York: Bloomsbury, 2018).
9   This is a very simplified definition of constructionism. For delving deeper into the richness of this theory, see Seymour Papert, "Situating Constructionism," in *Constructionism*, ed. Seymour Papert and Idit Harel (Cambridge, MA: MIT Press, 1991).
10 For a fascinating discussion of the "fictive blocks" from previous stories we've experienced as material we incorporate in our new narratives; see Daniel Mackay, *The Fantasy Role-Playing Game: A New Performing Art* (Jefferson, NC: McFarland & Co., 2001).
11 "Gettysburg, Pennsylvania," *Wikipedia*, July 9, 2019, https://en.wikipedia.org/w/index.php?title=Gettysburg,_Pennsylvania&oldid=905475308.
12 "Wikipedia: Neutral Point of View," *Wikipedia*, December 14, 2016, https://en.wikipedia.org/w/index.php?title=Wikipedia:Neutral_point_of_view&oldid=75485520.
13 "Wikipedia: Wikipedians," *Wikipedia*, May 9, 2019, https://en.wikipedia.org/w/index.php?title=Wikipedia:Wikipedians&oldid=896208307.
14 Daniel Oberhaus and Emanuel Maiberg, "Nearly All of Wikipedia Is Written by Just 1 Percent of Its Editors," *Vice* (blog), November 7, 2017, https://www.vice.com/en_us/article/7x47bb/wikipedia-editors-elite-diversity-foundation.
15 "United States," *Wikipedia*, July 15, 2019, https://en.wikipedia.org/w/index.php?title=United_States&oldid=906423405.

Our Hidden Prime Directive: How Classism Teaches People to Leave Spaceships and Wizards out of the Classroom

Jennifer Pullen
Ohio Northern University

Creative writing is a young academic discipline, beginning with the Iowa Writers' Workshop in 1936. Only recently has its history, lore, and pedagogical methods been critically interrogated. Many have done excellent work regarding the ways in which the workshop method of teaching can exclude people from historically marginalized groups, and literature classrooms have suffered from many of the same problems. The canon wars of the 1980s and 1990s resulted in some diversification, though these discussions continue to be important and productive.

I am interested in looking at a relatively unexamined corner of the creative writing workshop: specifically, the ways its founding cultural moment, along with its ideological and artistic underpinnings, have resulted in a privileging of realism over genre fiction. That privileging is mirrored in literature courses. College classrooms have enormous implications for the Language Arts curriculum of secondary education, for it is those classes that train the English teachers of tomorrow. Elevating realism over non-realist literature in these courses parallels the broader social conversation about what books to teach in secondary schools. One great example of this is the intensely partisan discussion about teaching *Harry Potter* that began in the early 2000s.[1] This contributes to the sense that there is *Literature* for school, to be idolized and analyzed and imitated as creative writers, and *literature* comprised of genres and styles students want to read on their own. This creates a false separation between reading for pleasure and school. If we want young people to read thoughtfully and see the literary arts as a living breathing tradition they can participate in as writers, we must break down that separation. There are many genre novels of merit, both contemporary and historical, yet most are avoided due to the privileging of *realistic* literature over *genre* fiction.

Teachers at all levels have a responsibility to be literate in and teach a wide array of fiction. We must realize that the privileging of realism is inescapably bound up in issues of class and ideology disguised as neutral aesthetics. If we move past the inherited bias against genre fiction, we can increase student engagement while maintaining aesthetic and intellectual standards *and* abiding by the requirements of the Common Core.

I must begin by drawing a picture of the status of genre fiction in the literary community. Even though the current moment is friendlier than the past, the sense of genre fiction being the ugly stepsister of literary fiction persists. The need to either deride genre fiction or defend it is rife in the popular and trade press. The contentious conversation between the late Ursula Le Guin and Kazuo Ishiguro acts as a sort of case study. In March 2015, Ishiguro published *The Buried Giant*, and in an interview with *The New York Times*, he said he was afraid that readers would think his latest novel was fantasy.[2] Le Guin, an ardent defender of science fiction and fantasy, fired back, calling Ishiguro's book fantasy, but not very good fantasy. Ishiguro later said he was on the side of faeries and dragons, not against science fiction and fantasy at all, and Le Guin misunderstood him.[3] The press, from *The New York Times* to *The Atlantic*, continued the fight, and Ishiguro's statement, regardless of what he meant by it, displays the bias against genre fiction.

Another example of a *literary* writer trying to write *genre* fiction while refusing to claim the label can be found in the upheaval surrounding Ian McEwan's *Machines Like Me*. In a 2019 interview McEwan said, "There could be an opening of a mental space for novelists to explore this future … in actually looking at the human dilemmas."[4] He was explaining why his book was not science fiction, yet anyone with a passing knowledge of the genre would know his statement is ignorant. Science fiction has been preoccupied with exactly that, the human dilemma of artificially created life, since at least Philip K. Dick's *Do Androids Dream of Electric Sheep* (1968).[5] The argument could be made that it has been since Mary Shelley's *Frankenstein* (1818).[6] To claim science fiction hasn't been addressing the human implications of artificial life ignores more books, stories, and films than could be listed here. *Both* Ishiguro and McEwan commit a "stacking the deck" fallacy, excluding everything they think is good from genre fiction, thereby making it impossible for genre fiction to be good. However, they are not the problem so much as *symptoms* of it. Defining genre fiction through its least stellar examples would be similar to defining realistic fiction through Nicholas Sparks.

As a result of this fallacy, creative writing workshops and literary magazines have a long history of hostility toward genre fiction. Science fiction and fantasy writers of America's list of literary magazines friendly to genre fiction, while not providing the longer list of those that are not friendly,[7] and even specialty MFA programs that focus on the craft of genre fiction much as a studio program in the visual arts might focus on becoming an accomplished painter, are evidence of the stigma. There is no MFA specifically for realistic fiction because it is treated as the default. Many of the specialist MFA programs are in popular fiction, often seen as synonymous with *commercial fiction*. This distinction, according to Lincoln Michel, is a false one. Many so-called popular fiction novels are not popular, or trying to be, but are very dense and sell few copies, while many realist literary novels, supposedly non-commercial, sell many copies. In 2015, the bestseller lists included twenty-five "fiction, general" books and only seven science fiction and fantasy books.[8] Popularity and high sales are exceptional for *any* book. Yet this illusory divide between what we think of as artistic and entertainment affects what is taught in classrooms at all levels. It affects what work students read and are allowed to write in workshops. Genre fiction bans are commonplace, and many textbooks reinforce the ban.[9]

How did we come to this place? Part of the answer is found in the roots of creative writing as an academic discipline. After the Second World War, universities were flooded with ex-GIs, people who might never have been able to go to college if not for the GI Bill. These students often didn't know conventions of standard English. As a result, writing as a subject in and of itself first entered the college curriculum via composition. Simultaneously, creative writing sought to integrate itself into academia.[10] Consequently, creative writing tried to differentiate itself from composition, which was primarily aimed at the new GI "interlopers" into academia.

In his book *Workshops of Empire*, Eric Bennett describes the founding conditions of the Iowa Writers' Workshop. America was a nation afraid of cultural reform, utopianism, or collectivist ideas of any kind. Such ideas smacked of fascism and/or communism.[11] Concurrently, new tax regulations made it incumbent on the wealthy to find tax breaks. As a result, much of the funding for Iowa came from John D. Rockefeller. Crucial motivators for Rockefeller came from the argument that the new discipline would be housed in the Midwest, away from the liberal East Coast intelligentsia and that it wouldn't be tainted by communism, socialism, or collectivist reforms of any kind.[12] The founders of Iowa believed literature should focus on the growth of the individual. This was explicitly considered the definition of literary *high culture* and a defense against the glorification of the common people seen in communism.[13] This fear, as well as that of decreasing class boundaries in the form of the influx of GIs into universities and the influence of popular culture, incentivized founding and funding the Iowa Writers' Workshop[14] and solidified its conservative foundational ideology.

What does all this have to do with genre fiction? The criticism of being idea or ideology driven is used to condemn genre fiction. What began as a critique based on a fear of communism has been converted to an aesthetic criterion. Genre fiction is also devalued due to its supposed popular quality. What is that but a new guise for the anxiety of a ruling class as manifested in the arts?

Even though much genre fiction is not part of low culture, to the postwar audience it seemed to be. Hugo Gernsback, one of the fathers of science fiction, founded *Amazing Stories* in 1926. Robin Roberts argues one of the effects of *Amazing Stories* was the propagation of the pulps, an entire industry of cheaply printed and mass-produced magazines with lurid covers, primarily marketed at young men.[15] They came to be deeply associated with the Second World War GI.[16] The lurid covers were only partially reflective of their contents. Even books that had formerly been considered respectable, like Orwell's *1984*, were given pulp covers. Anthony Enns explains how the stigma of the pulps was so great that genre publishers struggled to expand into hardback or obtain a place on bookstore shelves that was not next to pornography. Ray Bradbury was one of the first pulp writers to get wider critical acceptance and a hardback edition in the United States. This successful transition earned him the label "The Poet of the Pulps."[17] While clearly intended as a compliment, it implies that he is an exception to the rule.

The fear of social agendas in genre fiction, as well as a fear of mass culture and a desire to separate "high" and "low" literature, is an inherited prejudice from the nineteenth century. The first science fiction novel is widely believed to be Shelley's *Frankenstein* (1818). It contains themes and ideas that still preoccupy science fiction writers today, from what it means to be an artificial being, to what it means to be human, and the impact of science and technology on society and the individual within it. *The War of the Worlds* (1897), by H. G. Wells, hypothesized what might happen to society if humans weren't dominant.[18] He prefigured many eco-science fiction writers, who ask, "[W]hat if humans aren't the most important beings in the universe?" Additionally, folklore as a discipline began in the nineteenth century, spawning proto fantasy novels and much twentieth-century and contemporary fantasy fiction, and folklore and fairy tales have always been deeply social and political endeavors.[19] The social implications led to many reformers who identified with Marxism, like William Morris, choosing to write proto fantasy.[20] Morris's interest in utopia, medievalism, and folklore is characteristic of much twentieth-century genre fiction. There was intense pushback against not only these writers' ideas, but what they were publishing. All of the aforementioned novels demonstrate that genre fiction has been politically engaged and artistically varied since its beginnings.

In fact, the very notion of the fantastical was political in nineteenth-century England and entangled with issues of class.[21] According to Felicity Hughes, from the eighteenth century into the nineteenth, as the novel was coming of age as a form, writers struggled because "the novel was engaged in a struggle to live down the stigma of being a 'low' form, not art but entertainment."[22] The rules of what counted as artistically worthy were not yet agreed upon. Many nineteenth-century authors, like George Eliot,[23] have had their non-realist work forgotten.[24] No one had yet invented a label for realist vs. non-realist work. As mass-printed material became more available, class divisions within the novel began, mostly driven by ideas about *who* was reading *what*.[25] In the twentieth century, the pulps contributed to the disparagement of genre fiction, while in the nineteenth century, it was the penny dreadful. According to Judith Flanders, the penny dreadful put dramatic events, magic, and imaginary technology into simple prose, drawing upon the same content as Bram Stoker, Shelley, and Wells, but with dramatically different results. They came to be associated with the working poor, the dirtiness of city slums, loose sexuality, and alcoholism.[26]

As Britain, with its emergent middle class, tried to decide what being a part of this socioeconomic group looked like, the idea of childhood as a protected time began to take hold as a crucial divide between the classes.[27] As a result, the middle class began to decide what constituted children's literature.[28] By the late nineteenth century, fantasies belonged in the realm of children,[29] and this attitude toward the genre prefigures the debates surrounding books like *Harry Potter* in modern schools to this day.

The nineteenth-century cultural concerns surrounding class, the novel, and early genre fiction are also directly connected to the way creative writing is taught in America. Henry James, a transition figure between the nineteenth and twentieth centuries, wrote "The Art of Fiction," still widely assigned in MFA programs. He argues that fiction is only artistically valuable and good insofar as it succeeded in imitating life.[30] James claims that novels rise above mere low-class entertainment and become art only when realistic.[31] When fantasy is placed in opposition to realism, it implies the *only* serious fiction is realism.[32] As teachers, do we not want to bridge the gap between the interests of our students and the literary forms we want to teach? What if that gap is socially constructed? The nineteenth century and the GI Bill both created the cultural conditions and aesthetic assumptions that have alienated our literary interests from students'. Genre fiction offers opportunities we risk missing out on if we accept these inherited biases. By teaching genre fiction in the creative writing classroom, we can help students learn to write the best versions of what they love rather than leave them without guidance.

The legacy of the bias against genre fiction can now be seen in the way elements of the literary world fight over whether or not genre fiction can be art or if certain pieces of art are genre fiction. These skirmishes show how we labor under the burden of the past. The popularity of *Harry Potter* and other fantastical YA fiction reflects the belief that genre fiction is childish. Hughes describes how many authors of sophisticated fantastical fiction, historically and contemporarily (from Lewis Carroll to Le Guin), published much of their early work as children's literature because of those very assumptions.[33] This echoes the broader conversation about the place of genre fiction in schools.

As a specific example, *Harry Potter* is both defended and derided in educational communities. Detractors object on religious grounds. Proponents assert that fantasy helps kids enjoy reading and *Harry Potter* encourages kindness and respect for others.[34] Both sides assume children will be seduced by fantasy and fiction has the obligation to teach good or bad behavior. The debate about *Harry Potter* in high schools derives from the same assumptions present in the college classroom. Mary Elizabeth Garcia argues that *Harry Potter* can be used to segue college students into serious adult literature.[35] This argument contains within it the idea that fantasy is for children and is *literature* appealing to mass culture, valuable insofar as it can be used to get young people interested in *Literature*. Such ideas, commonplace in the college classroom, are not directly taught so much as unconsciously absorbed. This aesthetic trickles down from publishing to universities to secondary education.

Lynn Neary describes the use of *Harry Potter* in the classroom as evidence of the de-evolution of the reading public; kids aren't moving on from children's literature, and schools aren't assigning as many classics for adults. She reports a conversation with some college students: "Every single person in the class said, 'I don't like realism, I don't like historical fiction. What I like is fantasy, science fiction, horror and fairy tales.'" A teacher said, "There's something wonderful about the language, the thinking, the intelligence of the classics" implying that one reads YA fantasy and science fiction or "the classics" and nothing in between.[36] This ignores the sophisticated history and present of genre fiction.

What about moving students from *Harry Potter* to genre classics like Shelley's *Frankenstein* or even twentieth-century classics like Le Guin's *The Left Hand of Darkness*, a novel about a planet whose inhabitants are non-binary.[37] The classics that are being so mourned include *To Kill a Mockingbird*, *Oliver Twist*, and *Anna Karenina*. Why not assign classics that are the ancestors of what students love? Books performing similar analysis of class, gender, or race, in sophisticated prose? Why not help students see that *Twilight* is a descendant of *Dracula*[38] and only one (not very good) book from a tradition of vampire novels including Octavia Butler's *Fledgling*?[39] Why not give students the opportunity after reading *Dracula* and *Fledgling* to try their hand at writing vampire stories with equally literary qualities?

If you, as a teacher, are concerned about your students not moving on from YA, why not assign contemporary adult genre texts representing the best in their field? If the goal is to get students to read complicated books for adults, why not assign ones that draw from the same well, albeit in more challenging ways, as *Harry Potter*? The twenty most assigned books in high school, according to the Center for Learning and Teaching of Literature, are *Romeo and Juliet*, *Macbeth*, *The Adventures of Huckleberry Finn*, *Julius Caesar*, *To Kill a Mockingbird*, *Of Mice and Men*, *The Scarlet Letter*, *Hamlet*, *1984*, *Animal Farm*, *Fahrenheit 451*, *The Great Gatsby*, *The Bell Jar*, *The Catcher in the Rye*, *Wuthering Heights*, *The Complete Poems of Emily Dickinson*, *The Diary of Anne Frank*, *Lord of the Flies*, *The Odyssey*, and *All Quiet on the Western Front*.[40] Several trends can be observed from this list. Obviously, there is little racial diversity among the books' authors. Additionally, there are only three genre fiction novels, all written by men—two by Orwell and one by Bradbury. The "classics" considered valuable *Literature* haven't changed much. Orwell and Bradbury are the exception to the rule, the writers of genre fiction who aren't really genre writers, echoing back to when Bradbury was singled out as "The Poet of the Pulps." Can students be blamed for wanting to read *Harry Potter* and other YA when little of what they are taught to see as literature for adults contains content they are interested in? When it is assumed that literature with complicated and sophisticated prose looks like the canon approved by Henry James and the Iowa Writers' Workshop? Students need both classic and modern examples that illuminate the long and vital tradition their favorite books exist within.

I don't fault high school teachers for the books they teach—college faculty teach students what counts as *Literature* and what doesn't. Change needs to happen in both K–12 and higher education. If we want students to become engaged, lifelong readers, and to cease propagating the class-based assumptions of the

Victorians and their descendants, we need to break down the false separation between books we *like* and those we *admire*. Why not assign Shelley, Le Guin, and N. K. Jemisin? Jemisin is a novelist and psychologist whose multiple award-winning fantasy and science fiction novels tackle issues of race, colonialism, gender, and sexuality.[41] Her work is anything but easy or for children. Patrick Rothfuss's *The Name of the Wind* contains a main character who attends a magic school, goes into debt to attend, and struggles with bullying.[42] All of the aforementioned books can be connected both to the YA that students are said to love and works of what is considered classic literature, from folk ballads and the *bildungsroman* (Rothfuss), to the war novel (Jemisin). When teachers avoid genre fiction because they say it isn't *Literature*, they participate in long-held class-based assumptions. By not being literate in genre fiction, we miss out on assigning both historical and contemporary books students will love while also engaging with important issues.

If we want engaged college *and* high school students, we cannot ignore the literature they love. Simultaneously, creative writing in the classroom would benefit from the same buy-in. Taking the work students want to write seriously and talking about worldbuilding or character development in fantasy fiction rather than dismissing it empowers students to create art that matters to them. We can engage students in critical thinking about literature and creative writing more readily if the texts we assign connect to the books they already read.

In this way, creative writing of genre fiction can be a fascinating addition to the Language Arts classroom, dovetailing with the Common Core, which calls for eleventh- and twelfth-graders to demonstrate knowledge of the "foundational works" of literature primarily produced from the late eighteenth to the early twentieth centuries. Genre fiction is a crucial part of that foundation, and creative writing can be used to demonstrate knowledge, such as the use of "narrative techniques" mentioned in writing standards. I teach an environmental literature course where we read literature from Walt Whitman to eco-science fiction and scientific articles. Students write a utopian or dystopian story diagnosing a problem or proposing a solution to a social/environmental issue. They then write a reflective essay explaining how they are using literary techniques and scientific information, followed by an annotated bibliography, and are usually willing to put more work into this assignment than a standard analytical essay. Genre fiction, because of its tendency towards rhetorical storytelling, is especially well suited to this synthesis of fiction, nonfiction, aesthetics, and research. The Common Core requires students to learn all of the above, but it does not "define how the standards should be taught or which materials should be used to support students."⁴³ If we can engage students, teach them about literary history, connect literature to real problems, and meet Common Core standards all at once, why wouldn't we?

Social protest and countercultural movements—the very ideas feared by the founders and funders of the Iowa Workshop—are central preoccupations of genre fiction from the Victorian era on. It is no wonder, then, between the working class, mass culture associations, and the feared specter of social reform that genre fiction was not originally—and still often isn't—welcome in classroom. Teachers at all levels have a responsibility to assign works reflecting the real diversity of literature, both in terms of authors and types of texts. When we don't assign genre fiction, we are continuing a legacy of literary standards based on classism. If we don't let students write fantasy, or don't provide guidance to help them do it well, we are reinforcing outdated prejudices.

It is past time we acknowledge that the current contested status of genre fiction in creative writing and literature classrooms is not the result of ideologically neutral aesthetics but is instead one more uncomfortable legacy of the history of the discipline of creative writing and literary culture—one that should be left behind.

Notes

1. Trisha Tucker, "What Do Protests about *Harry Potter* Books Teach Us?" *The Conversation*, June 25, 2017, http://theconversation.com/what-do-protests-about-harry-potter-books-teach-us-79327.
2. Alexandra Alter, "For Kazuo Ishiguro 'The Buried Giant' Is a Departure," *The New York Times*, February 15, 2015, https://www.nytimes.com/2015/02/20/books/for-kazuo-ishiguro-the-buried-giant-is-a-departure.html.
3. Siam Cain, "Writer's Indignation: Kazuo Ishiguro Rejects Claims of Genre Snobbery," *The Guardian*, March 8, 2019, https://www.theguardian.com/books/2015/mar/08/kazuo-ishiguro-rebuffs-genre-snobbery.
4. Tim Adams, "'Who's Going to Write the Algorithm for the Little White Lie?' Interview with Ian McEwan," *The Guardian*, April 14, 2019, https://www.theguardian.com/books/2019/apr/14/ian-mcewan-interview-machines-like-me-artificial-intelligence.
5. Phillip K. Dick, *Do Androids Dream of Electric Sheep?* (New York: Doubleday, 1968).
6. Mary Shelley, *Frankenstein or the Modern Prometheus* (New York: Oxford University Press, 2008).

7   Caran Gussoff, "Lit Fic Mags for Spec Fic Writers 101: Five Things You Have to Know," *SFWA*, November 26, 2013, https://www.sfwa.org/2013/11/lit-fic-mags-spec-fic-writers-101-five-things-know/.

8   Lincoln Michel, "When Popular Fiction Isn't Popular: Genre, Literary, and the Myths of Popularity," *Electric Literature*, April 2, 2016, https://electricliterature.com/when-popular-fiction-isnt-popular-genre-literary-and-the-myths-of-popularity/.

9   There are more textbooks on creative writing that try to weigh in against genre fiction than I can count. Even some of the more balanced ones, which I myself have used, still decline to teach it. Books including *Creative Writing: Four Genres in Brief* by David Starkey or *The Art and Craft of Fiction: A Writer's Guide* by Michael Kardos. They decline to teach genre fiction, for various reasons, mostly claiming that it is just so different from literary fiction, they couldn't possibly teach it.

10 Donna Strickland, "Taking Dictation: The Emergence of Writing Programs and the Cultural Contradictions of Composition Teaching," *College English* 63, no. 4 (2001): 457–79.

11 Eric Bennett, *Workshops of Empire: Stegner, Engle, and American Creative Writing During the Cold War* (Iowa City, IA: University of Iowa Press, 2015), 32–3.

12 Ibid., 10–13.

13 Ibid., 46.

14 Ibid., 33.

15 Louis Menand, "Pulp's Big Moment," *The New Yorker*, January 5, 2015, https://www.newyorker.com/magazine/2015/01/05/pulps-big-moment.

16 Robin Roberts, *A New Species: Gender and Science in Science Fiction* (Champaign, IL: University of Illinois Press, 1993), 40–65.

17 Anthony Enns, "The Poet of the Pulps: Ray Bradbury and the Struggle for Prestige in Postwar Science Fiction," *Distinctions That Matter: Popular Literature and Material Culture* 13, no. 1 (2015), https://journals.openedition.org/belphegor/615.

18 H. G. Wells, *The War of the Worlds* (London: Orion Publishing Group, 2010).

19 Marina Warner, *Once Upon a Time: A Brief History of Fairy Tale* (New York: Oxford University Press, 2016).

20 William Morris, *News from Nowhere* (New York: Penguin Classics, 1994).

21 Michael Saler, "'Clap If You Believe in Sherlock Holmes': Mass Culture and the Re-Enchantment of Modernity," *The Historical Journal* 46, no. 3 (2003): 599–662.

22 Felicity A. Hughes, "Children's Literature: Theory and Practice," *ELH* 45, no. 3 (1978): 542–61.

23 George Eliot, *The Lifted Veil and Brother Jacob* (New York: Oxford University Press, 2009).

24 Hughes, "Children's Literature," 543.

25 Ibid., 544.

26 Judith Flanders, "Discovering Literature, The Romantics and the Victorians: The Penny Dreadful," *The British Library*, May 15, 2014, https://www.bl.uk/romantics-and-victorians/articles/penny-dreadfuls.

27 U. C. Knoepflmacher, "The Balancing of Child and Adult: An Approach to Victorian Fantasies for Children," *Nineteenth-Century Fiction* 37, no. 3 (1983): 497–530.
28 Ibid., 498.
29 Hughes, "Children's Literature," 544.
30 Ibid., 545.
31 Henry James, "The Art of Fiction," *Washington State University*, May 16, 2019, https://public.wsu.edu/~campbelld/amlit/artfiction.html.
32 Hughes, "Children's Literature," 551–5.
33 Ibid., 552–8.
34 Kate Pastoor, "Magic in the Classroom: The Controversial *Harry Potter*," *Prized Writing: UC Davis*, 2002, https://prizedwriting.ucdavis.edu/magic-classroom-controversial-harry-potter.
35 Mary Elizabeth Garcia, "*Harry Potter* Course Leaves Students Spell Bound," *News Center: UC Santa Cruz*, June 5, 2018, https://news.ucsc.edu/2018/06/harry-potter-class.html.
36 Lynn Neary, "What Kids Are Reading in School and Out," *All Things Considered*, June 11, 2013, https://www.npr.org/2013/06/11/190669029/what-kids-are-reading-in-school-and-out.
37 Ursula Le Guin, *The Left Hand of Darkness* (New York: Ace Books, 1987).
38 Bram Stoker, *Dracula* (New York: W. W. Norton, 1996).
39 Octavia Butler, *Fledgling* (New York: Seven Stories Press, 2005).
40 New York City Department of Education, "20 Most Taught Books in High School," *The Center for Learning and Teaching of Literature*, 2014, http://schoolsstg.nycenet.edu/NR/rdonlyres/A8C1D948-3E8D-4DAF-B56D-9C0553901ACB/0/MarkFederman_BoysEmpowerment316final.pdf.
41 N.K. Jemisin, *The Fifth Season* (New York: Orbit Books, 2015).
42 Patrick Rothfuss, *The Name of the Wind* (New York: DAW Books, 2008).
43 Core Org, *Common Core Standards*, http://www.corestandards.org/read-the-standards/.

Break Stuff: The Necessity of Mistakes and the Risks That Cause Them in Creative Writing

Michael Dean Clark
Azusa Pacific University

A common misconception about creativity is that inspiration is the central engine of invention. Put another way, artists depend on capturing capricious moments of clarity to inspire what will become their art. There are, however, three things wrong with this way of thinking as it relates to teaching language arts. First, it's impossible to teach inspiration. Second, most students don't see themselves as artists, and even those who do don't believe they understand storytelling the way the authors they read do. And finally, this lightning in a bottle theory is actually completely incorrect.

The core of creativity isn't inspiration but refashioning failed attempts to create meaning into successes.

Unfortunately, there are two large barriers to students learning this lesson. The first is they fear failure. This fear results from a system in which learning is keyed to their reflecting knowledge and skills primarily through standardized measures, and in which classroom grades are more punitive than diagnostic in practice. Second, the curricular demands placed on the ELA classroom are greater and more diverse than almost any other subject matter. Various and sundry skills in reading, writing analytically and creatively, literary analysis, information and visual literacy, rhetoric, and research and test-taking skills, among others must be covered over the course of the secondary educational path.

Laid end to end, the number of concepts to cover is daunting and requires a breakneck pace to merely address it all with space for necessary reteaching. Add in days lost to testing and other external curricular demands and it's no wonder creative writing seems impossible to engage—a challenge made even more difficult by an overwhelming emphasis on expository academic writing and functional texts in service of standardized testing results that reflect in school ratings and public opinion.[1] This cycle of teach and test, painted with the insinuation of continual high stakes, trains students to drill down on information that best helps them avoid failing and let the rest go.

Failure in the Classroom, or How to Win at Losing

To address this, students' fear of failure must be converted into a personal comfort with initial failings as pathways to success and combined with a classroom culture that celebrates unsuccessful attempts as necessary to learning. Creative writing, it turns out, is perfectly situated for this kind of work when constructed around collaborative projects and grades that assess engagement with the process rather than the subjective quality of the final product.

Before looking at three specific creative writing units designed with productive failure in mind, I'll offer a few notes on the forces that must drive this kind of work. For the sake of this chapter, this information will be presented with lesson design in mind. However, all of these precepts must be translated into student-friendly terms in order to build a culture that leans into learning from one's mistakes. Fear of failure drives student passivity or disengagement, stifling learning. In this regard, a few specific practical and philosophical shifts should be made in how the class experience is designed.

The first rule of bringing creative failure into the classroom must be shifting the orientation of assessment from product-oriented thinking to participatory process-based frameworks that are contextual, active, social, communitarian, and reflective.[2] Grading, in the case of an example I'll present later, the subjective quality of a novella written collaboratively by an entire class over the course of a single week would be counterproductive madness. Rather, if students see their efforts to engage and contribute rewarded—particularly their responses to failed attempts—they'll feel supported in taking risks rather than merely looking for the teacher's validation of their correctness. And, in practical terms, instructors can assess the learning that comes from these efforts with simpler, targeted demi-rubrics that include participation and contribution along with quality. For more on this, see John Belk's chapter.

Another foundation for building class experiences around failure is applying an active, team-based framework that positions students, in constructivist terms, as makers rather than receivers of information. Assessing student learning as a product of their process rather than the product itself and insinuating the desirability of creative failures radically alters their perception of how they're supposed to learn. At the same time, this shift also repositions the teacher as a guide rather than information dispenser. As Paul Vermette and Chandra Foote explain, "Cooperative learning structures that expect the students and teachers to be partners in learning convey the spirit sought by constructivist educators ... to take risks, to see from different perspectives, to engage in provocative thinking, and to re-analyze and/or reorganize content are all student outcomes."[3] Teachers must see themselves as facilitators and resources for using technology, grammar, and techniques of writing, operating more like interactive maps to the process than messengers delivering judgment regarding the acceptability of students' output.

All of this upheaval, along with the discomfort that inevitably accompanies telling young learners the failure they were taught to fear now means to be their friend, requires clear and user-friendly work processes. This work must be done in advance and will be the most direct and extensive way teachers guide students to self-directed exploration of what they can learn. To accomplish this, designate distinct roles for students to perform, simplify how they'll share their work in both technological and interpersonal ways, and develop clear group norms regarding how failure will function as fuel for improvement.

Finally, it helps to submerge standards rather than highlight them in the work process. Nothing feels less like making art than an assignment with Common Core or state standards codes attached to it. Furthermore, typical secondary pedagogy places such a heavy emphasis on connecting every lesson to specific standards and those standards to standardized testing and the results of those tests to perceived academic achievement that nothing will undermine making failure a virtue more than tying creative work to prescribed learning outcomes in early and overt ways. Hold off making these connections until late in the sequence or, even better, after the project is done as part of critical reflection exploring what students have learned.

With this framework for successful failure in mind, the following are three potential lesson sequences emphasizing student-driven, process-oriented creative writing experiences in which doing the wrong thing for the right reasons is a feature and not a flaw in the system. Furthermore, all of this can be accomplished while meeting several content standards and presenting multiple opportunities for identifying and exploring the elements of literature in students' own work that will later provide critical conceptual understanding of the same elements in other texts.

Novella in a Week

You read that subtitle correctly. At the end of a five-day school week, this process takes a class of students from a general understanding of what a novella is to having completed one as collaborative authors. Add a couple of class sessions on the back end and they can assess their own work with the same critical lenses they apply to others. And yes, I wouldn't see it as possible either if I hadn't done it myself with groups of ninth-graders when I taught high school English. Also, there is a certain amount of elasticity required in the teacher's role here, allowing for creativity that may not work out in the story while also keeping your students from traveling paths that derail their own contributions or, more likely, their classmates'.

If you hold loosely to the need to shape the product itself, though, this process offers many teachable moments merely reading and responding to others' stories just can't. And, dare I say, it may just be fun. While they're at it, students learn what it takes to construct a complex narrative,[4] making it easier for them to analyze others moving forward.

Day One

In order for the launch of this process to work, try to hold this session on a Monday and split your class into groups of two or three on the preceding Friday. After making groups, determine a genre of storytelling for the story they'll tell and have students consider it over the weekend as a way of priming the pump for the first session's work. They do not have to have a specific story in mind, as that's the point of Session One; just consider what goes into stories in that genre.

The first class should be an open brainstorming conversation you drive and chart visually so students can follow along. This is also where you must model the energy you want to see in your students while also ensuring key elements of storytelling get discussed in order to make decisions regarding the class novella. These elements include setting, primary characters, primary underlying tension, and a basic plot development of the story split into the same number of chapters as groups in each class. This is critical in setting up necessary notions of sequencing to ensure their story makes sense.[5]

A note on the teacher's role here: make all of the decisions students reach visual on the board or screen, leaving revisions and changes to these notes visible rather than erasing them so students can see the process as messy but developmental. Also, you can model productive failure here by inserting suggestions you know connect but won't work if students try them. Maybe suggest a love interest where there isn't one or an element of setting that's out of step with the one students have selected. This will create opportunities where they can correct you as needed and see you embodying the notion of productive failure you say they need.

The novella's chapters should fall along the basic elements of Freytag's five-part pyramid-shaped story diagram for ease, with one chapter serving as the opening exposition, one the pivot, one the climax, and one the resolution of the story. The rest, then, are distributed based on the needs of the chosen narrative representing the familiar concepts of rising and falling action. If the class is under twenty-six students, arrange them in groups of two and make the chapters four-to-five double-spaced pages. For larger classes, groups of three with six-page chapters will allow for everyone to write an equal amount and keep the total page count within the general expectations of the form.

In the last ten minutes, assign each group a chapter or allow them to select their own based on your best sense of what will allow students to feel settled in the section of the story they'll write. Then, for homework, have them collect research content to help build their chapter. Provide specific expectations for what kind of research would be most helpful and make it due the next day. Also, be aware that you will not be able to accomplish everything in this first session. This is built to a fifty-five-minute period, and the best you can do is help them create a framework for more specific thinking. That's enough, though, given that not having all the answers is part of the creative process and will lead to useful moments of failure in the next few sessions.

Day Two

Where the first session of this process is expansive in terms of wrangling ideas, the rest of the week grows increasingly focused and student-driven. The second session revolves around students planning the individual plot arcs of their chapters and deciding how to divide their work. During this session, you should roam, checking in regarding students' plans and answering any questions they have. Also, encourage groups to speak with those writing the chapters on either side of theirs—the first and last chapter groups can check in with each other—to get a sense of how they'll need to connect to the parts of the story most directly connected to theirs. This will drive home notions of story continuity and maintain each group's contact to the overall narrative.

For homework, each group member will write their section of the chapter into a shared Google document. This work can be done asynchronously or together over the afternoon and evening and allows them to continue their conversation as they complete a rough draft before the next session. It also allows students without a home computer to use campus resources. In service of the project's learning goals, provide a universal set of chapter requirements so students must use particular elements of storytelling, ensuring they engage the content and the construct.

Day Three

This session is devoted to identifying as a class any plot holes or issues in the development of the larger story and then returning to small groups to make necessary revisions based on this discussion. To facilitate this work, have each group summarize their chapter's story. As with Day One, you should make their discussion visual, charting the arcs and tension points of each chapter and asking pointed questions about elements that could be problematic in overall terms. But as you ask, encourage students to ask their own questions and keep notes for their own chapters. In the last ten minutes of class, have groups check in with those on either side of them again to nail down any particular issues and then send them out to revise their chapters based on what they learned. This allows for seeing the unavoidable failure to "know" how to adjust to the work of the other groups and means all will need to revise, which teaches the general need for this work in the writing process.

Day Four

The second-to-last session is a crowd-sourced effort to edit the entire novella for continuity and a chance for students to apply their growing understanding of the elements of fiction in peer reviewing each other's chapters. To keep this manageable and as effective as possible, have groups respond to the two chapters surrounding theirs. Provide a guide for what to look for in each other's sections and encourage students to offer suggestions for how other groups can improve in terms of their story arcs and in connection with the novella's larger narrative. This work will inform final revisions each group will complete as homework before the final session of the writing process and culminates a practical cycle focused on the importance of revision and editing for the sake of a story's quality.[6]

Day Five

Publication Day! When students arrive, invite them to add their chapters into a single, shared Google document. To ease this process, place chapter headers with corresponding numbers for the various chapters and have students add a title and their names to each. After that is complete, the class will select cover art and a title for the novel. This is a great time to move the discussion of the story out to the larger elements of literature they have engaged in over the course of the week while also celebrating the creation of something tangible they all had a part in making. At session's end, publish the book by "sending" a PDF copy to the class for them to read.[7]

After publication, spend time flipping their use of the story by making them critics of it. Because they wrote it, students will not feel shut out like they do with published stories by professional authors. Have them identify elements of literature in their own words, discuss ways chapters work or don't, unpack particular challenges they had during the project, and identify errors or places they'd improve if they were still working on the text. This is where inevitable discontinuities—rain in one chapter but not the next, inexplicable disappearances of characters, obvious plot holes, etc.—become powerful opportunities to teach elements of fiction. Adding this extra reflective time to focus allows students to use their own work to make sense of what you are teaching them and allows you to link this process to how they will engage literature and writing for the rest of the year.

Meme-oirs

A more contained project than the Novella in a Week is the Meme-oir. As an entrée to considering narrative nonfiction, an underutilized tool for teaching more academic expository forms, this sequence has students tell an important story from their lives in memes or GIFs they collect online. This process should take three or four class sessions with one take-home project completed in stages on nights one and two. Over that time, students will engage elements of storytelling while comparing the needs that come with various expressions of the same ideas in contexts ranging from print to micro-blogging to visual culture.[8] Meme-oirs also offer a novel way of drawing students' existing knowledge base into the academic conversation around some particular conventions of writing.

The assignment is simple: students take a meaningful moment from their lives, boil it down in its entirety to a thread of five Twitter-appropriate tweets, and then convert those into five memes with no more than five to seven words to act as context for each one. At the end of the process, they exchange their Meme-oirs with others and try to translate the story the author is telling into a complete idea. This work circles back into a discussion of what it takes to write a story, particularly in terms of the transitions writers use[9] and what they need as readers and writers to better understand it all.

I would be remiss if I did not acknowledge that there are some particular limitations to this process that require negotiation. However, if the experiment is positioned in the context of productive failure, those limitations become unexpected learning sites. The first of these is the brevity of the form. At five tweets, students will only have 1,400 characters to tell their story. Aligning each tweet with one element of Freytag's model will help make this a bit easier and offer another approach to teaching elements of story. A second limitation is the practical impossibility of telling their story in five memes or GIFs. There is no comprehensive way to convey the story in five images and, at most, thirty-five words. Some elements will be lost or muted for the sake of getting the basics across. But this imposed "failure" will allow students to better see what is necessary for a fully fleshed memoir or personal narrative to work for an audience.[10] It will also create space for discussing what information audiences need for making sense of a story and what can be left off the page. With these elements in mind, here are the specifics of the Meme-oir sequence.

Day One

Begin the first day of the process discussing what a memoir is and how memes/GIFs work in general, accessing students' prior knowledge for both but more for the second. You will likely need to draw on a general understanding of the five elements of a story here, which should help with sequencing this unit into the best place in your year's calendar. Once this is done, provide students a series of tweets telling a story from their author's life in text only. Discuss those posts as "micro-memoirs" and break down how they work. Then have students replace certain ideas from the posts with memes/GIFs. This can be done collaboratively a few times and then on their own before they leave, affording you time to show students less familiar with the form how to search for memes by theme.

For homework, have students pick a personal story and make a list of its key elements along a plot map of some sort as the beginning of their own micro-memoir. Frame the stories as something that represents a challenge they've overcome or a goal they've accomplished despite failing along the way. Their plot lists should have eight or nine elements minimum and be due the next day. It's best if they are created in digital form, but handwritten lists will work at this point.

Additionally, give students the meme/GIF requirements for the Meme-oir this will become. Use memes as transitions, emotional responses, expressions of confusion or figuring something out, or a concluding note. This way they can brainstorm ideas while making their lists.

Day Two

With completed lists in their hands, walk students through an example you created of the type of Meme-oirs they are being asked to write. Your example should conform to the rules of communicating on Twitter and the specifics of the assignment, and making your story personally relevant and a little vulnerable would be a powerful model for helping students buy into the process. Show them how each required visual element can work, paying particular attention to ways of writing that set up and respond to the memes/GIFs as part of the story's development. Most importantly, don't just show them your finished product. Rather, illustrate the ways you had to correct, revise, and reconceive your Meme-oir as a model of failing productively.

Once you finish your sample discussion, give students the rest of class to work on their projects. Encourage them to create an outline of the story with memes/GIFs properly placed. Then they can start writing. Circulate and answer questions and encourage along, particularly students who struggle with writing. Their homework, then, is to finish their draft in connection with a final rubric but also with the knowledge they'll be able to revise the next day.

Day Three

For this session, students return with drafts for process points and then complete basic peer reviews in groups of two. Give them two basic tasks. First, have them analyze every meme/GIF individually for whether or not its purpose in the story is clear. Second, have them read each sentence of the text to evaluate whether or not it helps tell the story. For each they see as not helping, have them make a note regarding what is confusing or not working. When done, students have the chance to revise their Meme-oirs and then submit. This also allows for struggling students to have one more night to finish up as homework. The final version serves as their product and should be graded on a limited number of standards-based criteria of the teacher's choosing.

Day Four (Optional)

If you would like to extend the learning connected to the Meme-oir process, use an extra session to discuss—in small groups first, then as a class—what was difficult about the assignment and specific ways different students worked well with text and image. Also, discuss what you can and can't do with the Meme-oir that you can and can't in a traditional print memoir or personal essay. You can call out particularly good examples from student work to push the discussion toward what kinds of storytelling devices students may have employed but didn't. For further extension, you could assign the task of writing the same story in a 300-word text version and then perform a formal comparison of the two forms of their story.

Mad Lib Poetry

Teaching the parts of speech can be daunting and boring at once. And yet working with them is a requirement of most secondary standards collections.[11] Drawing on the popular word-replacement activity Mad Libs and earlier OULIPian exercises like N+7,[12] this process has students write a poem evocative of a specific setting using imagery, concrete details, and strong verbs to bring the place to life. Then, they trade their poems with three other students in class. Once they've traded, the students will replace all specific nouns, verbs, adjectives, and adverbs with functional variations in each of the poems they receive. When finished, they return their versions to the original authors and receive their own to compare and contrast the four separate versions of their poems. Once they have taken specific notes on what they see, the process ends with a class discussion about the elasticity of language as well as their understanding of the work that the various parts of speech do. This exercise can be repeated and unfolds over three days.

Day One

First, provide some existing poems to serve as a framework for the kind students will be writing. For the sake of this process, focus on short, evocative poems heavy on specific word choice and interesting phrasing. Some specific, accessible works that come to mind are Roethke's "My Papa's Waltz," "Gloves" by Kaveh Akbar, and "Heat Lightning" by Jen Stewart Fueston, but there are scores online to choose from as well. Discuss how language choices help make the poem what it is. Then show them how each of the four parts of speech (nouns, verbs, adjectives, and adverbs) can be replaced by modeling the work. Make sure you exemplify some productive failure by starting with functional replacements that can definitely be improved upon with more specific choices. The goal is to illustrate that the first word students think of isn't likely to be the most creative—an important notion that helps them understand the work of good writing.

Once you finish the first poem, do one or two more as a class and encourage students to throw out suggestions for replacing words. For homework that night, have students write their own poem. Give specific line count and text guidelines as a model to follow. You can have students identify the parts of speech in their own poems or have their peers do that when they work on replacements. This second option not only reminds students what they already know about parts of speech but also addresses relevant standards involving specific nuances of language use.[13]

Day Two

Begin the session by having students exchange poems with three classmates and start working on word replacements. This will work best if students use a platform such as Google Documents that can be shared with each other. If this isn't available, keep the poems short and have students print out or handwrite three extra versions of the poem to share. While they work, keep a list of the parts of speech and their jobs visible for student reference. The replacement process should be completed and the revisions returned to the original authors before the end of the session. Once that's done, have students write a quick, guided reflection on what they notice when comparing their work to alternate versions. They can begin this in class and finish as homework for submission the next day.

Day Three

End the Mad Lib poetry process on the third day with a class discussion about the parts of speech, focusing on what students learned about language and composing poems. To extend this conversation, have some students read their poem and their favorite alternate version aloud so the class can discuss them.

Finally, turn the conversation into an exploration of what does and doesn't work in this exercise. This can lead to teachable moments about the intent of the author, the power precise words have for shaping specific meaning, and purpose-driven differences between writing poetically and prosaically.

Conclusion

The concept of productive failure is more a posture toward learning than a particular process or product in the classroom. All three of these projects could be presented and graded as if a particular outcome is preferable, and thus more correct, than others. Taken a step further, all of the concepts in these units could be taught via identification and description, as is often the case in secondary classrooms. But that emphasis on knowing more than doing is a cultural imposition on classroom practice and student learning expectations—one that tends to limit avenues of deep, experientially situated intellectual growth. Engaging new concepts in ways that embrace constructing students' knowledge through creative acts and incentivize failure as necessary for both the creative and intellectual work they are doing can shift that culture in the best possible ways. Even if this approach is taken in a mere handful of strategically timed situations across a term, those experiences can drive home lessons generally identified as critical by standards systems and classroom educators alike. And it might just create more writers along the way.

Notes

1 Richard Beach, Amanda Haertling Thein, and Allen Webb, *Teaching to Exceed the English Language Arts Common Core State Standards: A Critical Inquiry Approach for 6–12 Classrooms*, 2nd edn. (London: Routledge, 2016), 223–4.
2 Maartje Buijs and Wilfried Admiraal, "Homework Assignments to Enhance Student Engagement in Secondary Education," *European Journal of Psychology of Education* 28, no. 3 (2013): 768.
3 Paul Vermette and Chandra Foote, "Constructivist Philosophy and Cooperative Learning Practice: Toward Integration and Reconciliation in Secondary Classrooms," *American Secondary Education* 30, no. 1 (2001): 33.
4 CCSS.ELA-LITERACY.W.9-10.3. All standards referenced in this chapter come from National Governors Association Center for Best Practices, Council of Chief

State School Officers, *Common Core State Standards for English Language Arts & Literacy in History/Social Studies, Science, and Technical Subjects* (Washington, DC: National Governors Association Center for Best Practices, Council of Chief State School, 2010).

5   CCSS.ELA-LITERACY.W.9-10.3.C.
6   CCSS.ELA-LITERACY.W11-12.5.
7   This meets the standards' demands that students use technology to consider the demands of publication. CCSS.ELA-LITERACY.W.9-10.6.
8   CCSS.ELA-LITERACY.W.9-10.6.
9   CCSS.ELA-LITERACY.W.9-10.2.C.
10 CCSS.ELA-LITERACY.W.9-10.9.A.
11 CCSS.ELA-LITERACY.W.9-10.3.D and CCSS.ELA-LITERACY.W.9-10.2.D.
12 The n+7 exercise is a product of the experimental French literary movement, OULIPO. In brief, it requires selecting an existing poem, identifying every noun in it, and then replacing each with the seventh noun after it in the dictionary in order to experience the elasticity of language and meaning. For a brief description with examples, see https://poets.org/text/brief-guide-oulipo
13 CCSS.ELA-LITERACY.RI.9-10.4.

8

Freedom in Limits: Using Demi-Rubrics to Evaluate Creative Work

John Belk
Southern Utah University

With the expansion of standardized testing at the K–8 levels and the rise of high-impact practices and outcomes-based learning across higher education, it is no surprise that secondary instructors have felt increasing pressure on all sides to quantify and normalize student evaluation practices. In English/Language Arts classrooms—particularly when creative writing assignments are involved—such pressure can feel disingenuous at best and restrictive at worst. After all, how does one standardize the judgment of an earnestly composed poem? This article suggests the use of demi-rubrics—non-quantitative grading heuristics that provide narrowly focused, outcomes-based evaluative standards—for use in secondary classrooms. As a hybrid assignment sheet and evaluative[1] mechanism, the demi-rubric provides standardized grading criteria at the conceptual and stylistic/mechanical levels while deliberately encouraging experimentation and play beyond the boundaries of those criteria.

This piece offers practical suggestions for the development and use of demi-rubrics in secondary classrooms and beyond. Drawn from scholarship in postsecondary Composition Studies, demi-rubrics narrowly focus evaluation on only a few specific criteria per assignment while otherwise encouraging a "pedagogical sandbox" environment that rewards innovation and play. This makes assignments easier to grade, requiring less time from the instructor because of the reduced evaluative criteria, while also increasing knowledge retention through narrowing student cognitive load. In doing so, demi-rubrics help create more inclusive evaluative practices for diverse student populations by establishing flexible borders for the sandbox rather than locking down the entire playground. Ultimately, the demi-rubric offers a way of balancing the accountability demands of standards-driven education without stifling what language acquisition, literacy, and composition scholars have termed a "pedagogy of play."[2]

Finally, it is not the purpose of this piece to interject in the long-standing debate over the efficacy of rubrics for instruction, evaluation, and/or assessment. Suffice it to say that rubrics hold great value when they are (1) tailored for specific, individual contexts[3] and (2) implemented by trained instructors.[4] Used appropriately, traditional rubrics provide greater clarity of expectations, greater evaluative consistency across students and classes, and greater transparency for secondary stakeholders such as administrators and parents. However, rubrics are not without well-documented shortcomings:[5] in particular, their flattening of "acceptable" language use; their sometimes-constraining emphasis on consistency and inter-rater reliability in evaluating writing; and their exchange of more holistic, humanistic (and perhaps human) evaluation practices for easily digestible quantitative measures. It is in addressing these shortcomings while preserving the positive aspects of traditional rubrics that demi-rubrics offer their most useful contributions.

What Is a Demi-Rubric?

To define what a demi-rubric is, I should begin by first providing a brief definition of traditional rubrics, which come in a variety of shapes and sizes reflecting the conventions and priorities of the disciplines in which they are used.[6] Across most fields, however, rubrics usually contain (1) criteria for evaluation, (2) a rating scale, and (3) explanatory indicators tied to that scale. A demi-rubric truncates 2 and 3, providing explicit criteria for evaluation while leaving the nuts and bolts of that evaluation deliberately vague. In much of the scholarship around using rubrics to evaluate student writing, such vaguery is viewed as one of the arch problems of poorly implemented rubric use.[7] However, in creative writing classrooms—and particularly secondary creative writing classrooms—the non-quantitative nature of demi-rubrics serves to open space for experimentation while still providing evaluative criteria for students to work within—or press against—as they write.

Demi-rubrics look like a slightly more complicated checklist[8] attached to a larger assignment sheet. They clearly delineate specific assignment criteria, grouping those criteria by the cognitive complexity of the task they require. For example, Table 8.1 shows a demi-rubric for a 3–5 poem portfolio required at the end of an introductory poetry unit. The various requirements are grouped vertically in conjunction with where their underlying objectives fall in Bloom's Taxonomy. For example, all Conceptual Requirements ask students to incorporate higher-order cognitive tasks that fall under the *create* and *evaluate* categories, such as evaluating how different line breaks might create different meanings or emotional connotations in their work. The Aesthetic Requirements ask students to *analyze* and *apply* their choice of poetic meters and forms in their own writing. And the Writing Requirements ask students to *remember* and *understand* basic mechanical elements of standardized American English in their poems.

One advantage of demi-rubrics such as the one above is they are both evaluative and pedagogical tools. The organization of the demi-rubric allows one to see at a glance how the learning outcomes of an assignment align with

Table 8.1 Sample Rubric

	Assignment Requirements	
Conceptual Requirements	**Aesthetic Requirements**	**Writing Requirements**
1. **Line and Stanza:** Your poems as a collection should display a purposeful use of line breaks, stanza organization, enjambment, and end-stops. 2. **Musicality:** All of your poems (even free verse) should experiment with musicality of language. 3. **Balance:** Your poems should balance the multiple layers of poetry we have discussed in class: the technical, aesthetic, emotional. 4. **Exploration:** Your poems should explore your subject matter, the language you use, and yourself.	1. **Special Form:** One poem should experiment with one of the special forms from our textbook or class discussion (e.g., cinquain, villanelle, ghazal, sestina). 2. **Free Verse:** One poem should experiment with free verse. 3. **Meter:** One poem should experiment with a formal meter. You can use a regular stress pattern (i.e., four stresses per line), or a full-blown metrical pattern (i.e., iambic pentameter). 4. **Radical Revision:** One poem should be a radical revision from an earlier draft (e.g., a haiku you turn into a sonnet).	1. One em dash 2. One end-stopped line 3. One slant rhyme 4. One creative gerund 5. One hyphen

the outcomes of the course and the larger curriculum. For example, if we look at the Common Core standards in Writing and Language for Grades 6–12, we can easily extrapolate from the demi-rubric how this single assignment emphasizes and even pushes the boundaries of the standards for (1) *Production and Distribution of Writing*, (2) *Conventions of Standard English*, (3) *Knowledge of Language*, and (4) *Vocabulary Acquisition and Use*.[9]

And this list is by no means exhaustive; the demi-rubric makes it easy to visualize how this assignment reinforces core standards for reading as well, such as analyzing the structure of a text and integrating content in diverse formats and media.[10] It also makes it apparent when an assignment asks too much and might be improved by narrowing its focus. Finally, using the demi-rubric, an instructor can also see if certain outcomes/standards are not being addressed and alter the criteria of an assignment to include them. For example, when adapting the demi-rubric from Table 8.1 for this essay, I realized it did little to emphasize revision, a major component of the Writing Core Standards. Of course, students did plenty of revision in class with multiple small activities and workshops, but it was simple enough to add an explicit "Radical Revision" criterion to the demi-rubric for greater emphasis on this key skill. Put another way, the visualization of the demi-rubric helped me see a gap in my own standards-based assignment design and remedy it.

Finally, because they eliminate quantitative evaluative markers—that is, they don't assign points to the various categories or criteria—demi-rubrics are ideal for the kind of holistic grading that encourages experimentation in creative writing classrooms. When presented with traditional rubrics, students tend to focus overwhelmingly on what is explicit in that rubric to the detriment of more creative approaches. This should not be surprising, as it is a means of reducing cognitive load for students dividing their attention between five, six, or even seven other classes. As Jeanetta Miller reminds us, "A student in survival mode looks for the most direct route to the target grade,"[11] eschewing experimentation and risk in favor of a solid B+. For students, "investing personal passion and imagination in simultaneous assignments from five or six disciplines must seem not only impractical but downright irresponsible,"[12] and so rubrics become an unwitting tool of triage, allowing students to quickly complete an assignment to a "good enough" standard in order to refocus their energy on other work. I suspect this is especially true in high school creative writing classes in particular, where students under high cognitive loads prioritize other classes deemed "more important" by counselors, parents, and college admissions officers.

Demi-rubrics, however, encourage experimentation without sacrificing the valuable scaffolding of traditional rubrics. Through their clear design and criteria, demi-rubrics remain a tool for student self-monitoring and self-assessment of important components of writing, which is perhaps the most pedagogically significant function of traditional rubrics.[13] But demi-rubrics do so while holding space open for creative, process-oriented approaches to the assignment: instead of grammar and mechanics being evaluated on a numerical scale based on errors present or absent in a final draft, students are given five mechanical tasks to demonstrate in their writing but are left to their own creative devices for how and where to achieve those tasks. The end result is the same—students must still demonstrate effective use of a semicolon or hyphen—but the focus is shifted. Demi-rubrics reframe our evaluative practices from punishment to reward: instead of reducing points for grammatical "failures," we reward creative grammatical successes, emphasizing the process of writing rather than punishing an "inadequate" product.

In short, demi-rubrics straddle a line between existing evaluative mechanisms: they are more complex and more thoughtfully derived than simple checklists while being less restrictive and complicated than traditional rubrics. Because of their simplicity, demi-rubrics are an effective evaluative tool for creative work especially, but that design also makes them a useful tool for standards-based assignment development, showing at a glance how a given assignment aligns with or fails to address particular learning outcomes. Finally, demi-rubrics balance assignment scaffolding with open-ended requirements and criteria, encouraging multiple paths to achieving specific learning outcomes and refocusing instructor evaluative practices from product (What did a student achieve here?) to process (How did they achieve it?). But demi-rubrics offer another advantage for evaluating creative work in secondary environments: they shift the emphasis of grading away from assessment and reporting, reframing the act as a conversation, a point further unpacked in the next section.

Why Demi-Rubrics: Grading by the Numbers or Grading for Learning?

Traditional rubrics emerged primarily as a way to streamline evaluation of student writing, offering quantifiable and specific criteria that can be easily and quickly judged and marked.[14] In creative writing particularly, rubrics offer a measure of academic rigor and respectability that—in best-case scenarios—reinforces the disciplinarity and teachability of the subject.[15] After all, if we can clearly identify what makes a piece of writing "good" in the context of our classrooms, we can better teach "good" writing and demonstrate the effectiveness of our teaching to various stakeholders in empirical ways. Such rigor and quantifiability is especially important at the secondary level, with increased focus on standards-driven education, one-size-fits-all assessment, and heightened empirical accountability. In short, if grading at the secondary level is becoming more about bureaucratic accountability than student learning, then rubrics offer an alluring shortcut to such labor.

However, if grading is about more than simply communicating student successes and shortcomings to various administrative stakeholders—if it is about actually and significantly improving student learning and writing—then perhaps there are better tools. While the advantages of using rubrics have been well documented,[16] they are still prone to three main drawbacks in terms of improving student learning: (1) overly rigid evaluation criteria/practices, (2) overly complex evaluation criteria/practices, and (3) unrealistic evaluation criteria/practices that emphasize product over process. Furthermore, recent scholarship has begun to question the objectivity and rigor that rubrics promise, with significantly varied findings on evaluative reliability and validity.[17] This is not to add to what Jinrong Li and Peggy Lindsey call the "cautious or even hostile" voices suggesting that rubrics create more problems than they solve,[18] but instead to offer demi-rubrics as a localized solution to some of these drawbacks for secondary creative writing classrooms.

To begin, where traditional rubrics focus on attaching quantitative values to various standards for student writing—an approach that necessarily precludes conversation[19]—demi-rubrics instead open space for conversation. Consider the "Line and Stanza" criterion from the poetry demi-rubric in Table 8.1: "Your poems as a collection should display a purposeful use of line breaks, stanza organization, enjambment, and end-stops." The use of the word "purposeful" here is deliberately vague, allowing students a number of ways to achieve the criterion. Furthermore, students submit a brief cover letter with each assignment where they reflect on how they achieved or struggled with particular criteria from the demi-rubric (see Appendix 8.1). This helps guide and simplify commenting, as I can respond directly and conversationally to what a student was trying to do, giving constructive feedback for improvement or praising a job well done. This also helps me provide more tailored feedback for each criterion than merely assigning a score, an especially pressing need in creative writing classes where student writing is much more likely to stretch discursive norms.

Such a conversational approach to commenting leads to the next advantage demi-rubrics offer over traditional rubrics: they can simplify the evaluative process, ultimately creating less—or at least simpler—grading work. By encouraging conversational evaluation and placing the onus of carrying that conversation on the student, demi-rubrics give specific targets for our comments. Put another way, demi-rubrics provide scaffolding for both student writing and instructor response. To continue the previous example, a student's cover letter might indicate they chose to break the third stanza of their poem in an unusual fashion to place emphasis on a particular word. My comment, then, can simply explain why this was successful or not while still praising their creative attempt at experimenting with line breaks. In effect, demi-rubrics, especially when used in concert with reflective cover letters, allow students to tell *us* what to focus on, thereby softening the most intellectually and emotionally demanding part of grading.[20]

In addition to simplifying the grading process, demi-rubrics also offer a more realistic framework than traditional rubrics for evaluating writing. After all, when was the last time you used a rubric to evaluate a piece of writing in your day-to-day life? It is more likely you made an informed but non-quantitative judgment against a set of personal criteria (e.g., "I thought the last season of *Game of Thrones* was lackluster primarily because of inconsistent character development"). This of course leaves the door open for conversation. Your friend disagrees and says Dany's arc was always meant to end as it did. Perhaps you both agree on a crude ranking ("Well, it was better than season seven; I'd give it a B-"), but in reality, evaluations of creative work in the real world are much less statistically rigorous, reliable, and valid than evaluative rubrics in education might lead us to believe. The fact is, traditional rubrics at the secondary level evolved to facilitate a certain philosophy of grading more concerned with gathering and communicating data than improving student learning. Such an approach is not without merit, as we do not teach in a vacuum, and we should be accountable for the learning we help facilitate. But it does muddy the waters between evaluation and assessment, shifting the focus of our labor from improving student performance to reporting on it. Demi-rubrics give us a mechanism for remaining accountable—we can easily show alignment between the criteria from a demi-rubric and the board-approved standards of our curriculum—while refocusing the realities of our day-to-day work back to teaching and learning.

Finally, demi-rubrics help create more inclusive evaluation practices by allowing students agency in focusing the instructor's evaluative gaze. By foregrounding a conversational approach to commenting, demi-rubrics help shift the discussion away from specific scores as well as from "right" and "wrong" toward "effective" and "ineffective," respecting students' rights to their own language[21]—a key concept in college composition instruction that need not be antithetical to secondary creative writing classes. This allows teachers to set evaluative criteria, but it allows students an opportunity to explain their attempts to meet those criteria, giving voice to their decision-making and encouraging reflection on their writing process. After all, if writing, and especially creative writing, is truly an exercise in "ill-structured problem solving,"[22] the imposition of unnecessarily rigid evaluative criteria is doomed to exclusionary failure by privileging certain communication and problem-solving practices over others, doubly disadvantaging students from minority and socioeconomically challenged backgrounds. However, if we view writing as Joseph Petraglia suggests—as instrumental, transactional, and rhetorical[23]—then the demi-rubric's conversational approach allows for a much more inclusive evaluative framework that (1) values new/creative ways of communicating and problem-solving and (2) is driven by students themselves.

Conclusions

By providing clear assignment criteria without quantitative evaluative baggage, demi-rubrics offer productive limits for writing assignments that paradoxically encourage creativity and experimentation. This makes demi-rubrics ideal for secondary creative writing settings, where external standards necessitate clear assessment protocols for amorphous skills such as "creativity" that are difficult to evaluate, much less assess. In short, demi-rubrics offer the best of both worlds, providing the scaffolding of traditional rubrics while encouraging the open creativity of more holistic approaches to grading writing.

This is not to say demi-rubrics are without drawbacks. Their lack of quantitative evaluative mechanisms certainly reduces statistical reliability, particularly inter-rater, and validity compared to traditional rubrics. However, I am inclined to view this positively, particularly for secondary creative writing. After all, the purpose of rubrics with high inter-rater reliability is that they can be used by any teacher in any writing classroom to achieve roughly the same evaluative results. But *should* that be the case for creative writing? Should we—regardless of background, values, experiences, and education—evaluate creative works with such uniform precision? Perhaps the greatest asset of the demi-rubric, then, has nothing to do with grading or evaluation or assessment at all;

perhaps its greatest value lies in its ability to refocus our own presuppositions about what "good" creative writing is and what such writing—in the hands of our students who are so full of possibility—can do to make the world better.

Notes

1. For clarity, I distinguish between evaluation and assessment in this piece as follows: evaluation is the practice of measuring student knowledge/skill in a particular domain for the purpose of certifying competence (i.e., grading) while assessment is the measuring of student learning/performance for the purpose of improving pedagogy.
2. The most comprehensive resource on pedagogy of play research for K–12 instructors is Harvard's Project Zero Resource page "Pedagogies of Play," *Project Zero*, Harvard Graduate School of Education, https://pz.harvard.edu/projects/pedagogy-of-play.
3. Chris Anson, Deanna P. Daniels, Pamela Flash, and Amy L. Housley Gaffney, "Big Rubrics and Weird Genres: The Futility of Using Generic Assessment Tools across Diverse Instructional Contexts," *The Journal of Writing Assessment* 5, no. 1 (2012).
4. Jinyan Huang, "Factors Affecting the Assessment of ESL Students' Writing," *International Journal of Applied Educational Studies* 5, no. 1 (2009): 4.
5. Maja Wilson, "Why I Won't Be Using Rubrics to Respond to Students' Writing," *English Journal* 96, no. 4 (2007): 62–6; John R. Boulet, Thomas A. Rebbecchi, Elizabeth C. Denton, Danette W. McKinley, and Gerald P. Whelan, "Assessing the Written Communication Skills of Medical School Graduates," *Advances in Health Sciences Education* 9, no. 1 (2004): 47–60; Andrew D. Schenck and Eoin Daly, "Building a Better Mousetrap: Replacing Subjective Writing Rubrics with More Empirically-Sound Alternative for EFL Learners," *Creative Education* 3, no. 8 (2012): 1320–5; Amy E. Covil, "College Students' Use of a Writing Rubric: Effect on Quality of Writing, Self-Efficacy, and Writing Practices," *Journal of Writing Assessment* 5, no. 1 (2012).
6. For more on rubric differences across disciplines—and why generic rubrics are ineffective as a one-size-fits-all measure for both assessment and evaluation—see Anson et al., "Big Rubrics."
7. Jinrong Li and Peggy Lindsey, "Understanding Variations between Student and Teacher Application of Rubrics," *Assessing Writing* 26 (2015): 78.
8. For years, rubric design specialists have been arguing *against* "checklist" rubrics because they often create unclear expectations, muddied understandings, and little objective consistency for evaluative criteria. However, as I will show in this piece, demi-rubrics can avoid these pitfalls while still embodying a belief that

creative writing is markable beyond simple value judgments and, by extension then, teachable. For more on this debate, see Susan M. Brookhart, *How to Create and Use Rubrics for Formative Assessment and Grading* (Alexandria, VA: ASCD, 2013), 76; Merilee Griffin, "What Is a Rubric?" in *Assessing Outcomes and Improving Achievement: Tips and Tools for Using Rubrics*, ed. Terrel L. Rhodes (Washington, DC: AAC&U, 2010), 9; Fay Weldon, "On Assessing Creative Writing," *International Journal for the Practice and Theory of Creative Writing* 6, no. 3 (2009): 168.

9   Outcomes have been excerpted from the 2010 *Common Core Standards for English/Language Arts and Literacy* found here: http://www.corestandards.org/wp-content/uploads/ELA_Standards1.pdf

10 Ibid.

11 Jeanetta Miller, "Weaving Imagination into an Academic Framework: Attitudes, Assignments, and Assessments," *The English Journal* 99, no. 2 (2009): 68.

12 Ibid.

13 Kendall L. Bradford, Amanda C. Newland, Audrey C. Rule, and Sarah E. Montgomery, "Rubrics as a Tool in Writing Instruction: Effects on the Opinion Essays of First and Second Graders," *Early Childhood Education Journal* 44 (2016): 464.

14 Susan M. Brookhart and Fei Chen, "The Quality and Effectiveness of Descriptive Rubrics," *Educational Review* 67, no. 3 (2015): 343–44.

15 Alicita Rodriguez, "The 'Problem' of Creative Writing: Using Grading Rubrics Based on Narrative Theory as Solution," *New Writing: The International Journal for the Practice and Theory of Creative Writing* 5, no. 3 (2008): 168.

16 Heidi Andrade, "Using Rubrics to Promote Thinking and Learning," *Educational Leadership* 57, no. 5 (2000): 1–18; Heidi Andrade and Ying Du, "Student Perspectives on Rubric-Referenced Assessment," *Practical Assessment, Research and Evaluation* 10, no. 3 (2005): 13–11; Todd H. Sundeen, "Instructional Rubrics: Effects of Presentation Options on Writing Quality," *Assessing Writing* 21 (2014): 74–88; Brookhart and Chen, "The Quality and Effectiveness"; Anders Jonsson and Gunilla Svingby, "The Use of Scoring Rubrics: Reliability, Validity, and Educational Consequences," *Educational Research Review* 2, no. 2 (2007): 130–44.

17 Ali Reza Rezaei and Michael Lovorn, "Reliability and Validity of Rubrics for Assessment through Writing," *Assessing Writing* 15 (2010): 18–39; Kerry Hunter and Peter Docherty, "Reducing Variation in the Assessment of Student Writing," *Assessment and Evaluation in Higher Education* 36, no. 1 (2011): 109–24; Huang, "Factors Affecting the Assessment of ESL Students' Writing"; Peggy Lindsey and Deborah J. Crusan, "How Faculty Attitudes and Expectations toward Student Nationality Affect Writing Assessment," *Across the Disciplines: A Journal of Language, Learning, and Academic Writing* 8 (2011): 1–35.

18 Li and Lindsey, "Understanding Variations," 68.

19 Wilson, "Why I Won't Be Using Rubrics," 65.
20 My own informal observation since implementing demi-rubrics and cover letters is that my average commenting time has dropped from 12 minutes per essay to 9 minutes. Across a full college-level teaching load, this has shortened my total grading time from 18.5 hours per assignment to 14 hours—no small reduction, especially when considered across an entire semester with five major assignments where this change has saved me on average 22.5 hours of total grading time over the course of a full academic term.
21 Conference on College Composition and Communication, "Students' Right to Their Own Language," *College Composition and Communication* 25, no. 3 (Fall 1974): 1–32.
22 Joseph Petraglia, "Writing as an Unnatural Act," in *Reconceiving Writing, Rethinking Writing Instruction*, ed. Joseph Petraglia (London: Routledge, 1995), 80.
23 Ibid., 81.

Part Two

Creative Foundations: The Benefits of Prioritizing Creative Nonfiction in the Secondary Standards-Based Classroom

Sara C. Pendleton
Grace Brethren Senior High School

Creative nonfiction is seldom prioritized in the secondary standards-based classroom. If taught, it's usually the bonus unit at the end of the school year once other units, usually with more easily quantifiable benefits, have reached completion. However, my research and practice demonstrate that creative nonfiction should function as the foundational unit that all other writing builds from in English Language Arts classrooms. Although creative nonfiction can be daunting to educators without a background in creative writing, this chapter will equip even the most hesitant teacher as a practitioner of this method. In order to find success with this methodology, integrating hospitality into one's pedagogy, implementing a writing process, and facilitating collaboration are essential. The most salient evidence of student success is found when transitioning students from the creative nonfiction unit into formal, research-based writing units. My findings demonstrate that students who experienced the creative nonfiction unit were far more confident writers than those in previous semesters who did not have the same foundational unit.

Pedagogy

Five major premises inform my pedagogy: demonstrating hospitality, valuing student experiences, prioritizing student choice, promoting an educator-as-facilitator perspective, and providing opportunities for collaboration. While these foundational pieces originate with various educational theories, when successfully combined, the subsequent classroom environment is electric.

Hospitality comes first, through physically welcoming students into my classroom. Before I started teaching, my friend Heather shared with me that she shook every student's hand during every class to gauge their mood each day. I followed her model and then continued with a posture of intellectual hospitality[1] where I seek first to understand without being combative or dismissive when interacting with new theories, people, and opinions. I promise intellectual hospitality to my students and also commission them to follow a similar practice.

Once this is explained, I detail various writing assignments students will compose in my class, informing them that they will propose topics and pitch them to me for each essay they write. I encourage them to choose topics they're actually interested in. At this point, I offer a brief monologue acknowledging the value of big topics/texts like *Hamlet* but explain that I prefer they write on makeup production ethics or steroid use in the Major Leagues. I highlight that I care about their experiences and interests outside the classroom and want to grant them opportunity to research what interests them. I explain that they'll be able to collaborate with each other almost every day through table discussion, debates, and peer reviews. This helps them understand that I run my class as a workshop, seldom lecturing. I want students to engage the process with the necessary scaffolding to foster curiosity and discover their own voices.

That said, I cannot take credit for these methodologies. Theorists have assigned the act of valuing prior knowledge to feminist pedagogy, where "[w]e developed a scale to measure teachers' commitment to four facts of women's studies pedagogy described by feminist pedagogic theorists: creation of participatory classroom communities, validation of personal experience, encouragement of social understanding and activism, and development of critical thinking skills/open-mindedness."[2] Students enter a classroom with differing experiences and burdens; thus, it's critical to actively engage students' differences. Furthermore, bell hooks's research in pedagogy establishes similar findings regarding valuing previous experience, giving students freedom of choice and promoting an educator-as-facilitator classroom. When teachers relinquish authoritative control and give students the opportunity of choice and freedom, the results are higher comprehension levels and superior student-teacher relationships.[3] Jarring as this may be to some, allowing students to take ownership of their own education provides a much richer academic experience while also preparing them for college and beyond. As hooks contends, most students are capable of rote memorization, but through challenging them to do more, they think more, thus creating more interactive classrooms.

Finally, the aforementioned pedagogical perspectives are also found incorporated into constructivist pedagogy, a theory with five major premises: respecting student background through individual attention; fostering group dialogue and collaboration; facilitating planned and unplanned discussion around domain knowledge; providing students opportunities to engage in purposeful tasks that determine, challenge, reinforce, or add to prior understanding; and developing students' understanding of their own learning processes.[4] Following these guidelines in the secondary ELA classroom creates a more collaborative space where prior knowledge is highly valued while students corroborate previous viewpoints with new knowledge.

Process

Given that teacher-student collaboration works best when the instructor does not hold fast to her desire to maintain authority and control, a democratic classroom is one of the best climates for collaboration to authentically and properly mature. In a shared study, college writing instructor Missy Nieveen Phegley and high school writing teacher Janelle Oxford connect their separate classroom environments and demonstrate that collaboration and the implementation of social networking can enhance students' writing and educational journeys. They highlight the many social benefits of shared work: "Collaboration such as ours allows students to engage with others unlike themselves as they consider how their writing affects various readers."[5] Their research concluded that collaboration helps students at all stages, regardless of specific grade levels or regions. Collaborative experiences pair less advanced writers with more advanced writers, allowing their writing to mature while their understanding of each other expands. If a teacher establishes collaboration as the cultural norm and positions writing as process and not product, eventually students will be less apprehensive about sharing their "imperfect" work with peers. Although I avoid quoting Anne Lamott directly in class, identifying that we all should have "shitty first drafts" is a notion specific to this perspective and must be identified in the writing classroom.[6]

In terms of a process orientation to writing, Donald Murray also encourages educators to value process over product. He found that "instead of teaching finished writing, we should teach unfinished writing, and then glory in its unfinishedness. We work with the language in action. We share with our students the continual excitement of choosing one word instead of another, of searching for one true word."[7] Murray breaks composition into three stages—prewriting, writing, and rewriting—with prewriting taking up 85 percent of the process. Emphasis is placed on prewriting and rewriting as having greater value than drafting. In the classroom, Murray contends that "[t]o be a teacher of a process such as this takes qualities too few of us have, but which most of us can develop. We have to be quiet, to listen, to respond. We are not the initiator or the motivator; we are the reader, the recipient."[8] Educators must be supporters of the writing process rather than judges, because writers are not composing as a means to an end; rather, they are authentically writing to either express, experience, or argue. This does not mean high school teachers should discontinue grading essays, as we have an obligation to provide feedback and evaluation for students. However, through drafting and student-teacher conferences, targeted questions, and collaborative responses intended to inspire better writing, teachers also inspire better grades. This practice is especially important when asking students to write about their personal experiences.

Implementing a well-articulated writing process is essential. In a perfect world, students would start their freewrites the day a paper is assigned, then progress to brainstorming, drafting, revising, and editing intuitively. The reality, though, is they are not trained to identify the necessity of process. For example, at Back to School Night each year, I tell parents I am trying to avoid the 11:00 p.m. knock on their bedroom door, asking for help on a paper due the next morning. Many parents harbor just as much writing anxiety as their children, so the more opportunity provided for students to practice process, the less pressure they experience when they work at home. And yet students seldom follow my advice initially without process benchmarks in place for them. For this reason, I guide them through the different steps of the writing process for each assignment. While this might seem like an extensive list, it is incredible to watch students grow through this process. In addition, my grading has become far easier because many sets of eyes have seen each paper prior to my assessment.

Nonfiction as Foundation

Creative nonfiction utilizes literary techniques to illuminate true stories—different from a more rigid model found in thesis-driven writing, creative nonfiction gives permission to employ onomatopoeia, metaphor, and descriptive language. The integration of such techniques often requires the writer to tap into his or her creativity. Beginning the semester with creative nonfiction poses a challenge initially, because, up to this point, I find that most students have not written creatively since grade school. Upon entry into junior and senior high, their focus has had to be on research-based expository writing. Although such writing is valuable in academia, it is not the only valuable genre. Furthermore, identifying the importance of personal story is necessary to help students recognize other expository writing as valuable. It never takes much coercing, as many students initially think creative nonfiction is easier than research-based writing and willingly jump in. Ironically, they usually find that writing creative nonfiction can be painful or exhausting in a way academic forms are not. This, I explain, is because of the deeply intimate critical thinking demanded of a writer when he or she composes nonfiction work. That said, when we write our own stories, the benefit readers experience is exponential because we are moved by each other's stories. Like any teacher who tries to stay connected to high school pop culture, I reference reality television as much as possible. I ask them, "Why do you think America is so obsessed with reality TV?" Usually my students are quick to answer, as they often recognize this obsession in their own life. After some group collaboration, each class typically lands on something like this: we are moved by true stories. (Huzzah! One point for the teacher who connects these ideas to *The Bachelor* or *Keeping up with the Kardashians* in class.)

After this, I transition to reading a nonfiction piece with my students, usually an essay written by a woman who opted for an abortion after finding out that her child would have numerous postnatal medical issues. Since I teach at a private Christian school, many of my students' pro-life convictions run deep. Prior to distributing the essay, I ask my students to write on a slip of paper what kind of person might have an abortion. As I walk around the classroom, I see words like "irresponsible" or "high schooler" or "slut" written on their pages. After giving sufficient time, I ask them to pause and actively engage intellectual hospitality.

After passing out their copies, I have them annotate the piece with hand-drawn emojis before calling on students to read aloud in turn. They discover the author is married, has other children and a full-time job as a lawyer, and sends her young children to soccer camp each summer while worrying about scraped knees and grass stains. They read about the agonizing pain she experienced when the baby seized inside her and the similar excruciating pain she felt at night, staring at her ceiling while contemplating whether or not to abort her baby.

The purpose of this activity is not to convince students of specific political viewpoint but rather to complicate their own black-and-white thinking; I strive to demonstrate the way stories can disrupt unconscious biases we seldom engage with. When asked, all students claim that the narrative evokes empathy within them. Specifically, it speaks a different narrative than they expect and alters an otherwise unconscious bias and single-story that many of them possess. After this, I ask my students to write their own nonfiction essays and push their readers out of monotony by using the power of story.

Practice

Like many educators, and specifically those in the secondary standards-based classroom, I must establish scaffolding for my students to write with specific process and intention. Left to their own writing process, they will seldom begin any earlier than just before the deadline. With this in mind, I assign every aspect of the writing process as classwork or homework, guiding students through the process of freewriting, brainstorming, outlining, drafting, editing, composing a final draft, and approaching revision. When I describe this method to other teachers, their first concern is all the grading associated with multiple levels of scaffolded homework. However, I don't grade it all. I give work credit/no credit some days, leave it unchecked others, and occasionally collect it and provide thorough feedback. Students don't know how each assignment will be evaluated, so they are motivated to do them all. I always collect drafts and final submissions for feedback, as those benchmarks ensure comprehension. However, with assignments like brainstorming, I'm not concerned with specific student practices. Clusters, lists, or full-text plans are all appropriate and personal choices. Students also enjoy more freedom while writing creative nonfiction. Thesis-driven essays require a more prescribed outline and essay format with source requirements, but creative essays allow students to discover a process and format that works best of them. Once they identify this, I encourage them as much as possible, because empowering students along their own paths is critical in helping them fall in love with learning.

Many scholars and writers acknowledge the benefit of writing specifically about experience. Julia Cameron's *The Artist's Way*[9] prescribes mandatory "morning pages" in which writers write something each morning: summaries of the previous day, a dream, a past experience, etc. Additionally, writing about our lives helps us to heal from trauma and painful experiences. Cameron acknowledges that "expressive writing is known to help assuage psychological trauma and improve mood. Now studies suggest that such writing, characterized by descriptions of one's deepest thoughts and feelings, also benefits physical health."[10] When I first ask students to write overcoming something in their lives, most begin with lists including losing the state football championship game or overcoming stage fright at the fall talent show. However, once prompted to ruminate on more personal options, some consider writing about their parents' divorces or a mother's suicide attempt. I always write on the board, "What story inside of you needs to be written?" Sometimes students aren't ready to dig deeply into their psyche, but those who do describe the process as liberating. Giving students a platform to process prior pain is crucial to their development and something we have the honor of doing in ELA classrooms. While a chemistry class is incredibly important, it does not give students the opportunity to process their father abandoning the family, their grandparents dying, or their sister experiencing sexual assault. ELA does.

Allowing students to write creative nonfiction as the foundational unit of study empowers them as practitioners. When given authority over their own story, they build writing muscles and achieve higher levels of critical thinking, and this confidence often transfers to our next unit on rhetoric. While there are many differences between creative nonfiction and persuasive writing, they share a core principle: put something that matters on paper. Students need a platform of authority, and we must empower their attempts to build confidence in their discourse.

Unit Creation

When I developed my curriculum, I was most excited about the creative nonfiction unit. I wanted to present authors and texts that matter; after all, nonfiction is the biggest tool in demolishing unconscious bias and single-story thinking. While I wanted to simply assign readings from the likes of Amy Tan, David Sedaris, and Anne Lamott and just sit in a circle discussing how incredible each is, the standards-based classroom doesn't always lend itself to such dreams. However, standards are only intimidating when we don't look at them with specific contextual pragmatism. In this unit, I address Common Core State Standards[11] with ease by incorporating narratives, argument, precise wording, and textual support into most assignments. The wonderful opportunity provided by teaching standards through creative nonfiction is that students can be less jarred by the conduit; if I taught figurative writing and style while teaching the thesis-driven research paper, students would likely be overwhelmed and resent both. However, when I ask them to describe their personal story with exceptionally figurative language, they engage more willingly, I suspect, because they've lived it already. They know what the banana bread smelled like, or what it felt like when they got caught cheating on a test, or exactly where they were when they learned they got the scholarship. In contrast, they don't always know how to identify the rhetoric of the food industry with figurative language, because they aren't yet aware of how they have experienced it. However, once they begin practicing the standards-based skills in a creative nonfiction unit, students are much quicker to apply those skills to the papers in coming units.

Conclusion

When I was in high school, many of my teachers utilized a form of teaching Paulo Freire identified as banking method of instruction. They taught, I memorized, and they tested me. However, a few teachers opposed such pedagogy and required much more from me. They emphasized curiosity, questioning, and working collaboratively. These are the teachers I remember most fondly—the ones who most impacted my trajectory, then and now. This is what creative nonfiction can do in your classroom: it can change your students. Ultimately, that's what we all want as educators. In my class, and especially during our unit on creative nonfiction, I know I can impact my students most positively by integrating hospitality into every lesson and then requiring them to share responsibility for their own growth.

Notes

1 Diana Pavlac Glyer, "Intellectual Hospitality," *Azusa Pacific University*, July 21, 2015, www.apu.edu/articles/intellectual-hospitality.
2 Francis L. Hoffmann and Jayne E. Stake, "Feminist Pedagogy in Theory and Practice: An Empirical Investigation," *NWSA Journal* 10, no. 1 (1998): 79.
3 bell hooks, *Teaching to Transgress: Education as the Practice of Freedom* (London: Routledge, 1994).
4 Victoria Richardson, "Constructivist Pedagogy," *Teachers College Record* 105, no. 9 (2003): 1623–40.
5 Missy Nieveen Phegley and Janelle Oxford, "Cross-Level Collaboration: Students and Teachers Learning from Each Other," *The English Journal* 99, no. 5 (2010): 27–34.
6 Anne Lamott, *Bird by Bird: Some Instructions on Writing and Life* (New York: First Anchor Books, 1994), 21.

7   Donald M. Murray, *A Writer Teaches Writing: A Practical Method of Teaching Composition* (New York: Houghton Mifflin, 1968), 4.
8   Ibid., 5.
9   Julia Cameron, *The Artist's Way: A Spiritual Path to Higher Creativity* (New York: Tarcher/Putnam, 2006).
10 Tori Rodriguez, "Writing Can Help Injuries Heal Faster," *Scientific American*, November 1, 2013, https://www.scientificamerican.com/article/writing-can-help-injuries-heal-faster.
11 CCSS.ELA-LITERACY.W.11–12.3: Write narratives to develop real or imagined experiences or events using effective technique, well-chosen details, and well-structured event sequences; CCSS.ELA-LITERACY.W.11–12.3.B: Use narrative techniques, such as dialogue, pacing, description, reflection, and multiple plot lines, to develop experiences, events, and/or characters; CCSS.ELA-LITERACY.W.11–12.3.D: Use precise words and phrases, telling details, and sensory language to convey a vivid picture of the experiences, events, setting, and/or characters.Standards taken from National Governors Association Center for Best Practices, Council of Chief State School Officers, *Common Core State Standards for English Language Arts & Literacy in History/Social Studies, Science, and Technical Subjects* (Washington, DC: National Governors Association Center for Best Practices, Council of Chief State School, 2010).

10

Unruining Poetry

Tim Staley
Oñate High School

The Hook

Somebody taught me how to read and it was amazing—for about five minutes. Once they identified me as a reader, they fired on me like a Panzer tank: answer these questions about what you read, write an essay about what you read, diagram what you read, read for this many minutes, underline what you read, summarize what you read, discover the theme of what you read, write little notes in the margins of what you read, write in the style of what you read, compare and contrast what you read, extract the figurative language from what you read—the demands went on and on and on. The experience I describe here is not unique; turning what student's read into a task is classic English teacher artillery.

Similarly, students learning poetry are asked to rhyme before they've truly befriended any syllables, before they've been properly swooned by pronunciation. Somewhere along the line, bless their hearts, the traditional methods of teaching poetry have ruined the form. The first time I was taught poetry in high school I had to memorize and recite the General Prologue to *The Canterbury Tales*. Jumping through that hoop taught me more about rote memorization and public speaking than poetry. I became a poet despite that assignment. I became a poet because poetry is where you get to be funny, say what you want, and nothing has to make sense. For me poetry has always been a break from the boring stuff. My goal is to help students see it that way, and even with such a great goal, I still get lots of pushback.

Let's start with some snappy comebacks to our students' most common complaints about reading poetry:

Student: I don't get it.
Teacher: Lower your standards.
Student: It's too dark.

Teacher: Death is the only mystery left.
Student: It's boring.
Teacher: OK.
Student: I don't understand.
Teacher: It's not rocket science.
Student: I don't like it.
Teacher: No poet in the history of poets ever sat down to write a poem designed to torture you.

Why do we hear these complaints from our students? Is it because they're told poems can have multiple interpretations, but the only interpretation that's ever on the test comes from their teacher? Is it because poetry, especially in our hands, has the reputation of being even more torturous than normal English class activities? Is it meter? Is it the Petrarchan sonnet? Is it the sestina? Is it all those Greco-Roman allusions? Perhaps it's just plain old fear—fear that students might not know the right answers, especially when the answers that matter in poetry can't be found on an answer key. (Perhaps this also frightens the teacher.) Furthermore, just because a student has a feeling of understanding about a poem, what have you done to instill in them the confidence they'll need to share that feeling with you or their peers?

The techniques outlined in this chapter are designed to bolster your students' poetic confidence by demystifying poetry. If poets do anything, they play with language—aggressively—to make it suit their needs. By providing students an opportunity to engage in that play, we give them incentive for engagement. And isn't engagement the prerequisite for every Common Core standard? Our students don't come with a built-in desire to out-benchmark every benchmark, but they do come with a desire to play. Don't worry though. These playful activities comprehensively build skill development aligned to the Common Core State Standards for English Language Arts.[1]

The Ear

There's a poster in my classroom with this Robert Frost quote: "The ear is the only true writer and the only true reader." Even though analyzing the impact of language that's "particularly fresh, engaging, or beautiful" is part of our reading standards,[2] we haven't spent enough time cultivating our students' ears. What if we let them decide for themselves which sounds they found pleasurable and which they didn't? The alphabet holds the notes the poet gets to play. Those sounds are the colors on the poet's palette and contribute to the reader's joy. If the poet uses more than one language, they get even more notes to choose from, thus increasing the odds of readers' joy. I like to play this up, as many of my student are more comfortable with Spanish than English. You don't have to be an expert with a language to hear it as resonating sounds; in fact, the more you know a language the harder it is to linger in the aural pleasure zone. Why have our students never filled pages with sounds the way they've filled them so freely with the scribbles of a crayon?

Poet Connie Voisine was one of my teachers in graduate school. One day she said, "Poetry is half ideas, half music." It turns out the ideas half is easier to swallow under the influence of the music half. Imagine if you told your students, "We're not going to talk about the ideas half, what things mean. We're just going to listen to the music half. There's no quiz, no vocabulary, no discussion questions. All I want to know is where you hear pleasure." When they tell you, clearly and persuasively, where they're hearing pleasure in a text, they're building skills aligned with our Speaking and Listening standards[3]—and goodness, what a surprise, no torture was involved.

Did anyone ever sit you down and teach you how to watch a TV show? Did anybody give you a lecture on how to enjoy a movie? Perhaps this is why you like watching movies and TV shows. In this regard, do your poetry lessons serve to empower students' aesthetics, or is your aesthetic overpowering theirs? After all, how much did you really learn about sex from your sex education teacher? I saw an interview with Erica Jong[4] in which she said, "[T]he passion to write is allied to the passion for sexual pleasure." To bleach poetry completely clean of this headiness is to ruin it. It's best to shut the textbook and open the poetry volume, but as an unadulterated fan rather than a teacher. And make sure the poetry book you choose doesn't have a harpsichord on the cover.

On Prompts

When you share a poetry prompt with students, remember that no great poem was ever written from a prompt. It's the reverse of that. A poem was concocted and its recipe was shared as a prompt, but you'll never be Chef Boyardee if you're just opening and reheating the contents of someone else's can. *Poetry Everywhere*[5] is the best book of prompts I've ever found, but let prompts be for the students who have no idea what to write about and need practice. For the students who do know, get out of their way.

I'm a fan of timed freewrites. Students respond well to timed writing because they're already so accustomed to scheduled bells. Timed writing is like forcing yourself to barf for eight minutes straight, substituting your words for bile. You know you successfully scratched your subconscious when your handwriting can't be contained between the lines of your notebook. It's important to write alongside your students and share what you wrote, especially if it stinks. Timed writing helps build writing stamina, which comes in handy during in-class essays or the essay portion of standardized tests. I prefer freewriting on paper, rather than a device, because paper never interrupts the person using it.

On their way out of class, I encourage students to throw away their freewrites. I'm teaching them a process while trying to counteract the notion that everything they write is precious. If any administrator asks about this practice, I'll point them to the writing standard[6] that describes the developing and strengthening of writing by rewriting or trying a new approach. During class I encourage students to share aloud, but I don't penalize them if they refrain. Imagine at the end of your poetry session asking students what grade they deserve, and you put that in the grade book without question. How might their conjuring and emotional ownership of grades affect their engagement with your lesson? Students enter my classroom fully capable of judging adults; why not give them experience of judging themselves? Why not allow them to self-correct, evaluate their own precision and be honest with themselves in terms of their patience, creativity, and effort? These are the first skills poetry demands.

There's testimonial evidence that writing our thoughts down can maybe make us feel a little better about our problems. Sometimes, however, if you don't want to compose verse based on your deepest, darkest terrors, then don't. That's poetry's best feature. You can write about what you want, however you want, to whomever you want. The teacher of poetry is there to guard these features while simultaneously revealing all poetry's devices. These devices, or tricks as I call them, include but are not limited to, concrete nouns, verbs that kick butt, lineation, figurative language, rhyme, alliteration, repetition, paradox, image, syntax, hyperbole, reticence, synecdoche, and diction. When poets choose a word they sometimes bring its history of meaning to the table. A discussion about how words are used differently at different times aligns with life *and* a language standard.[7] Every piece of literature you teach contains literary techniques which are meant to be used, not just observed. We're not museum docents; we're bad magicians who give away every trick.

Approaching Poetry: Writing and Risk

While attending his "Five Powers of Poetry" seminar, I heard Tony Hoagland say, "No form of writing risks ambiguity the way poetry does." Readers of poetry get uncertain about what they should be getting from it, and that's what gives it life. Don't be certain about poetry the way you're certain about the construction of thesis statements or the identification of dangling modifiers. Don't be certain about poetry the way a Teacher's Edition makes you certain. When reading poetry with students, laugh it off when you're lost or at least admit it. I read poetry every day and I don't "get" half of it. I usually find pleasure in my ear, or in an image, or a turn of phrase, but "getting it" is never my main concern because it's not always meant to be "got" in the same ways as other types of writing. Poetry is often about going out on a limb and enjoying the precarious position and potential fall. Teaching poetry should reflect this riskiness.

My main goal is to give students the tools, language, and confidence to go deeper into the poetry they are already attracted to. Instead of telling my students to take off their headphones, I ask them what they are listening to. A minute or two later I have their song's lyrics on the big screen, and the poetry they are passionate about becomes the lesson. With lyrics, it's easy to find something to say about the poetry tricks being employed. You can have students identify the figurative language, for example, or have them tell you how language in any particular line is functioning.[8] At the very least it can lead to a discussion about the dangers of abstraction or the ways clichés are made new. If there's nothing of poetic value in the song, then ask the students for another one. One thing about students, they have no shortage of songs.

Maybe you're worried the lyrics your students like aren't safe for school. Maybe they're not. You have to decide what you're comfortable with, of course. Keep in mind though that un-safeness is part of what attracted your student to it in the first place. It's my love for poetry coupled with my desire to trust student instincts that makes me teach this way.

The most useful poetry volume I've ever used in the classroom is *Nice Hat, Thanks*[9] by Joshua Beckman and Matthew Rohrer. These poets took turns writing lines to make really, really short poems. For example, the title, *Nice Hat, Thanks*, is an entire two-line poem. They were having fun, and students can tell. Making students collaborate the way Beckman and Rohrer did is one of the few times I ever "force" them to do anything. By mimicking different authors, students are able to build their repertoire of writing strategies. Even uptight students relax a little when they partner up to write really short, loose poems. This is a good place to include a poetry trick or two. I will instruct students to write a two-line poem that uses half rhyme and a simile, for example. This is a playful, engaging way to demonstrate understanding of figurative language and interpret figures of speech.[10]

I encourage you to find the poetry you find pleasure in. Read it before work, instead of the news. When you bring it to your students, step back and give them—through your silence—the breadth to discover the poem's saturnalia for themselves. If you must, reveal some of the poem's tricks. Or you can just share it and step back. Poetry should be a break from the typical horrors of high school. Do you really have to blackmail your favorite poems with discussion questions? Do you really have to make them fit in a formula? Will you really get fired if you let a poem bloom—just this once—unsupervised? When it comes to a poem, my goal isn't to lead a conversation, but to join one. The good news is that all the activities I've described relate to the Common Core if you just take a few steps back from it and boil it down to its biggies: Reading, Writing, Speaking, and Listening. We do many little things to help students grow in these areas; it starts on the first day when we learn their names. We greet them openheartedly and with a smile. Why not greet poetry the same way?

Approaching Poetry: Reading Diverse Voices

One day I was looking at all the thin spines of my poetry collection and realized 90 percent of the poets were men, mostly white. It's natural to gravitate toward poets who talk your talk, but as a supplier of poetry it's important to offer many different voices. I muted my inner poetry snob and tried some superstar poets like Rupi Kaur and Courtney Peppernell who continuously outsell the prized poets of academia.[11] I discovered so many great poets once I opened my borders. Some of my favorite women poets, all of whom I've shared with my students, are Lynn Strongin, Diane Wakoski, Morgan Parker, Mary Ruefle, and Fanny Howe. You could go look up these poets, but that won't give you the pleasure of discovering them through your own curiosity, and that could lead to a certain staleness when you bring them to your students. Anthologies are a good place to find new poets to love. Consider finding an anthology of poets from your state. Another great place to stumble upon new poets is the website Poetry Daily (poems.com). All the poems they post are pulled from recently published journals and collections, and they maintain an extensive archive. My students start with the poem that was posted on their birthday. My first question: "How'd you like it?"

Caveat Emptor

To honor poetry is to sometimes separate it from history—even your own. Instead of just reading poetry and learning poetry terms, my students experience the confidence that comes through filling up one piece of notebook paper after another with their own lines. Those big shots in our literature books aren't the only ones who get to play. Breaking a line starts the game. I'm not promising any of this will work for you; however, implementing any sliver of my tone may make a few of your students comfortable enough to prompt themselves to write in their free time. Trying a hair of my style may make a few of your students curious enough to seek out poetry after they graduate. Maybe they'll even reach for a pen and paper the next time they're upset, instead of reaching for something less healthy. Hopefully my students will forget I wore the same brown pants for six weeks, but may they never forget the confidence I gave them in their own voice, their own ear, and their own words.

Notes

1. National Governors Association Center for Best Practices, Council of Chief State School Officers, *Common Core State Standards for English Language Arts & Literacy in History/Social Studies, Science, and Technical Subjects* (Washington, DC: National Governors Association Center for Best Practices, Council of Chief State School, 2010).
2. CCSS.ELA-Literacy.RL.11–12.4: Determine the meaning of words and phrases as they are used in the text, including figurative and connotative meanings; analyze the impact of specific word choices on meaning and tone, including words with multiple meanings or language that is particularly fresh, engaging, or beautiful.
3. CCSS.ELA-Literacy.SL.11–12.1: Initiate and participate effectively in a range of collaborative discussions (one-on-one, in groups, and teacher-led) with diverse partners on Grades 11–12 topics, texts, and issues, building on others' ideas and expressing their own clearly and persuasively.
4. Erica Jong, "Erica Jong Interview: Sexuality and Creativity," *Louisiana Channel*, Louisiana Museum of Modern Art, June 28, 2017, https://www.youtube.com/watch?v=eMQMMfCL0Fo.

5   Jack Collom and Sheryl Noethe, *Poetry Everywhere: Teaching Poetry Writing in School and in the Community* (New York: T&W Books, 2005).
6   CCSS.ELA-Literacy.W.11–12.5: Develop and strengthen writing as needed by planning, revising, editing, rewriting, or trying a new approach, focusing on addressing what is most significant for a specific purpose and audience.
7   CCSS.ELA-Literacy.L.11–12.1: Demonstrate command of the conventions of standard English grammar and usage when writing or speaking.
8   CCSS.ELA-Literacy.L.11–12.3: Apply knowledge of language to understand how language functions in different contexts, to make effective choices for meaning or style, and to comprehend more fully when reading or listening.
9   Joshua Beckman and Matthew Rohrer, *Nice Hat, Thanks* (Amherst, MA: Verse Press, 2002).
10 CCSS.ELA-Literacy.L.11–12.5: Demonstrate understanding of figurative language, word relationships, and nuances in word meanings.
11 Carl Wilson, "Why Rupi Kaur and Her Peers Are the Most Popular Poets in the World," *New York Times*, December 15, 2017, https://www.nytimes.com/2017/12/15/books/review/rupi-kaur-instapoets.html.

11

The Poetry of Math and Science

Kelli Krieger
Union-Endicott Central School District

Men love to wonder and that is the seed of science.

— Ralph Waldo Emerson[1]

I tell my students that the best scientists and engineers are more poet than empiricist. I say this because true scientific discovery takes not only intellect and training, but also creativity and a willingness to work outside of the lines. Furthermore, what good is a scientist who only does what's already been done? True discoverers and creators, whether scientists or poets, need to travel beyond the realm of the already known. They need to go to new places, to dark places, to unknown places; they must travel inward and outward to look at the ordinary in extraordinary ways.

If you've been in the secondary classroom in the last ten years, then you know how difficult it is to get students to go to those places. Correct answers and quick results matter more than creative thinking and risky intellectual behavior. America's post-9/11 obsession with STEM only exacerbates the situation. Students flock to the science and technology electives not necessarily because their hearts, or even their minds, direct them there, but because their parents and guidance counselors tell them STEM is the pathway to college and career prosperity.

This move toward STEM is a cultural shift underpinned by political and economic interests. We could talk about that all day long, but I'd rather make my peace with STEM and the hard sciences in the form of this chapter. Specifically, I'd like to show humanities teachers how to move STEM from the science shelf to the shelf with the poets and the artists. I was explaining my ideas to a colleague who said, "Oh, I've heard of that. It's called STEAM." The colleague smiled and walked away as I sat back down, frustrated because STEAM has replaced STEM as a ubiquitous term that can mean almost anything. The new letter in the lineup—"A"—is a stand-in for Art or the Arts. The ambiguity and enormity of "the Arts" allows us to interpret the new term in any number of ways. Third-grade teachers might ask students to identify the parts of a cell and then paint that cell in either a realistic or interpretive manner. A ninth-grade English teacher might ask the AP physics teacher down the hall whether or not the science in HG Wells's *The Invisible Man* is legitimate or just gibberish. The English teacher and the science teacher might then have students conduct experiments based on Wells's "fictional" writing. Exactly which index of refraction will allow a rod immersed in a liquid-filled flask to appear invisible? Students might then do some further research on their own and discover Japanese companies experimenting with the same principles Wells pondered in an attempt to create invisibility cloaks similar to those featured in the *Harry Potter* series. Those students might then write both fiction and nonfiction pieces sharing their discoveries with the rest of the world.

The possibilities for combining STEM and ART—in my case, STEM and creative writing—are enormous and exciting but also time-consuming and problematic. Teachers need time to think and plan and work together. For most teachers in American classrooms, space for this type of professional collaboration just doesn't exist. It seems that, despite our country's constant innovation in industry, public schools still linger in an industrial-era paradigm ruled by schedules and assessments. Finland has a different view of how teachers should spend their time. *In Finnish Lessons 2.0*, education specialist Passi Sahlberg contrasts the stark difference in the number of classroom instructional hours for teachers in Finland versus US counterparts: "Finnish primary teachers teach about 590 hours annually while American primary teachers teach roughly 1,131 hours annually."[2] Finnish teachers spend hundreds of non-classroom hours collaborating with colleagues and generally working toward improved student experiences. Can you imagine how much American educators could accomplish if we had access to these unfettered hours? What could the ELA teacher do? How many creative endeavors could we engage in? How much could we shake up the STEM world?

Realizing schools are run by "not" teachers, I'll proceed in a way that addresses the very[3] real obstacles and pressures American teachers navigate every day. Of course, ELA teachers face unique challenges, including an inordinate amount of time reading student work. To each and every English or humanities teacher reading this chapter, I feel you, and I hope my ideas and experiences will help you in your own classrooms. Despite the title of this chapter, I'm not so much interested in STEAM as I am thinking and writing about science and the world with a poet's heart.

In the spring of 2018, at least partially out of spite for the seemingly endless funding for STEM programs, I wrote and won a grant from the Craig Newmark Foundation that allowed me to implement a new creative writing unit: "The Poetry of Math & Science." In my grant, I requested a medical quality brain model, a box full of clay, and copies of Sir Isaac Newton's *Philosophiæ Naturalis Principia Mathematica*. In this chapter, I'll share the results of my experiment along with other classroom-tested ideas designed to inspire curiosity and joy by bringing STEM and creative writing together!

But wait. How is it possible to be creative when we have state tests and standards staring us down? As Chris Drew posits earlier in this book, creative writing isn't something we have to treat as a separate learning event. On the contrary, creative writing is a natural and dynamic means by which to engage topics inside and outside the English classroom. Before I dive deep, let me give you some basic information about me. I teach secondary English in an urban high school in central New York that graduates around 300 students each year. My department has ten full-time ELA teachers. In New York, all students must take the ELA Regents exam prior to graduation. We administer the test to juniors and those who fail can retake the exam in subsequent administrations. This year, I taught AP English Language, English 10 Honors, English 12, and Graphic Novels. I also spent one period a day at our Project-Based Learning (PBL) campus where I teach sophomores. In general, I have made a deliberate choice to bring STEM and creative writing into all of my classes. I just don't always make a big deal about it.

This chapter is for the classroom teacher who works every day to infuse lessons with meaning and excitement. It's for all teachers who have ever felt frustrated with district manifestos privileging one discipline over another. It is a bridge between the English teacher in room 416 and the Applied Biology teacher in room 413.

The Poetry of Math and Science

Have you ever read Wordsworth or Shelley or Coleridge? What about Whitman or Poe? For that matter, what about Sir Isaac Newton? The physicist and mathematician responsible for some of the most important advances in modern science wrote about planets and curves and optics and force. His thoughts on mathematics, physics, and natural philosophy emanated from his own wonderment with the world. Newton wanted to know more about the universe, so he conducted endless experiments. Isn't that exactly how poets operate? Isn't that also exactly the behavior we want to foster in our students? Curiosity and the desire to understand the world drive us to ask questions and find connections. Poetry and other forms of creative writing allow students to both wonder and wander on the paper laid out before them. Sometimes that paper is blank, but sometimes it's covered in wild-looking scientific equations.

Sir Isaac Newton, the Nature Poet[4]

Whether you studied Newton in college or not, you know him. He's one of those figures in Western civilization that permeates every aspect of our daily lives. *Principia* focuses primarily on Newton's Three Laws of Motion:

1. A body at rest will remain at rest, and a body in motion will remain in motion unless it is acted upon by an external force.
2. The force acting on an object is equal to the mass of that object times its acceleration.
3. For every action, there is an equal and opposite reaction.

Newton's laws are so well known that in 2014 Pfizer incorporated the physicist's first law into a campaign for their anti-arthritis drug, *Celebrex*. The pharmaceutical giant proclaimed, "It's simple physics. A body at rest tends to stay at rest while a body in motion tends to stay in motion."[5] I wonder what Newton would say about his first law showing up in a drug ad. I also wonder what he would think about the idea of "simple" physics. When Newton wrote his laws in the late 1600s, his eyes were heavenward.

Newton wrote about objects, planets, and forces, filling the pages of *Principia* with drawings and angles and formulas, as in Figure 11.1.

As it turns out, the invisible forces of advanced physics and mathematics are beautiful when laid out on paper.

Newton's principles are advanced. For many of these classroom activities, understanding the scientific principles is irrelevant, so please don't let the text scare you away. This is an opportunity for students to play with the science, to be friends with it.

PROPOSITION XLII. THEOREM XXXIII.

All motion propagated through a fluid diverges from a rectilinear progress into the unmoved spaces.

CASE 1. Let a motion be propagated from the point A through the hole BC, and, if it be possible, let it proceed in the conic space BCQP according to right lines diverging from the point A. And let us first suppose this motion to be that of waves in the surface of standing water; and let *de, fg, hi, kl*, &c., be the tops of the several waves, divided from each other by as many intermediate valleys or hollows. Then, because the water in the

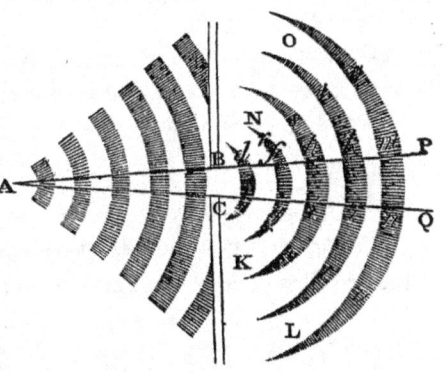

Figure 11.1 Sample page from Newton's *Philosophiæ Naturalis Principia Mathematica*, 1687.[6]

Sir Isaac Newton and Blackout Poetry

Step One: Rip out the pages of the book. Let your students put their hands on the paper. The edition that I purchased through my Newmark grant has rough-hewn fibers, so the act of parsing the pages provides a distinct tactile experience. Ask your students to select one page and then return to their seats.

Step Two: Have students sit in silence for five minutes and admire the beauty of the page. Just about every page of *Principia* includes variables, sentences, lines, angles, and formulas, so looking at it is not like looking at a page torn out of a novel. Cue students and help them to explore the page. Students can focus and unfocus their eyes. They may turn the page upside around; they can read single lines over and over. It's important that students do no writing until the five minutes expires. They can, however, underline or circle details. This extended looking allows them to notice patterns in the author's craft such as repetition, word structure, and geometric angles.[7]

Step Three: At the end of the observation, ask students to reflect on what they noticed and write out their thoughts. I often cue them. What did you see at the end of the five minutes that you didn't see at the beginning? Which of the writing methods changed your perspective most? Turning the paper? Unfocusing your eyes? How did looking at the page for this extended period of time affect your understanding of Newton's principles? It's critical that students don't stop writing. I tell them the first words that come out of their pens are not necessarily the best ones. Writing primes the brain for more writing. If students get stuck, they can repeat a line until they get unstuck.

The purpose of this reflection is to give students a space in which to think about what they know now that they didn't before. It's also an opportunity to commune with their own thoughts on the page and begin to develop a sense of themselves as writers. This practice can be awkward at first, but it can also lead to important revelations about the text and writing. The associates at the Institute for Writing and Thinking (IWT) at Bard College in the Hudson Valley refer to this as process writing and consider it a crucial aspect of thinking and composing. Institute associate Alfred E. Guy writes: "Process writing invites a reflective stance that, besides being useful also nurtures something beyond."[8] This writing helps writers pull together the discoveries from the writing activities. It's basically another chance to consider what is happening and what is possible.[9]

Step Four: It's important to bring individual observations into the community space. At this point I use a simple technique I learned at IWT. I ask students to bracket off at least one sentence to share with the class. After a few moments, they share that sentence and only it. No editorializing, preambles, or apologies. Just reading exactly what is on the paper. This method encourages full participation and is especially helpful for students who find it difficult to speak in class.[10]

As students share, the discussion often becomes more organic and spirited conversation ensues. This is the moment when students surprise each other with their discoveries. You have several options at this point:

1. Create traditional blackout[11] poetry. Using their reflections, students return to their pages from *Principia* and create poetry from Newton's words. One suggestion I make is that they circle words they want to emphasize. They then go back with a marker and "blackout" unwanted words. Some students opt for a basic blackout while others use the non-poem space to create an image supporting the new poem. Students can use colors other than black when creating their poems.

In my class, one student noticed that Newton used the word "drops" six times on one page so she outlined each occurrence. She then formed downward arrows of varying widths and lengths. The only other words the student left unblocked were "The planet" (Figure 11.1).

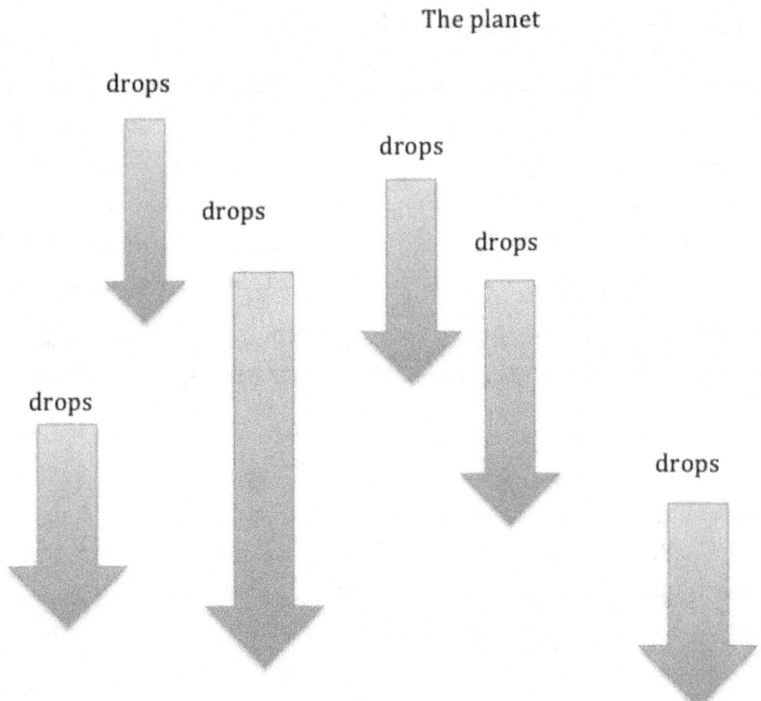

Figure 11.2 Student illustration of Newton's word choices.

2. Introduce students to creative nonfiction. Students focus in on words, drawings, or formulas from Newton's work and then turn those findings into short writing pieces that examine and convey complex ideas and information.[12]

For example, one student, who also happened to be a varsity golfer, noticed how Newton used vectors to talk about force. This student, whose overall GPA hovered in the low 2.0 range, wrote a one-page short story about the old English guy who wrote a book about how to golf. During the five-minute stare down, this student found the lines in Newton's diagrams mimicked the way they think about using a five iron to smack a golf ball. Sharp angles, long lines, massive force. Action and reaction. The student also incorporated the entire first law, including the portion that the Celebrex commercial neglects: "A body at rest will remain at rest, and a body in motion will remain in motion *unless it is acted upon by an external force.*"

3. Create mixed media pieces. *Principia* is a big, thick book so there will be many extra pages. Let students play with them.

One of my students took his original page, several extras, a pair of scissors, a glue stick, and markers and headed to the corner of the room. When he emerged, he had an entirely new creation based on his interpretations of Newton's text. The student focused on the sharp lines on his page, then cut up several of the extra pages in various, hard-angled geometric shapes, colored those shapes, and glued them onto his original sheet. The shapes formed an old man with a walking stick.

4. Hold a written conversation with the scientist(s). Have students use direct quotes from the text to create newly imagined conversations.

One of my shyest students surprised me by creating a dialogue between Kim Kardashian and Sir Isaac Newton. Apparently, Kim was intrigued by Newton's wardrobe choices. In this conversation, Newton was a big fan of "long angles" and well-tailored "radii." As I read through this student's creative piece, I imagined additional lessons for future classes. For example, why not give students background information on the scientists and philosophers who informed Newton, including Euclid, Haley, Hobbes, and Descartes, and then have a gathering of those scientists in the form of a group poem? I imagine students isolating specific words from their assigned scientists and then putting them into conversation on a giant sheet of paper. It might also be fun to have students verbalize the poem as they develop their imagined experience.[13]

(Descartes): The senses deceive
(Hobbes): The privilege of absurdity

Perhaps what we need is

(Euclid): A moment of universal silence.

Newton is not the only ingress for creative writers into the land of the hard sciences. Poets and artists have a love of the human form, as do biologists. As part of my Newmark project, I asked for and received a rather expensive—and accurate—model of the human brain. Similar to touching the pages of *Principia*, students need to put their hands on the model of the brain and then write about it. We embarked on the following adventure: Blindfolds and Metaphors.

5. Introduce Blindfolded Sensory Writing. Blindfold students and have them run their hands over and around the brain model for a specific amount of time. Remove the blindfolds, and have students write about the experience.

I purchased a gigantic remnant of red material from my local fabric shop and just ripped long pieces for my blindfolds. You can also just ask students to close their eyes, but that's not nearly as fun. Give students a set amount of time for their tactile observations of the brain model. The model comes apart so you can give students just the inside or outside or the entire thing. When time is up, ask students to describe what they felt. They can write with anatomic specificity or metaphorically. What does the brain remind them of? A landscape? A map? A building? You can also challenge students to create specific metaphors. For example, how is a brain like a house? One additional possibility is to record students during the tactile experience and then let them use the recordings to inform their writing. One student wrote about the brain as a beehive while another called it a cold piece of plastic. I'm still not sure if that second one was meant to be literal or metaphoric. Regardless of intent, the student had an up close and personal experience with STEM and creative writing, and in doing so, generated new knowledge. But what's the point? Why bother reading Newton and touching brains?

Bringing STEM and creative writing into the same space isn't merely hitting Common Core standards in preparation for state exams. It's challenging students to look at old curiosities from new angles. It's deep learning and problem solving. It's shifting paradigms and seeing education as an integrated biosphere rather than individual and unrelated microcosms. It's English informing science and vice versa. Making connections among texts is a form of deep analysis that demonstrates understanding and creative thought. When we show students that diverse subjects can coexist, we help them see just how exciting and unexpected the world can be. We also help them see beyond the bounds of standardized tests and college preparation. Like Newton and his laws, creative writers leverage their sense of wonder and curiosity to reimagine the world every day.

Before I leave you, I'd like to circle back to the example in my introduction about H. G. Wells's *The Invisible Man*. We only taught the book for one year. Our department chair at the time meant to order 200 copies of Ralph Ellison's *Invisible Man*, but he ordered *"The" Invisible Man* instead. I really did go to the AP physics teacher to ask about the science jargon in the book. He asked for a copy of the pages and told me he would get back to me in a few days. What he did instead was invite me and my adorable freshmen into his senior AP physics class, wrote out the relevant passages on his chalkboard, and then demonstrated the principles of refraction at the front of the room. He then asked my students to conduct the same experiment at the lab tables. None of us could believe it. Depending on the viscosity of the liquid, the rod in the beaker actually "disappeared." Wells's *fictional* musings were scientifically sound.[14]

I think every one of those students signed up for AP physics in their heads that day. The excitement in the room was palpable. The following day, two students came in with an article about Japanese researchers developing their own version of an invisibility cloak. Another student made a connection to Stealth Bomber technology. I didn't assign these additional references. Students were just so curious and excited about the experience that they wanted to look further. The motivation was intrinsic, the curiosity unstoppable. We were supposed to take a quiz the next day, but we wrote stories and reflected on our experience instead, because that's where the real learning was lurking. In his book, *Wild Curiosity: How to Unleash Creativity and Encourage Lifelong Wondering*, Erik Shonstrom argues, "Curiosity is subversive at its core. It leads not just to authentic learning—curiosity liberates us."[15] It fires up our brains and our imaginations. The intellectual experimentation that takes place when we combine the seemingly disparate worlds of creative writing and STEM frees us from our own preconceived notions of what knowledge looks like. It pushes us beyond the highly controlled curricula of public education and encourages us to think differently.

Notes

1. Ralph Waldo Emerson, *The Complete Works of Ralph Waldo Emerson: Society and Solitude*, vol. 7, University of Michigan Online Library, accessed January 5, 2020, https://quod.lib.umich.edu/e/emerson/4957107.0007.001?rgn=main;view=fulltext.
2. Passi Sahlberg, *Finnish Lessons 2.0: What Can the World Learn from Educational Change in Finland?* 2nd edn. (New York: Teachers College Press, 2015).
3. As Mark Twain famously said, "Substitute 'damn' every time you're inclined to write 'very;' your editor will delete it and the writing will be just as it should be." I usually get out my red pen when students use "very" in their writing. I tell them strong verbs are better than lazy adverbs. However, in this case, "very" feels necessary in emphasizing the mountainous hurdles teachers negotiate daily. Forgive me, Mark Twain.
4. Disclaimer: not all of Newton's theories and practices have survived modern scrutiny. For example, Einstein's Theory of Relativity challenged and eventually replaced Newton's Theory of Gravity.
5. Celebrex, "Body in Motion," television advertisement, 2019, https://www.ispot.tv/ad/7V7z/celebrex-body-in-motion.
6. Isaac Newton, *Philosophiæ Naturalis Principia Mathematica* (Gravesboro, CA: Snowball Publishing, 2010).

7   CCSS.ELA-LITERACY.RI.11–12.6. All Common Core standards from: National Governors Association Center for Best Practices, Council of Chief State School Officers, *Common Core State Standards for English Language Arts & Literacy in History/Social Studies, Science, and Technical Subjects* (Washington, DC: National Governors Association Center for Best Practices, Council of Chief State School, 2010).
8   Alfred Guy, *Process Writing: Reflection and the Arts of Writing and Teaching. Writing Based Teaching: Essential Practices and Enduring Questions*, ed. Teresa Villardi and Mary Chang (Albany, NY: State University of New York Press, 2009), 69.
9   CCSS.ELA-LITERACY.W.11–12.1.
10 CCSS.ELA-LITERACY.SL.11–12.1.
11 Blackout poetry, as described here, is also commonly referred to as "erasure poetry."
12 CCSS.ELA-LITERACY.RI.11–12.3.
13 CCSS.ELA-LITERACY.W.11–12.3.
14 H. G. Wells, *The Invisible Man* (Amazon Kindle Edition, 2012), https://www.amazon.com/Invisible-Man-Herbert-George-Wells-ebook/dp/B0082Q69I6.
15 Erik Shonstrom, *Wild Curiosity* (Washington, DC: Rowman and Littlefield, 2016), 157.

12

Making Writers Out of Readers: Using Creative Writing to Deepen Literary Analysis in Secondary Settings

Heather J. Clark
Covina Unified School District

Creative writing has become the driving force I use to teach the literary analysis skills demanded by California and national English Language Arts standards. This idea of English as a skills class rather than the study of particular content became clearer to me the first year I taught AP courses than it had been in all the years I'd taught before that. While my colleague who teaches AP US History focuses on covering all of her content before the test and has rubrics for free response questions that assign points for mentioning specific details, my AP Language and Literature students must learn to analyze any text excerpt provided. Beyond that, they must not only identify the author's choices but also analyze their impact. It was that emphasis on authorial choice—combined with implementing Framework for 21st Century Learning outcomes and my constructivist mentality—that helped redefine my discipline and led me to develop a practice of making students authors in order to help them become better readers.

Spend any time teaching literary analysis to high schoolers and you will hear complaints of English teachers inventing literary content and themes for students to analyze in texts rather than the original authors including that material on purpose. Ask them what's symbolic about the green light in *The Great Gatsby* and you'll get something like, *It's just a light Daisy and Tom use to find their house from the boat that Gatsby can see from his house. It doesn't mean anything else.* If they cannot see it concretely, they assume it's not there. Forcing them to make the same choices as the authors we read and analyze, then, challenges their preconceived ideas of both literary analysis and creative writing by encouraging them to access relatively untapped creative abilities and consider writing from the perspective of an author rather than just a reader.

I first developed this practice in my AP Literature class simply because the course focuses entirely on literary analysis and affords me the freedom to design my own curriculum. My academic year begins with a Short Story Workshop unit focusing on one facet of literature per week that leads nicely into implementing creative assignments employing each literary device we study. However, after finding success with this idea, I have since begun integrating creative writing to teach analysis skills in my non-AP classes with equal success, and I am confident this practice can be used successfully in any setting.

Before discussing the specifics of how this unit employs creative writing to improve student skills, there are a couple of key elements informing the process I should touch on. First, I view my teaching role as facilitating natural learning within an interactive constructivist philosophy. Neubert and Reich nuance this thinking by focusing on the impact our cultural contexts have on how we approach material: "we are always already observers, participants, and agents even before we begin to reflect upon these roles" and our "observations are always imbedded in the cultural contexts in which we act. And they depend on our participation in communities of interpretation."[1] Through this lens, my assignments help students learn to purposefully use their experiences and those of their learning community to increase their own skills. In this case, creative assignments allow them to experience being an author, observe others becoming authors, and transfer those skills to analysis.

Advances in technology have only encouraged me to push further into constructivist methods. Content knowledge, referring to "the facts, concepts, theories, and principles that are taught and learned in specific academic courses,"[2] is no longer something our students rely on us to deliver. They have access to the information at their fingertips but still need us to help them see what knowledge is important to learn, how to evaluate sources, how to approach new perspectives, and what to do with what they have learned. The Framework for 21st Century Learning,[3] which is integrated into the Common Core State Standards, addresses this in the following way: "[S]tudents, who will come of age in the 21st century, need to be taught different skills than those learned by students in the 20th century, and the skills they learn should reflect the specific demands that will be placed upon them in a complex, competitive, knowledge-based, information-age, technology-driven economy and society."[4] Constructivist approaches are more effective for this because they turn students into makers of meaning instead of collectors of information.

California's Common Core Reading Standards are divided equally between literature and informational texts, while the Writing Standards are two-thirds informational/argumentative and one-third narrative. However, the high-stakes tests eleventh-grade students complete generally have just one passage of fiction for reading analysis and no prompts asking students to write fiction. While Common Core Writing Standards require other departments to have students write, the tests are still divided between ELA and math sections, which continues to push the majority of the pressure for reading/writing skills onto ELA. Additionally, the difference in testing pressure between 1999, when I started teaching, and now means current students only know an educational system where a focus on state testing causes a fear of answering incorrectly instead of viewing wrong answers as paths toward better conceptual understanding. Educational psychologists refer to this "rigidity or mental set that locks thinking so an individual cannot see alternatives" as "functional fixedness."[5] At the same time, ELA curricula are increasingly encouraged to focus on informational reading and writing, which also places the emphasis on correct answers, or at least ones that can be proven/argued in expository or technical forms.

Due to the impact of high-stakes assessments, many district-level interpretations of the standards have resulted in a move away from creative applications. This reduction of creative work, ironically, has a negative impact on students' ability to meet those very standards. Without writing creatively, students lack a key component in the mental framework required to analyze authorial choices, the purposes they serve, and whether or not those choices are effective. Also, they don't have spaces to fail productively—a key element in learning. Giving students the opportunity to become authors and make choices in their storytelling renders the authorial process more visible and allows students to see depth they couldn't access before experiencing it themselves. For example, this deeper learning occurs when students construct a character rather than simply identifying the traits of one they read about. Additionally, because ELA standards do include literary analysis and narrative writing, the activities I use for the purpose of improving analytical skills also address standards often pushed to the edges of the curriculum.

Along with the Common Core standards, many teachers also focus on their lessons' Depth of Knowledge (DOK). DOK is similar to Bloom's Taxonomy but focuses more on the complexity of tasks rather than merely what the task is. There are four levels of knowledge: (1) recall and reproduction, (2) basic application of skill/concept, (3) strategic thinking, and (4) extended thinking.[6] Teachers are expected to achieve Levels 3 and 4 in significant ways within each unit. When it comes to literature, comprehending it is a Level 1 skill, while drawing inferences about an author's purpose or analyzing relationships between elements of literature are all Level 3, and writing a play that includes stage notes achieves Level 4 because it requires synthesizing two forms of information.[7] Creative writing, then, requires strategic and extended thinking, an important distinction for those who see storytelling as a filler task lacking depth or importance.

With this framework in mind, the Short Story Workshop unit provides a solid foundation for discussing the use of creative writing to teach the primary elements of literature—a unit that often starts the school year in most ELA curricula. The primary goal is to begin the year analyzing a variety of literary elements in short stories before moving on to analyzing longer works. I chose some alternate readings outside of my textbook to include a more diverse range of authors because while ELA standards specify skills rather than content, part of the job of an ELA teacher is to build empathy by extending students' understanding of the world while also allowing them to see themselves reflected in the works they read.

The entire unit spends a week on each of the following elements: plot, character, setting, point of view, symbolism, and tone/style/irony, and then ends with a focus on theme before bringing all the elements together in the final week. Each week follows the same basic format. Monday's lesson emphasizes analyzing stories for a literary element and assigning a creative activity. Tuesday through Thursday the focus is on discussions of the works they read that compare a theme or topic treatment by different authors and contain elements from all four DOK levels working from comprehension to deeper analysis. Thursday also includes sharing their creative work with classmates and discussing its impact on their ability to analyze authorial choices in the week's stories. Then, on Fridays they complete an academic writing assignment using a literary analysis-driven prompt addressing the element of the week, which is where they practice informational writing standards[8] as well as the literary analysis[9] that originally inspired this writing-based approach. The key to success with this method is clearly explaining what each aspect of the week's work should accomplish, ensuring teacher clarity that assists students in purposefully connecting the skills they're learning.

One of the most effective creative experiences students have during workshop comes in the second week's unit on character, which includes reading analysis focused on the topic and developing a character in writing, both of which are addressed in our standards. The creative activity for this element is taken from role-playing games. First, students generate a character via predetermined traits on a form—honesty, dexterity, self-centeredness, etc.—by rolling dice to determine the relative strength of these characterizing elements. During this part of the activity, students work through the form and I walk around the room, helping them interpret how the characteristics they've randomly generated work together to create a personality. For example, a character with high levels of empathy but a low action resolve will be frustrated when others are mistreated but likely do nothing about it, or a character with a high level of action orientation but a low athletic ability will attempt many physical activities but not be great at any of them.

When everyone is ready, I present a series of situations and students discuss how their characters would respond. The situations range from what type of student they'd be to what role they'd have in a zombie apocalypse. They share these responses with their table groups and then the class. It is an engaging activity with a lot of laughter, but the skill of mentally combining multiple personality traits to determine how fictional characters respond is DOK Level 3. Additionally, as students often begin by explaining how *they* would respond to that situation instead of their *character*, it provides ample opportunities to normalize productive failure in a low-stakes activity as we work as a class to determine how *characters* would actually respond.

To conclude the day, I ask students to use what they now know about their character to write a one-paragraph description as if they were describing a friend to someone who didn't know them. This helps students synthesize all of the day's experiences and later allows them to better analyze the seemingly erratic and impulsive decisions of the main character in "Saving Sourdi" by May-Lee Chai. I encourage these connections in the discussions, which result in more students using them in the academic writing assignment—exactly what I want to have happen, because transferring these strategies leads to better character analysis.

All assignments in the eight weeks of this unit are formative, asking students to develop and practice their analytical skills, and grading them strictly would undo the work of learning to trust productive failure as part of their process. This unit is so early in the school year that I generally grade for how much effort and risk they've put into their attempts to analyze at the depth I ask for. This way, I can provide feedback identifying what they're doing well and help them adjust attempts toward improvement rather than focusing on where they have missed the mark. Later, I continue to respond to effort, creativity, depth, and risk in creative assignments while shifting to assess literary analysis assignments against holistic rubrics.

Setting is often one of the more difficult aspects of literature for students to analyze because they see it as a background detail, so I piggyback on the character work from Week Two by introducing the concept of setting as character in Week

Three, first assigning a basic character analysis of the settings from stories read previously in the unit to initially engage the idea. This capitalizes on background knowledge from the previous week while also requiring students to "analyze the impact of author's choices regarding ... where a story is set."[10] This week's creative writing activity is one I uncreatively call Setting Stories. It repositions setting as an integral plot element rather than mere background information for students. Additionally, they write a whole story this week, which requires use of all the skills detailed in the Writing Narratives standards[11] rather than merely those for setting, making it a DOK 3 assignment.

We begin together by brainstorming several settings on the board. At this point, only I know we will continue to generate ideas until potential settings outnumber students. Pushing them to continue providing ideas results in some wonderfully random settings, like the inside of a goldfish bowl, for instance. Then, we define a basic plot structure for a story together: the major conflict, character names, how the story ends, and so on. Maybe it's just my students, but these stories almost always include a love triangle and someone dying. These story elements are created after the settings, because I don't want them consciously or unconsciously tailoring their setting to logically match the story.

Then, I reveal the assignment: they all must use this same plot structure to write their own story, but each will use a different setting so we can see how the elements of setting impact story development. On Thursday, they read their setting stories to their table groups, each choosing one to be shared with the class, and we end with a DOK Level 3 or 4 discussion analyzing the choices each student-author made because of their setting, which helps me make the value of the experience more visible.

This week, we work collaboratively to create meaning students then integrate into their personal learning, a prime example of the constructivist philosophy in which "[t]he interconnection of our roles as observers, agents, and participants represents one primary circle in interactive constructivism's account of the cultural construction of realities."[12] This happens because we begin with what they already understand about character and plot structure and then extend those elements together into setting. They have independent but parallel experiences as they process writing their own stories, and we discuss as a group both their narratives and the works we read, allowing them to crowd-source a deeper understanding of the concepts before the individual academic writing task assessing their personal progress. This method of students using their collective understanding and experiences through creative writing to improve personal analysis skills is how this unit works overall, but this week is especially cohesive.

Consider this specific example: the class with the goldfish bowl setting also had a story set in outer space. The student with the goldfish bowl wrote from the perspective of a fish owner anthropomorphizing her fish's actions into a love triangle story as she watched them swim, while the student with the outer space setting transported a typical high school drama into a future community on the moon. When we discussed how students had settled on telling their story, which included mentioning alternative narratives they discarded, the concept of how setting shapes a story became clearer. In conjunction with this, we read Hemingway's "Soldier's Home" and discussed how the protagonist struggles with his hometown not feeling like home after returning from the war in Europe, and I consistently directed the discussion back to how the setting impacts his decisions and emotions. After we shared our setting stories, we returned to discuss whether alternate settings could have achieved the same tension in "Soldier's Home," the contrast helping them understand the influence the chosen setting had on the story. When they completed the academic writing that week, I was pleased to see them using language and insight in their setting analysis that their previous writing didn't contain, even if that language still lacked depth.

Moving back to the unit structure, in the fourth week we again use what we've learned about character analysis as we focus on point of view. First, we discuss how our interpretation of any story has to consider the narrator's reliability and whether the author uses that POV primarily to conceal or reveal. This also addresses the following standard: "[A]nalyze a case in which grasping point of view requires distinguishing what is directly stated in a text from what is really meant."[13] To conclude, they write two Double-Nickels telling the same story but from two different points of view, with bonus points for also using internal and external narration, a standards-based requirement that students "establish one or multiple points of view."[14] A Double-Nickel story restricts the writer to using exactly fifty-five words to tell a story and could also be used later as a unique way to assess student comprehension by imposing a fifty-five-word limit on summaries of larger works. The brevity of this form limits their feeling overwhelmed with writing the same story from two perspectives and, as an added benefit, gives me a framework for addressing wordiness in their essays later in the term. Another effective POV activity has students create social media posts about the story by imagining another character's point of view regarding major plot elements. Both options also require students to think about how they write in different modes and for different purposes or audiences.[15] Additionally, giving students purposeful practice in seeing narratives through someone else's eyes lays the groundwork for negotiating different student points of view in class discussions as we practice that life skill.

One of the works we read for POV is "In a Grove" by Ryūnosuke. After their experiences writing Double-Nickels, students have a framework for understanding how the perspective of the story changes what is included. One student even made this connection in her literary analysis: "Like in the assignment, 'Double-Nickels,' there are perspectives that reveal two different descriptions of the situation." This is a perfect example of encouraging students' process at work and resisting a fixed mindset, because although this isn't a sentence she should include in later academic essays, it demonstrates that she is integrating her creative writing experience with her analysis, while also giving me the opportunity to provide productive feedback for how to make it more academic, because I have created the ability to see and readdress lacking understanding in real time.

The final week of the unit, then, is spent tying it all back together. By the third week of workshop, I stop hearing comments about how I'm inventing the choices authors make, and students' analytical writing begins to rely less on summary, demonstrating more sophisticated identification and analysis. So, at the end of workshop, I have each group pick one of the unit's stories and apply all of the elements of literature we have discussed in a thorough analysis. This final week is where they show me how their experiences have impacted their learning and affirm that they have shifted their thinking and are ready to engage longer works. Demonstrating all of those new abilities indicates that these deliberate acts of creating, the hallmark of the Short Story Workshop unit, are generally more effective in increasing my students' ability to competently and confidently analyze authorial choices, purposes, and effectiveness while also neatly addressing a number of additional state standards along the way.

Notes

1   Stefan Neubert and Kersten Reich, "The Challenge of Pragmatism for Constructivism: Some Perspectives in the Programme of Cologne Constructivism," *The Journal of Speculative Philosophy* 20, no. 3 (2006): 165–91.
2   "Content Knowledge," *Glossary of Education Reform*, Great Schools Partnership, https://www.edglossary.org/content-knowledge/.
3   The Framework for 21st Century Learning was developed by a group of government workers, educators, and major employers who started their work in the 1980s as they realized how changes in technology impact the skills necessary

for people to succeed in jobs and society. The 2010 Common Core State Standards called for integration of these twenty-first-century skills into K–12 curricula.

4   "21st Century Skills," *Glossary of Education Reform*, Great Schools Partnership, https://www.edglossary.org/21st-century-skills/.

5   Mark A. Runco and Ivonne Chand, "Cognition and Creativity," *Educational Psychology Review* 7, no. 3 (1995): 247.

6   Norman L. Webb, "Issues Related to Judging the Alignment of Curriculum Standards and Assessments," *Applied Measurement in Education* 20, no. 1 (2007): 7–25.

7   Karin Hess, "A Guide for Using Webb's Depth of Knowledge with Common Core State Standards," *The Common Core Institute*, 2013, https://education.ohio.gov/getattachment/Topics/Teaching/Educator-Evaluation-System/How-to-Design-and-Select-Quality-Assessments/Webbs-DOK-Flip-Chart.pdf.aspx.

8   *California Common Core State Standards* (Sacramento: California Department of Education, 2013). W2: Write informative/explanatory texts to examine and convey complex ideas, concepts, and information clearly and accurately through the effective selection, organization, and analysis of content.

9   CCCSS RL3: Analyze the impact of the author's choices regarding how to develop and relate elements of a story or drama (e.g., where a story is *set*, how the action is ordered, how the *characters*/archetypes are introduced and developed); CCCSS RL5: Analyze how an author's choices concerning how to structure specific parts of a text (e.g., the choice of where to begin or end a story, the choice to provide a comedic or tragic resolution) contribute to its overall structure and meaning as well as its aesthetic impact.

10 CCCSS RL3.

11 CCCSS W3: Write narratives to develop real or imagined experiences or events using effective technique, well-chosen details, and well-structured event sequences.

   a. Engage and orient the reader by setting out a problem, situation, or observation and its significance, establishing one or multiple point(s) of view, and introducing a narrator and/or characters; create a smooth progression of experiences or events.

   b. Use narrative techniques, such as dialogue, pacing, description, reflection, and multiple plot lines, to develop experiences, events, and/or characters.

   c. Use a variety of techniques to sequence events so that they build on one another to create a coherent whole and build toward a particular tone and outcome (e.g., a sense of mystery, suspense, growth, resolution).

   d. Use precise words and phrases, telling details, and sensory language to convey a vivid picture of the experiences, events, setting, and/or characters.

   Provide a conclusion that follows from and reflects on what is experienced, observed, or resolved over the course of the narrative.

12 Neubert & Reich, The Challenge of Pragmatism for Constructivism: Some Perspectives in the Programme of Cologne Constructivism.
13 *CCCSS* RL6: Analyze a case in which grasping point of view requires distinguishing what is directly stated in a text from what is really meant (e.g., satire, sarcasm, irony, understatement).
14 *CCCSS* W3a: Engage and orient the reader by setting out a problem, situation, or observation and its significance, establishing one or multiple point(s) of view, and introducing a narrator and/or characters; create a smooth progression of experiences or events.
15 *CCCSS* W4: Produce clear and coherent writing in which the development, organization, and style are appropriate to task, purpose, and audience.

13

Responsive Freedom: Creative Writing in the Advanced Placement English Literature and Composition Classroom

Amanda Clarke and Nan Cohen
Viewpoint School

A three-word/three-line poem after Toni Morrison and Jean Rhys; a backpack ode after Pablo Neruda and Tim O'Brien; a fake translation after Aleksandr Pushkin and Eeva-Liisa Manner; a ghost-logic short story after Ishiguro and Maria Elena Llano; a metafiction piece, narrated by a short story or a poem, after Douglas Adams and Marianne Moore.

Along with reading assignments, close reading practice, class discussions, small group activities, timed writing, writing workshops, peer editing, revised writing, individual and group reports, student-led debates, and formative and summative assessments, we incorporate with equal attention and intention these kinds of creative writing exercises into our Advanced Placement (AP) English Literature and Composition classrooms. As longtime AP teachers, we have seen the marked pedagogical and personal growth in students who share the identity of *writer* with the authors they study, and remain delighted with the energy, engagement, and enthusiasm these creative tasks elicit in them. On a practical level, we have found that engagement with creative writing encourages students to consider literature from the inside out by providing them with practice in making a range of decisions regarding structure, voice, tone, style, and subject matter as they craft their own pieces of writing. Indeed, our experience has shown us that such increased sensitivity to the myriad questions of craft produces stronger reading skills and, indeed, testing results.

But beyond the considerations of the possibility of enhanced scores on exams, we continue to integrate creative writing exercises in order to support the social and emotional development of the whole student. Indeed, we believe well-crafted creative writing assignments can enhance their reaction to the psychological strain of navigating an increasingly automated and emotionally anonymous world. Creative writing work can also address adolescents' sense of social dislocation, a feeling not unique to the twenty-first century but one that arises from adolescents' sense of impending adulthood, tempered by their awareness of their powerlessness in the world constructed by adults. As the Association of Writers and Writing Programs usefully articulates, "Many students feel that the world is not of their making, and not theirs to form or to reform. Writing classes often demonstrate the efficacy of the human will—that human experience can be shaped and directed for the good: aesthetically, socially, and politically."[1]

Creative writing in the classroom also supports the decentering of the European experience as the apex of the literary canon. We honor the emergence of a more diverse generation of students who, in David Fenza's words, "want to see literature about their diaspora, not the diaspora of others. They want literature about them and their families and not the ancestors of white, European, English-speaking peoples."[2] Indeed, the very activity of self-expression through inventive and sensitive play with human language reaffirms our existence as individual, autonomous thinkers and creators, each of whom has a uniquely expressive voice. But beyond the benefit to any single student or group of students, well-considered and thoughtfully constructed creative writing exercises support a range of critical social goals that underlie important values of our democracy: honoring and affirming the individual, celebrating the diversity of voices and heritage languages, and encouraging empathy toward and awareness of others.[3]

Despite the myriad positive outcomes of incorporating a wide and rich range of creative writing assignments in the AP classroom, writing in the creative mode tends to be slighted or ignored entirely in prevailing national standards. The Common Core, for example, lists as the main categories for its writing standards the following modes: argument, informative/explanatory, and narrative. While the inclusion of "narrative" signals its tacit approval of creative writing as a component of ELA, an examination of the sample activities from the Core's curriculum maps reveals bias toward analytical, informational, and argumentative writing over creative tasks.[4] Furthermore, the College Board itself, in the most recent AP English Literature and Composition Course Description, eliminated its previous reference to the suggested inclusion of "well-constructed creative writing assignments [that] may help students see from the inside how literature is written."[5] Indeed, the 2019 revision[6] of the document omits all references to creative writing, stipulating that "[w]riting assignments include expository, analytical, and argumentative essays that require students to analyze and interpret literary works."⁷ Thus, as mandated by official standards and the institution governing the articulation of AP Standards, writing is to be taught predominantly as a tool of argument and a means of exposition with little acknowledgment of its power as a process for creative self-expression and the imaginative exploration of tricks and strategies, forms and genres, decisions and revisions.

As noted earlier, we do not hew to ideology that marginalizes or diminishes the importance of creative writing. In the sections ahead, then, we will describe a number of creative writing activities we have used, and will continue to employ, in our courses. While current, dominant standards tend to marginalize or ignore creative writing skills in favor of argument and exposition, we have found that creative writing activities are often directly supportive of the outcomes and goals explicitly promoted by guiding governmental and discipline-specific institutions. For each of the three sample assignments that follow, we first include a brief summary of its rationale and effects and then provide references to the specific skills listed in the Common Core standards. While the creative writing activities draw out and refine skills articulated by such organizations as the National Council of Teachers of English, the College Board, and various state standards, we believe that cross-referencing to the Common Core will prove most useful to secondary teachers reading this essay who must engage these standards or others like them specific to their context. Instructions to students and suggestions for modifications and supplemental readings follow. Finally, we offer brief descriptions of ten additional exercises for teachers to consider using or adapting—or as inspiration for as-yet-unimagined assignments!

"Three-Word/Three-Line Poems": A Poetry Exercise for Beginning a Long Prose Work

We use this first sample exercise primarily when beginning a novel with students, although it could also work with plays or with an epic poem such as the *Odyssey*; the word sets provided were created for *Song of Solomon* and *Wide Sargasso Sea*. Students are given a choice of three-word sets we draw from the beginning chapters of the novel (e.g., *soar, house,* and *mercy* for *Song of Solomon*) and must write either a tercet or a longer poem in tercets using each of those words once in each poem or stanza.

If you create your own, consider choosing a mixture of nouns, verbs, and adjectives; words that can function as more than one part of speech; concrete and abstract words. As students read the novel, they are often surprised to see how their poems anticipated some of its chief themes, interests, and obsessions.

Nan first wrote a three-word/three-line poem in Sandford Lyne's class at the University of Virginia Young Writers Workshop. She often uses this as a first poetry exercise for groups of all ages.

Objectives

1. Students will bring their attention to words of particular significance in a literary work they are about to read.
2. Students will explore the connotations and associations of those words by using them in a poem.
3. Students will discover more about the uses of the poetic line break and stanza break through reading examples of tercets and writing their own tercets.

Common Core Standards

Because the exercise draws students' attention to words of heightened significance in the longer work, it supports their ability to analyze the impact of specific word choices and consider the impact of word choice on development of character, tone, and meaning.[8] It also allows them to practice deploying writerly choices of their own, including poetic techniques such as metaphor and simile.[9] Students' play with the repetition of single words in varying syntactic patterns and semantic uses engages their imaginative use of figurative language.[10] Furthermore, the focus on words thematically significant in forthcoming assigned literary readings encourages students' appreciation and comprehension of the power of well-selected lexical items.[11]

Supplementary Reading

Students might read some poems composed in tercets (Linda Hogan's "Lost in the Milky Way" and Natasha Trethewey's "Enlightenment" are both available online) and discuss how the stanza form directs the reader's attention, brings tone to the speaker's voice (imagine each poem composed in one long strophe; what's different? What happens in stanza breaks?), establishes patterns of thought, and also breaks them (where do ends of stanzas coincide with ends of sentences? Where do they not?).

Assignment

Poem Prompt: Choose one of the sets of three words below. Write a three-line poem in which you use each of these words in one line. (You can vary the forms of the words, if you like—conjugate the verbs, make singular/plural, etc.)

Suggestions for beginning:

Have the first word be an imperative verb (Give, Take, Listen …)
Write in the first person. Who is your speaker?

Think about the other elements of SOAPSTone (Speaker, Occasion, Audience, Purpose, Subject, Tone). What has just happened or is about to happen? To whom is your speaker speaking? (Etc.)

Extend the poem out to three or more stanzas, repeating each of the words (the same three you chose before) in each of the stanzas.

Sample

> There has only ever been one dress
> in which I felt myself safe—
> this blue dress made of water.
> My water dress swirled around my knees
> when I was five. When I outgrew it
> we laid it safe in a box in the attic.

Table 13.1 For *Song of Solomon* by Toni Morrison

soar	Key	Son	name	table
house	father	height	bone	mother
mercy	petal	wings	milk	flight

Table 13.2 For *Wide Sargasso Sea* by Jean Rhys

dress	Friend	daughter	name	song
safe	flower	name	pencil	mother
water	prayer	home	fire	hair

"The Things We Carry": A Prose or Poetry Exercise

Although Amanda created this sample exercise to use with Tim O'Brien's *The Things They Carried*, its elements are adaptable to other works or could be used as a freestanding exercise. Either before or after reading the book's first chapter—often anthologized as a short story—students are asked to unload their backpacks or purses, arrange the contents on the floor, and create a poem or prose piece that mimics the style and function of several of the paragraphs of O'Brien's chapter.

Objectives

1. Students will discover how characters, dramatic situations, and themes may be expressed, and implicit meaning conveyed, through objects and other concrete details.
2. (Prose version) Students will experiment with paragraph structure and transitions between paragraphs in their own writing.
3. (Poetry version) Students will experiment with lineation and stanza structure in their own writing.
4. (Poetry version) Students will become familiar with and practice the conventions of the ode.
5. (With "The Things They Carried") Students will practice identifying how both description and narration of action function to create what we recognize as "a story."

Common Core Standards

In the poetry version of this exercise, students' careful selection of detail supports several key Common Core standards regarding word choice and figurative language.[12,13] Furthermore, while the Common Core writing standard calling for students to practice "a variety of techniques to sequence events so that they build on one another"[14] refers to prose compositions, it can also apply to skills and decisions regarding the development and sequencing of the poetic line.

In the prose version of this exercise, students must make choices regarding genre, narrative voice, tone, structure, organization, all of which are highlighted in numerous Common Core standards.[15,16,17,18,19] If the assignment is to be presented visually as a reading over a video or series of photographs of the objects, students are honing use of digital texts as a creative means of production and distribution.[20]

Supplementary Reading and Activities

Students might read some poems centered on objects, such as Marilyn Nelson's "The Century Quilt," Robert Pinsky's "Shirt," or Charles Simic's "My Shoes." If choosing the ode option, explore the ode form at the website of the Academy of American Poets or the Poetry Foundation and read some of Pablo Neruda's *Odas elementales* ("Ode to My Socks," "Ode to a Large Tuna in the Market").

The website *The Burning House* (https://theburninghouse.com) challenges writers to take a photograph of one thing they would save from a burning house:

> It's a philosophical conflict between what's practical, valuable and sentimental. You're forced to prioritize and boil down a life of accrued possessions into what you can carry out with you. What you would bring reflects your interests, background and priorities. People's stage in life also dictates their selection. A father of five in his forties would grab very different things than he would have as a bachelor in his twenties. Think of it as a full interview condensed into one question.[21]

Students may also find inspiration in exploring American photographer Adrienne Salinger's images of 1990s teenagers in their bedrooms, surrounded by their possessions.

Assignment

Sit on the floor and unpack your backpack (or purse or locker), arranging the objects around you. Some questions for brainstorming: What do the contents of your backpack reveal about you, about teenagers (or sixteen-year-olds, or eleventh-graders), about your school and community, about the time and place in which you live?

Prose: Write a short story (or the opening paragraphs of one) modeled on "The Things They Carried" in which you reveal both an unfolding narrative and a compelling picture of a time, place, and situation. Optional presentation: record a narration of the piece over a short video (or series of still photographs) of the relevant objects.

Poetry: After exploring the ode form, choose one object from your backpack and write an ode to that object.

"Fake Translation": A Poetry Exercise

This sample exercise is based on fake translations (Nan first wrote one in a workshop with poet, editor, critic, and librettist J. D. McClatchy), which are effective for compelling students to examine their underlying assumptions about what a poem is and to think about how line breaks and stanza breaks work. Nan often uses Finnish poet Eeva-Liisa Manner's "Pelkoa"; its repetitions make students consider the function of repetition itself (what is important enough to repeat?), and its punctuation (including three questions and a phrase set off by a dash) draws their attention to the shaping power of punctuation. She also uses the short rhyming love poems in *Spring Essence: The Poetry of Hô Xuân Hương* (Copper Canyon Press), which includes the poems both in *Nôm*, the writing system for Vietnamese that uses modified Chinese characters, and in the modern Vietnamese alphabet.

Whatever source of poems you choose, make sure it is in a language that is not understood—ideally not even guessed at—by your students. And do have all students use the same poem; their responses will likely range from the comic to the melodramatic to the lyrical, and they'll be able to see what technical choices— lineation, stanza form, repetition, punctuation, and syntax, even though they will not be able to recognize the syntax of the source poem—are most significant, even though various writers will handle those choices differently.

Objectives

1. Students will unearth and examine implicit assumptions about what a poem is, what its subjects are, and how it changes from beginning to end.
2. Students will discover more about the function and power of syntax, repetition, lineation, and stanza form in poems.
3. Depending on the poem, they may also identify poetic elements they have already studied, such as rhyme, enjambment, apostrophe, and alliteration, and practice showing their understanding of the functions of such elements.

Common Core Standards

Even though students cannot literally read the text of the foreign-language poem, this exercise challenges students to apply their reading, decoding, and interpretation skills[22,23] to demonstrate an understanding of structure and the significance of syntactic choices as they "translate" the shape of the poem into an original written text.[24]

Supplementary Reading and Activities

Writing fake translations may whet students' appetites for doing real translations, which provides valuable opportunities to grapple with connotative meaning, tone, and other fundamental elements of literary analysis. Both fake and real translation projects pair well with the study of works in translation; we have used them with Franz Kafka's *The Metamorphosis* and while reading *The Vintage Book of World Poetry*.

Assignment

Examine a poem in a language you do not know, preferably one with few or no cognates in any language you do know. Try reading it aloud if you can. Notice what words or phrases occur more than once. Look at the sentences—short or long? Do they end at the same time as the lines, or do they strain against the regimentation of the line?

Type or write out the poem, leaving double spaces between the lines. Then translate it, preserving whatever elements you can tell exist (e.g., if the poem's third line is a question, the third line of your translation should be one too). On the first pass, match the original poem line for line (i.e., if its first stanza has five lines, yours should too; on a second draft, you may stray from that).

Have everyone read their translations aloud. What do they all have in common? What are their most significant differences?

If you decide to find the "real" translation, don't let it change your opinion of the poem you wrote in this exercise. It may be wonderful on its own!

Brief Descriptions of Additional Exercises

1. *Ekphrasis:* After exploring the poetic practice of ekphrasis (poems about or inspired by works of art), write an ekphrastic poem of your own. Sample ekphrastic poems: "Musée des Beaux Arts" by W. H. Auden, "The Kermess" by William Carlos Williams, "Night Magic (Blue Jester)" by Lorna Dee Cervantes, "Degas' Laundresses" by Eavan Boland.

2. *Ekphrasis on Newer Art Forms:* Write a poem on a movie, a television show, or a video game. Try writing in imitation of or homage to an ekphrastic poem you have read.
3. *Imitation Is the Sincerest Form of Flattery:* Let any poem you have admired (or any poem you have a quarrel with) inspire a poem. You might even include the epigraph "After X's Poem, 'Y.'" The UK's Poetry Society has a good page on this practice, focusing on Emily Mercer's poem "Canute's Wife (after Carol Ann Duffy)."
4. *Updating Is the Sincerest Form of Flattery:* Also on the Poetry Society Page is a link to Patience Agbabi's "Wife of Bafa," part of her book *Telling Tales*, a retelling of Geoffrey Chaucer's *Canterbury Tales* in different contemporary poetic modes. A video of Agbabi performing "Prologue (Grime Mix)," her version of the General Prologue, can be found on YouTube. Try updating a well-known poem from a century or more ago in a more contemporary style (slam poetry, rap battle, etc.).
5. *Backwards Update:* Most English teachers are probably familiar with the Pop Sonnets Tumblr and the books based on its translation of pop songs into Elizabethan language. Reading these can help accustom students to the syntax and vocabulary of Early Modern English; writing them gives students the opportunity for advanced play with language.
6. *Parody Is the Sincerest Form of Flattery:* Parodies are one of the most effective ways for students to demonstrate understanding of the subjects and conventions of different literary periods and authors—by subverting them! *The Faber Book of Parodies* contains both prose and poetry examples, such as Raymond Chandler's parody of Ernest Hemingway, "Beer in the Sergeant-Major's Hat."
7. *Flash Fiction:* Jerome Stern's pocket anthology *Micro Fiction* is a treasure trove of excellent stories under 300 words, any one of which could also (a) serve as a mini-lesson in fiction structure, characterization, setting, or tone and (b) inspire a writing prompt. Here's a favorite: Write a short-short story (no more than 300 words) that, like Stuart Dybek's "Flu," is a "How They Met" story. Make one up, or modify your own (could be how you met your best friend) or someone else's (parents, grandparents, Beyoncé and Jay-Z, etc.). ("Flu" is available online.)
8. *Flash Fiction and Prose Poems:* Is there a difference? How do we know? Compare a poetic short-short story like Molly Giles's "The Poet's Husband" with a prose poem like Russell Edson's "The Adventures of a Turtle." Write a companion piece, perhaps in the other genre.

9. *Ghost Logic* (adapted from Lisa Brown and Adele Griffin in *Don't Forget to Write*, ed. Jennifer Traig): Brown and Griffin observe, "A ghost is more interesting if he or she isn't all-powerful, but exists within a circle of specific abilities." For example, "the ghost only appears in photographs; the ghost can move through glass, but not wood; the ghost can appear in dreams." Make up three rules for a ghost and build a story around it. This is a helpful ancillary activity when reading a literary work that includes science fiction (Kazuo Ishiguro's *Never Let Me Go*) or the supernatural (Toni Morrison's *Beloved*, María Elena Llano's "In the Family").
10. *Metafiction*/Ars Poetica: After reading examples of metafiction (or metafictive elements in a longer work, like *The Hitchhiker's Guide to the Galaxy*) or *ars poetica* (Marianne Moore's "Poetry," Archibald MacLeish's "Ars Poetica"), write a short-short story with "the story" or "the main character" as the main character (in either first or third person), or a poem with "a poem" or "the poem" as the speaker. Or write a story or poem in the second person ("you"), addressed to a reader.

Notes

1 "Our History and the Growth of Creative Writing Programs," *Association of Writers and Writing Programs*, accessed March 27, 2020, https://www.awpwriter.org/about/our_history_overview.
2 Michael Melia, "Demand Booming on College Campuses for Creative Writing," *AP News*, April 7, 2017, https://www.apnews.com/286ad20c060f4e57b545d1dcd5793c44.
3 For a fuller treatment of teacher attitudes toward the imposition of limiting standards and its impact upon creative writing in the classroom, see the November 2014 edition of *The English Journal*, which has as its theme "The Standards Movement."
4 See Chris Drew's chapter in this book for further consideration of this perceived bias.
5 *English Literature and Composition Course Description. Effective Fall 2014*, The College Board, 2014, PDF, https://secure-media.collegeboard.org/digitalServices/pdf/ap/ap-english-literature-and-composition-course-description.pdf, 9.
6 *AP English Literature Course and Exam Description. Effective Fall 2019*. College Board, 2019, PDF, https://apcentral.collegeboard.org/pdf/ap-english-literature-and-composition-course-and-exam-description.pdf?course=ap-english-literature-and-composition.

7   Ibid., 7.
8   CCSS 11-12.4 in National Governors Association Center for Best Practices, Council of Chief State School Officers, *Common Core State Standards for English Language Arts & Literacy in History/Social Studies, Science, and Technical Subjects* (Washington, DC: National Governors Association Center for Best Practices, Council of Chief State School, 2010).
9   CCSS 11-12.5.
10 Ibid.
11 CCSS 11-12.4.
12 Ibid.
13 CCSS 11-12.2d.
14 CCSS 11-12.3c.
15 CCSS 11-12.3.
16 CCSS 11-12.3a.
17 CCSS 11-12.3b.
18 CCSS 11-12.3c.
19 CCSS 11-12.3d.
20 CCSS 11.12.6.
21 "The Burning House," *Tumblr*, accessed March 27, 2020, https://theburninghouse.com/.
22 CCSS 11-12.4.
23 CCSS 11-12.5.
24 CCSS 11-12.3.

14

From Queen to Court Jester: Writing Multigenre Papers alongside My Students

Oona Marie Abrams
Chatham High School

This is a story about a teacher who often tries new approaches—but not too often. A teacher who, *too* often, bows to the idols of time, efficiency, and fear. A teacher who, more than she'd care to admit, sacrifices creativity on the altar of standardization. Writing this story is that teacher's attempt to exorcise the pedagogical demons that have haunted her for far too long.

In hindsight, telling this story in a linear fashion seems simple. In the spring of 2018, my Advanced Placement Literature students, most of whom had struggled throughout the year with analytical academic writing, improved notably when tasked with writing multigenre papers. In composing and structuring their multigenre pieces, they demonstrated writing that aligned with the New Jersey Student Learning Standards for English Language Arts,[1] which require that students use narrative techniques, structure narratives coherently, and achieve an intended tone.

But who wants to read a neatly packaged, bland, linear story? So this is also a story about the hidden curriculum, about the daily battles waged in my "heat-oppressed" teacher brain, about feeling trapped by what seem to be valid and acceptable practices that—when "practiced"—silence voices.

Innovation and joy sustain us on our teaching journeys and create cultures of design thinking in our classrooms. So this is not a story about rubrics or graphic organizers, outlines or annotated bibliographies. It's about my students and me, failing forward together, waiting for ideas to arrive, then taking off when momentum struck. Like the surface of a beautiful tapestry, its underside revealing a mélange of colorfully clipped and fringed threads, there's meaning above the messiness. So this story begins in medias res.

In April of 2018, my principal and supervisor ask the eleventh-grade teachers to meet and discuss our current college essay writing practices. I put it on my calendar and don't worry. I've got exemplars and planners and tip sheets galore. It is a matter of pride that my students leave class every June having drafted, revised, and finalized not one but *two* college essays. After two decades of teaching AP Literature and AP Language, I'm the college essay *queen*.

The meeting doesn't go well ... for me. Parents have expressed concerns that some eleventh-grade teachers are dedicating much more instructional time to college essay writing than others. As I sit in a circle with my colleagues and listen to them describe how they cover college essay instruction in their classes, I realize that "some" is a euphemism. I'm the only *one* of us who dedicates an entire instructional unit to this work. As a grade-level group, we decide we will all spend *some* time reviewing college essay prompts in class, but no one will assign or grade them. In the weeks that follow, I privately fume. Why is it that this *one* thing I do so well has to be taken away? It is the *one* steady piece of instruction I *don't* have to overthink. And now, I have to come up with something *new*.

Oh, the irony.

As a creative on every personality test I've ever taken, as someone who prides herself on "never teaching the same lesson twice," the college essay unit is my *one* easy thing. Until now, I haven't realized that it is my recycled secret, the unit I cling to with blind nostalgia. Now the Lazy Train is pulling out of Nostalgia Junction. What am I going to do for the last four weeks of school?

Multigenre papers had been on my radar for quite some time. As early as 2014, I'd seen other respected educators chatting about them on Twitter. In 2015, I'd edited Kelly Weber's article about multigenre papers for *English Leadership Quarterly*, in which the author described the nondirective teaching model, anchored in the work of humanistic psychologist Carl Rogers. Reinforcing how, in a multigenre writing workshop, "the instructor acts as a counselor or facilitator, helping students to process feelings and decide which steps to take and what to learn next .... The instructor asks questions and verbally reflects students' feelings and responses to help them gain insight."[2] Shortly after editing this article, I reached out to fellow English teachers whom I knew had assigned multigenre papers. I asked for samples of their students' work, which they immediately shared. Serendipitously, I landed in Sarah Andersen's workshop on writing multigenre memoirs at Nerd Camp Michigan in the summer of 2016. Moved to tears by her students' multigenre memoirs, I flew home to New Jersey with hope and promise in my heart. By the spring of 2017, I had a veritable font of resources to get myself started. But I was still hesitant to do so, because, I rationalized, I just didn't see a place in the year where multigenre work would "fit."

Still, over the summer of 2017, I read more about multigenre work in *Write Beside Them*, and in *Blending Genre, Altering Style*, leaving the two books brimming with marginalia and sticky notes. In *Blending Genre*, Tom Romano describes multigenre papers as works "composed of many genres and subgenres, each piece self-contained, making a point of its own, yet connected by theme or topic and sometimes by language, images, and content."[3] Then, I put the book away. For a year.

Now it is 2018, and I pull the same books down from the same shelf of my classroom closet and peruse my notes. *Love it!* I've flagged on a Post-it next to Penny Kittle's multigenre work. *Yes!* I've inscribed in purple gel pen on several sections of Romano's text. I sigh as I consider how and why these books have traveled back to my shelves for a year. *You're no Tom Romano*, echoes the voice of self-doubt in my mind. *You're no Penny Kittle.*

There has never been enough time to get to the "dreaming big" multigenre project at the end of the year. Until now. It's May, and there is no time to prepare the way I like to prepare, which is neurotically. I can't dust off the old college essay unit, so it's time to dust off these books and revisit all the resources I've put in storage for "the future." This time, when the voice of self-doubt begins to creep back into my consciousness, I gently escort it to the door. I make some decisions to move forward. I decide that in these final weeks of school, instead of college essays, we will write multigenre narratives grounded in topics of personal interest. We start by mining our writer's notebooks for ideas. I craft as my students craft.

I look through my notebook and harvest several topics. Then, I start my multigenre drafting with a manifesto about why English teachers specifically should not be assigned cafeteria duty. As I draft, I take a deep dive into the inequities that exist within my profession. I swim in the stressors of working motherhood, of packing school lunches, of cafeteria as metaphor. I write poems and scripts. I draft (then scrap) arguments. I create a visual diagram of the tables in the cafeteria, top ten lists of all the things I'd rather be doing than watching teenagers eat. Many of my students select topics about which *they* are passionate, which means that many pursue the same topic: the stressors of eleventh grade. I worry I will end up reading the same paper ad nauseam, but it's wasted worry. They all approach their topics from different angles. Some write editorials, others create storyboards, others "deep fried" memes, Buzzfeed-style quizzes, mock journalism. Some choose specialized topics outside my purview.

One May morning, I get so sick of looking at all the documents in my digital folder on screen that I print them all out and put them up on the white board. As my students enter the classroom, they're greeted with magnetic clips, masking tape, memes, poems, short prose pieces, scripts and Post-Its, layered, rearranged like some literary crime board. I share with them that I am hoping to find some cohesion, some semblance of structure and sequence. Making my process visible helps. That night, I go home and write this piece, which began as a quick write in my notebook:

> **Questions I Ask Myself on Wednesday, February 21, 2018, during Lunch Duty**
> Why doesn't that kid ever eat anything? Wouldn't it just be easier to actually do the homework right now instead of copying? What's the point of a 56-minute lunch period if you can't get some work done? Why does lunch need to be 56 minutes long? Why does this 56 minutes feel so much longer than any other 56 minutes?
> Why is that kid on a phone when the kid has a concussion and can't use a computer? Why is it not okay to use a Chromebook in class but okay to go on a phone at lunch? Why are they gathering around a phone and talking heatedly? Is it really any of my business? What if there's some fight later in the day today, and it turns out the fight started at lunch, and I was here and I could have stopped it? Will I be to blame? Would one of those kids be grateful if I intervene? Should I just casually meander my way over there?

I've hit the turning point in my process, where I have seen that the topic I started with has led me on a deeper journey. The cafeteria, my place in it, is representations of schools' complexities, of my multiple roles as an educator. Ultimately, I place this prose piece between a script and a poem in my final multigenre paper, and it creates the transition and cohesion I need. I share this process with my students. I am living in my pages, they in theirs.

The list for conferences on my whiteboard is populated every day of digital writing workshop, and the conferences feel different from many of the tense ones I've had during office hours this year. Students leave happy. I send them off to continue their work feeling great warmth. In retrospect, I don't know why this surprises me so much. They've likely been hoping for an experience like this since September, and I wince a bit as I mentally trek down Flashback Freeway with all of its cringe-worthy potholes.

Specifically, I had begun the year in the least inspiring way any teacher can kick off a semester: by administering a diagnostic assessment. Expository writing skills needed work, so I skipped the community building I usually did in the first few weeks of school. Instead, I spent the time reviewing skills such as quotation integration, choice and sequencing of evidence, and sentence fluidity—all worthy goals. What I didn't understand at the time is that all this efficiency was feeding the systemic beast that consumes through "standardization, compliance, and surveillance."[4]

I was selectively naive about this beast's existence, and I tried to balance my approaches to instruction and assessment. I assigned brief formative writing tasks, graded on my department's rubric, which allow me to turn around quick and actionable feedback. One night, I opened my email to an inquiry from my student Kevin, who asked what *exactly* he needed to *do* to get *all* the points on these writing tasks. Thanks to archives of saved student work from previous years, I sent Kevin exemplar "answers" that received a perfect score on the rubric. The email I sent Kevin was cursory and abrupt. In this moment, my protégé and I both personified what Warner claims to be a "deeply impoverished notion of what writing does and how it works."[5] I tried to provide a packaged solution for this student, whose thoughts were absorbed with devising workarounds and quick fixes to earn points, a ceaseless cycle that seduces many. "We treat formula as necessary when instead it is incendiary," Kelly Gallagher and Penny Kittle assert in *180 Days*. "It consumes the creativity, the voice, and the originality that students are capable of bringing into their writing."[6] In responding to Kevin with samples of work that scored an A on the rubric, I conveyed that his own capabilities as a writer were limited. It's time to undo some of that damage.

Now, in the spring of 2018, Kevin sits at his desk, typing away on his Chromebook, drafting his multigenre paper without stopping to ask me any questions. He writes long prose pieces, constructs poems, and creates infographics. I'll likely see him for an in-class conference tomorrow. There is no due diligence here for me and no standardization for him. As a veteran English teacher, expository writing has been my bread and butter for two decades. I am an expert at offering students "executive help"—correcting grammar, usage, mechanics and spelling. But so much of the nondirective approach to multigenre writing demands that students advocate for "instrumental" help. As Tom Newkirk underscores in *Embarrassment*, executive help is "dependency-oriented and aimed at 'fixing' a particular problem .... In instrumental situations, the student needs to be a more active participant."[7] While students are pros at the email or office hours "proofreading pop-in," they need a great deal of coaching to see me during class time, early in their writing process when their vulnerabilities are particularly evident.

As the lead learner, I need to redefine what the writing conference *actually* is. I try a new conferring approach, inviting students to meet with me in pairs or triads if they have a "common problem." They come together to see me at the conference table, thinking they have a common problem. (They usually don't, but there's safety in numbers.) Newkirk's advice on this issue encourages me: "A writing conference ... essentially models the prompts a more experienced writer does internally and automatically ... it models a set of questions or expectations, which the writer can, at some point internalize."[8] As I sit with writers and grapple with such complex issues as organization, tone, and purpose, others overhear the conversation, self-assess their work, internalize their own unique, iterative processes.

Sometimes, I don't know what the issue will be or how they will need my help, but I'm open. My words are more questions than answers, and I begin to experience and appreciate this truth: "Although the content of the conference is unpredictable, the language we use to solve problems with students carries our values and beliefs."[9] No longer queen of the college essay, I'm more of a jump-starting jester, playing the fool and landing on wisdom that's not packaged or prepared.

Across the room, Jennifer raises her hand. She needs to caption a photo. I'm flummoxed. I state the obvious. "So ... you are hoping to caption this and capture a mood ...?" Jennifer nods. We sit. Stare at the photo. Sigh. As a fellow writer, I can empathize and sit with her in her search for words. This is teaching, a quieter kind than I am used to. I count down from five in my mind, stay silent, and when I get to two, Jennifer speaks. "I think the most important thing in the picture is the portal window." I look at the photo for several seconds and then ask, "Why is that perspective important?" Jennifer answers, and from that speaking, she gleans what she needs to write her caption. My blank turn and inquiry helped her more than the other "help" I've grown accustomed to giving.

Students are creating work that I do not always feel qualified to assess. Sometimes, all I can say as they are creating is, *Wow*. I learn to ask more questions. *How long did it take you to do this? What materials did you use to make that?* I do not feel like a fraud—in fact, authenticity banks up my resolve. Not knowing all the answers turns me into a better listener. I affirm what they've already done and ask questions to help them extend and revise their work. I watch them return to their desks with heightened intent. I'm witnessing as an instructor that "story is more than a formula and writing is more than an activity."[10] We crowdsource for suggestions on drafts, offer organic feedback, return to our own work with new ideas and different approaches.

As I confer with students, I refer to our collective struggles and successes, describe our choices, our processes. I send them to each other for help much more quickly, work in more impromptu "turn and learns" when a topic emerges in a conference that might be for the good of all. Newkirk describes this experience as "a robust faith in processes of learning [which] allows us to manage difficulty and be alert to the often microscopic advances we or our students make."[11] What most impresses me as we draft together is that students are owning their work instead of renting ideas and approaches. We've arrived in writing territory that Warner describes as "deep learning, lasting, transferable knowledge, [that] requires each individual to reinvent the wheel for themselves."[12]

The final papers come in, a stack of seventy-five assignments I'm eager to read. I head for my porch at 5:00 a.m. and 9:00 p.m. every weekday in the second week of June. My cups of coffee cool and my glasses of iced tea sweat on the side table as I read. I see new sides to my students, richer facets of their lives they are revealing to me, and what I realize is that they have always been these amazing young people, waiting for the opportunity and agency to express themselves in this fashion. They've always been right here. Reading their multigenre work helps me see them more fully, to be more present in their lives. It also helps me appreciate the diversity of "range and content" outlined in the New Jersey Student Learning Standards for English Language Arts. They are spending dedicated time, both in school and at home, writing multiple pieces.

The comprehensive endnote reflections of my students, a requirement for their paper, make evident that this initiative has not been a waste of time or some hippy-dippy experiment. "This paper went from a simple documentation of my high school experience and transformed into a social activist piece while still maintaining my teenage experience," writes Mary. Her reflection reinforces Newkirk's assertion that "the capacity to improvise, to be open to possibilities in the act of writing, is critical to analytic fluency."[13] In the language of the writing standards, Mary learned to "adapt the form and content of their writing to accomplish a particular task and purpose."[14] As a high-performing student, Warren had seen most writing tasks in high school as standardized and requiring a "proper thesis." Entrenched in explicative criteria, this was one of his first experiences with writing choices, and he thrived when given permission to pursue his passion as a writer. "In writing multiple genres, I could represent a part of my life that I cannot express .... I had the freedom and control to work how I would like and on what I would like, although I had not initially wanted to share much of my feelings." To use the language of the standards, Warren was able "to communicate clearly to an external, sometimes unfamiliar audience."[15] Warren's endnotes are a reminder that student writers need encouragement and affirmation that "'real' lives need not be separated from their school lives."[16]

Collectively, the students' metacognition exemplifies why multigenre work was a worthwhile pursuit, and their reflections underscore Warner's ultimate premise in *Why They Can't Write*: "Rather than standardization, efficiency and proficiency, we should be concerned with choice, curiosity, risk, and the building of a critical sensibility."[17]

Writing a multigenre narrative alongside students strengthened and externalized my existing belief that "emotion is the engine of intellect."[18] Too often, in too many classrooms, including my own, students are asked to write things about which they care very little. This project gave us all permission to lead with our feelings and interests. Moving forward, it also encouraged me to bring the writer's notebook into my high school classes beyond just short daily entries. I now offer students opportunities to write beside texts such as poems, articles, and photographs, to value practice and play, and to see the writer's notebook as a tool rather than a product. Had I not undertaken this multigenre work in concert with student writers, I might not have witnessed and appreciated the extent to which "students want to write what they think they can't—and do it well."[19] The tall order of writing thirty-six college recommendations the summer following this unit was made much more pleasurable by having their multigenre work to reference.

My students and I came to see that writing our stories is "life work," in which we compose pieces to learn more about ourselves and our world. Fellow teachers may ask, "How do you find time to work this into the curriculum?" and I swear by the words of Kelly Gallagher and Penny Kittle in *180 Days*: "Teaching can feel like an act of rebellion."[20] Student writers deserve to create bodies of work that prove pleasurable, memorable, enriching, and restorative. Carve out time because your students' stories matter, because the work can not only be done, but done meaningfully, because engaging in the process as a writer yourself will make you not only a better teacher, but a better human being. Don't succumb to self-doubt and shelve your storytelling for a day when you're "ready" or "an expert." Spend your time generously, humbly, wisely, and well. Spend your time writing beside your students. Tell and retell, write and rewrite all the stories of your lives.

Notes

1   "New Jersey Student Learning Standards for English Language Arts," New Jersey Department of Education, accessed March 27, 2019, https://www.state.nj.us/education/cccs/2016/ela/g1112.pdf.

2   Kelly Weber, "Voice, Choice, and the Optimal Mismatch: Empowering Students' Voices by Making Them (Un)Comfortable with the Student-Directed, Multigenre Research Paper," *English Leadership Quarterly* 38, no. 1 (2015): 5–9, http://www.ncte.org/library/NCTEFiles/Resources/Journals/ELQ/0381-aug2015/ELQ0381Voice.pdf.
3   Tom Romano, *Blending Genre, Altering Style: Writing Multigenre Papers* (Portsmouth, NH: Boynton/Cook, 2000), x–xi.
4   John Warner, *Why They Can't Write: Killing the Five-Paragraph Essay and Other Necessities* (Baltimore: Johns Hopkins University Press, 2018), 133.
5   Ibid., 142.
6   Kelly Gallagher and Penny Kittle, *180 Days: Two Teachers and the Quest to Engage and Empower Adolescents* (Portsmouth, NH: Heinemann, 2018), 223.
7   Thomas Newkirk, *Embarrassment: And the Emotional Underlife of Learning* (Portsmouth, NH: Heinemann, 2017), 69.
8   Ibid., 143.
9   Gallagher and Kittle, 16.
10 Penny Kittle, *Write beside Them: Risk, Voice, and Clarity in High School Writing* (Portsmouth, NH: Heinemann, 2008), 154.
11 Newkirk, 88.
12 Warner, 169.
13 Newkirk, 142.
14 "New Jersey Student Learning Standards."
15 Ibid.
16 Maria Colleen Cruz, *The Unstoppable Writing Teacher: Real Strategies for the Real Classroom* (Portsmouth, NH: Heinemann, 2015), 126.
17 Warner, 159.
18 Kittle, 39.
19 Ibid., 125.
20 Gallagher and Kittle, 225.

15

Crafting Online Worlds as Literary Response

Stacy Haynes-Moore
The University of Iowa and the Cedar Rapids Community School District

Sometimes changing students' learning outcomes means a major shift in the class culture. When I started studying teacher Becca Knowles's tenth-grade language arts classroom,[1] she and her "struggling" students were in the process of ditching routines of short answer prompts and five-paragraph essays. Becca joined as a participant in my university research, and together we explored a new approach to curriculum—one in which she would continue explicit literacy instruction yet make room for student creativity and ownership of learning. Old world out, new world underway. In our project, Becca and her sophomores began reading the dystopian novel *The Hunger Games*,[2] and as part of their studies they crafted original characters and "stepped into" these roles for an online writing role-play. Students' storytelling, coupled with the twists and turns of Collins's novel, led to a collaborative and reimagined version of the narrative.

Prior to developing her plans for the role-play, Becca acknowledged that many of the LA-10 class's students disliked language arts classes. One of her students, Travis, told me that he and his classmates were "not good readers" and described himself as a student daunted by writing tasks. "I don't like writing. I'm not good [at it]," he said. Becca's introduction of the online role-play, grounded by a creative and student-centered approach to writing, generated newfound engagement that she leveraged to extend students' academic practices: reading closely, writing frequently, discussing in depth, developing editing skills, and experiencing writing as a recursive process. Becca's unit plans encouraged playful interactions with literature, implementing lessons framed not only by language arts standards but by pedagogical appreciation of the way creative and collaborative learning can empower students as readers and writers.

Spring semester for Becca's students at Trident High marked the start of their storytelling role-play. Each day, for more than a month, Travis and his classmates pressed through Becca's door, scooped up books and laptops, and secured spots with one another to plot scenes. Collaborations were social, lively, and productive, evidenced by clarified sentences, fine-tuned story details, and a general increase in the volume of writing. Students received instantaneous peer feedback as the digital space afforded them freedoms as online authors; they could continuously share, discuss, and revise, taking part in a synchronous participation that made their story world a messy and entertaining playground, a space to explore writing strategies and their immediate impact on audience.

Recursive writing became accepted and expected in Becca's class. Face to face, their laptops prepped for peer conversations, students became discerning readers and editors and fans of each other's fiction. Hearing scenes read aloud was useful, as words and sentence sounds cued the writers to discover their errors in mechanics, usage, or grammar. Their class activities varied during daily routines. While some students independently read the novel, others might team up and focus on revisions for the role-play, leaving Becca opportunities to conference with individuals to hone skills or nurture confidence as writers. Peer conversations, readings, and drafting collaborations complemented Becca's direct instruction; her lessons ranged from vocabulary strategies to applications of literary devices.

Research Context

I frame my research with a sociocultural lens, drawing upon theories of Bakhtin and Vygotsky to examine how issues of student identities, participation, and culture surface and operate in language arts instruction. My research and work with Becca's classroom reflect my curiosities about the complex ways that adolescents respond to literature and demonstrate literacies within digital spaces.[3] Studies of digital storytelling used in school classrooms[4] and research of adolescents' online role-play[5,6] or digital gaming[7] describe communities of participation that are rich with literacies and imagination.

Online worlds are spaces that invite and extend opportunities for students to collaborate and create. Research suggests adolescents join online together around shared interests or hobbies to participate in activities from photo-sharing and music production to reviewing fashion or YouTube.[8] Though adolescents' uses and choices of digital platforms and tools evolve, their online participation is steady,[9] as is the reported value of shared meaning-making for whatever teens might decide to play, produce, or discuss.[10] Situated online, there is relevance in the communal activity and a heightened engagement to participate[11] in the space, all of which present opportunities for educators.

Classroom Context

Before launching the digital role-play project, it was unusual for Becca to ask her students to write creatively because it was a little outside her comfort zone. On its surface, the writing assignment was atypical, given the course's emphasis on academic skills. Expository form was generally the key to assignments, but Becca's role-play challenged students to explore authors' technique through a narrative structure.

As earlier noted, Becca's class was defined as "remedial." Students enrolled based on their marginal proficiencies on state assessments, and the course provided them a daily double-dose of language arts activities. I learned that students' dislike of LA-10 stemmed from what they felt was a merciless cycle: read books, complete worksheets, answer questions, make PowerPoints, take tests, and take computerized assessments. Students said they respected Becca, yet LA-10 was an academic hoop. Read novels? Boring. Analyze themes? Irrelevant. Write essays about any of these things? Meaningless.

Newer to teaching this "remedial" curriculum, Becca realized around midwinter that she was "in trouble" with the school-provided lessons and she needed change to engage and support her students in learning. With her principal's approval, she purchased a classroom set of the novel *The Maze Runner*[12] to develop a month-long unit on dystopian literature. She planned for students to read and use the text to identify narrative elements, draw evidence into class discussion, and write multi-paragraph essays. Becca explained that she pushed students forward academically and there "was some success in reading" the novel. However, as the chapters concluded, Becca's worries increased. She reported to me that "[students] don't want to do anything. I'm frustrated. They're frustrated."

Organizing the Story World

I asked: *Would you consider trying something different with the way the students respond to literature? How about asking students to write creatively?* She agreed. Sticking with their study of dystopias, I located a classroom set of *The Hunger Games*, and we structured Becca's spring reading and writing unit around

Collins's text and a creative writing role-play, drawing from my previous research of an online book club, Goodreads. Its members produced a role-play writing game in which they imagined characters, developed scenes, and then performed their characters online in a sequence mimicking the novel's storyline.

For Becca's class instruction, we framed learning objectives with Common Core standards for language arts[13] (Table 15.1) and focused our initial efforts on frequency of reading and writing practices to extend students' understanding of text structure, theme, and characterization, as well as helping them develop and apply literary techniques in their own writing.

By the end of the unit, however, we recognized myriad ways standards could frame and guide the students' role-play activity with even greater depth—in short, we connected the reading of literature with playful writing, and we did not find academic challenge and creativity to be mutually exclusive.

Table 15.1 Language arts standards that frame the role-play

Activity	Standard
Student will compose an imagined narrative.	CCSS.ELA-LITERACY.W.9-10.3 Write narratives to develop real or imagined experiences or events using effective technique, well-chosen details, and well-structured event sequences.
Students will practice and produce writing that applies elements of narrative technique.	CCSS.ELA-LITERACY.W.9-10.3.A Engage and orient the reader by setting out a problem, situation, or observation, establishing one or multiple point(s) of view, and introducing a narrator and/or characters; create a smooth progression of experiences or events. CCSS.ELA-LITERACY.W.9-10.3.B Use narrative techniques, such as dialogue, pacing, description, reflection, and multiple plot lines, to develop experiences, events, and/or characters. CCSS.ELA-LITERACY.W.9-10.3.C Use a variety of techniques to sequence events so that they build on one another to create a coherent whole. CCSS.ELA-LITERACY.W.9-10.3.D Use precise words and phrases, telling details, and sensory language to convey a vivid picture of the experiences, events, setting, and/or characters.
Students will develop a unified story for an audience of peers, doing so within an online forum.	CCSS.ELA-LITERACY.W.9-10.4 Produce clear and coherent writing in which the development, organization, and style are appropriate to task, purpose, and audience.

Activity	Standard
Students will engage in writing processes that include revision, editing, and rewriting.	CCSS.ELA-LITERACY.W.9-10.5 Develop and strengthen writing as needed by planning, revising, editing, rewriting, or trying a new approach, focusing on addressing what is most significant for a specific purpose and audience.
Students will use a digital space where they will exchange information and ideas to craft and develop a shared story.	CCSS.ELA-LITERACY.W.9-10.6 Use technology, including the Internet, to produce, publish, and update individual or shared writing products, taking advantage of technology's capacity to link to other information and to display information flexibly and dynamically.
Students will use events and details from *The Hunger Games* as a foundation for their own, original creative writing.	CCSS.ELA-LITERACY.W.9-10.9 Draw evidence from literary or informational texts to support analysis, reflection, and research.
Students will write daily and for both shorter and extended periods of the class time.	CCSS.ELA-LITERACY.W.9-10.10 Write routinely over extended time frames (time for research, reflection, and revision) and shorter time frames (a single sitting or a day or two) for a range of tasks, purposes, and audiences.
Students will communicate with one another to shape the story's direction, events, characters, and outcomes.	CCSS.ELA-LITERACY.SL.9-10.1 Initiate and participate effectively in a range of collaborative discussions (one-on-one, in groups, and teacher-led) with diverse partners on Grades 9–10 topics, texts, and issues, building on others' ideas and expressing their own clearly and persuasively. CCSS.ELA-LITERACY.SL.9-10.1.B Work with peers to set rules for collegial discussions and decision-making (e.g., informal consensus, taking votes on key issues, presentation of alternate views), clear goals and deadlines, and individual roles as needed.

Source: Common Core ELA Standards (www.corestandards.org/ELA-Literacy/CCRA)

We used the book club's format and game rules as a handy outline to structure the role-play. Becca reviewed several free web and blog spaces to house the students' story and decided on Schoology, a setup that allowed her to organize the web homepage with a list of designated writing prompts, similar to a list of chapters that preview the content of a novel. Becca borrowed the general rules from the book club, which explained the role-play activity in this way:

> Starting within the next few days, we will be hosting an enormous Hunger Games roleplay, in which 24 members will create 24 tributes and be thrown into an arena …. [i]n that time you will be able to:
> - Roleplay your chariot rides & interviews
> - Be given a training score
> - Make alliances with members of your choice
> - Fight and run and hide and kick-butt in the arena …
> Moderators (organizers) will act as GameMakers & Sponsors, reigning all sorts of havoc upon you (and supplying you with necessitates, depending on your given training score). Tributes will be killed off in a poll, made by GameMakers. This is where your alliances really come in handy, since you can gang up on a certain tribute. Of course, inactive Tributes will be killed off in a GameMakers attack.
> All the fine details (rules, guidelines, arena, etc.) will be supplied once we have our 24 Tributes …. See you in 24 hours, and may the odds be ever in your favor![14]

Becca's role as the game moderator was to establish the rules, determine the project time frame, and select scenes around which students would write, including the "Introduction of Characters," "Run for the Cornucopia," "Pre-Game Warmup," "Tributes Fighting to Stay Alive," and "The Final Battle."

Shaping the Characters

As students began to read and discuss *The Hunger Games* in class, Becca also launched their writing role-play and asked students to invent unique characters that they would use to narrate story scenes. With excitement, they stepped into their author roles to outfit their characters with names such as Revan, Bob Billy, Lightning Bolt, and T_Mac. Students developed backstories about character talents and hobbies, families and friendships, strengths and weaknesses.

Becca added prompts each week and students' scenes unfolded. For example, for "Post Four: Into the Capitol" she asked students to provide a travel narrative from their characters' perspectives regarding the following:

1. Their travels into the Capitol.
2. The decision on whether they and their fellow tributes would be trained together or separately and the reason for the decision, including which tributes they considered to be "Career Tributes" and why.
3. Their biggest fear before entering the games.
4. A description of their stylist team, how/what they thought of their makeover, and a description of the costume the stylist designed for them.

5. A description of the skill they planned to show off to the Gamemakers and how their interaction with the Gamemakers went during the individual showcase of skills.

As one student posted about her character's sprint to reach the Cornucopia to secure food, another student simultaneously posted his character's race to the Cornucopia and the discovery of camping gear. Writers' subsequent scenes involved each other's characters in dialogue and action, and in this way students' individual scenes mixed and meshed with classmates' scenes toward a unified storyline.

Collaborating as a Class

Becca emphasized teamwork throughout lessons. She organized students as pairs or small teams to brainstorm upcoming story conflicts and make decisions about characters' next actions. Her direct instruction reading the novel helped students recognize how Collins's story centers on battles of external and internal conflicts; students realized their characters, too, should face similar challenges and solutions. As authors, they plotted obstacles and designed moments of bravery. They collaborated to write scenes in which characters survived severe weather, consumed magical potions, and stumbled across hidden shelters.

Students also worked together to revise drafts and edit. Reading their posts aloud garnered feedback, even peer applause, though some class conversations were neither easy nor easily facilitated, especially as characters competed against one another to survive the games. Even these story moments were teachable, though, and Becca guided the class through navigating social and emotional conflicts of characters and peers.

Students didn't always agree with each other or Becca. For example, around the fourth week of role-play, as she mapped instruction to the role-play resolution, Becca told students they would soon begin to select which characters to remove—to kill. This is a significant detail that occurs in *The Hunger Games*. Becca outlined for students that during their remaining classes for the role-play, they would vote one character to be killed, doing so until only one character remained alive to be crowned the winner of the role-play game. She explained that the students whose characters were cast off would write their own character's death scene and then join her as a game moderator for the remainder of the activity.

There was silence as she announced this direction. Then, rebellion. "No one gets kicked off," her students pleaded. "No one is killed." Students were adamant and argued that Becca's decisions were unfair to them and mean-spirited for characters. Instead, students offered a counter: they would all write scenes to complete the final storyline and together plot scenes against the evil President Snow. In this way, instead of removing one on their own, they would imagine a resolution in which Snow dies and the students' characters would claim victory.

To Becca's delight, her students cared about their characters, cared about crafting the story, and wanted to write. She agreed to alter her instructions and used students' feedback to rewrite guidelines to close the project. Instead of killing their characters, students would write the next scenes to demonstrate acts of compassion, teamwork, problem-solving, or ingenuity. Weekly, the class would read these character installments together and cast votes for "best" scene writings, awarding points to student writers. Whoever claimed the most points would be crowned the winner and earned the privilege of authoring the final scene to defeat President Snow.

On the class's final day of role-play, students shared posts, voted, and tallied points. Each student earned at least one peer's vote for excellent writing, but it was Travis, the reluctant LA-10 writer, who received peer recognition as the most skilled. His peers crowned him the role-play game winner and gave him the honor of authoring of the final scene.

Concluding the Games

In post-project discussions, it was clear students valued the opportunity to write with imagination and network with classmates. Becca's embrace of creativity as a response to literature worked for her students' practices in reading and writing. Situated in the online role-play space, students demonstrated abilities to apply literary technique, revise and edit language, and design a text from beginning to end. Frequency of writing, peer collaboration, and Becca's direct instruction illuminate a classroom experience supportive of skill development as well as nurturing for students' engagement in literacies. Notably, the celebrations of characters and scenes altered at least a few students' negative self-perceptions as capable writers. Maybe they *did* like writing, *and* they were good at it after all.

Notes

1   Becca Knowles, her tenth-grade students' names, and Trident High School are pseudonyms per research guidelines of the Institutional Review Board.

2   Suzanne Collins, *The Hunger Games* (New York: Scholastic Press, 2008).
3   Stacy Haynes-Moore, "Trading Spaces: An Educator's Ethnographic Exploration of Adolescents' Digital Role-Play," *Journal of Language and Literacy Education* 11, no. 1 (2015): 35–46.
4   Henry Jenkins and Wyn Kelley, eds., *Reading in a Participatory Culture: Remixing Moby-Dick in the English* (New York: Teachers College Press, 2013).
5   Rebecca W. Black, "English Language Learners, Fan Communities, and Twenty-First Century Skills," *Journal of Adolescent and Adult Literacy* 52, no. 8 (2011): 66897.
6   Jen Scott Curwood, Alecia Marie Magnifico, and Jayne C. Lammers, "Writing in the Wild: Writers' Motivation in Fan-Based Affinity Spaces," *Journal of Adolescent & Adult Literacy* 56, no. 8 (2013): 677–85.
7   James Paul Gee, *Good Video Games + Good Learning: Collected Essays on Video Games, Learning and Literacy* (New York: Peter Lang Publishing, 2013).
8   Mizuko Ito et al., *Hanging Out, Messing Around, Geeking Out: Living and Learning with New Media* (Cambridge, MA: MIT Press, 2010).
9   Jean M. Twenge, Gabrielle N. Martin, and Brian H. Spitzberg, "Trends in US Adolescents' Media Use, 1976–2016: The Rise of Digital Media, the Decline of TV, and the (Near) Demise of Print," *Psychology of Popular Media Culture* 8, no. 4 (2018).
10 Monica Anderson and Jingjing Jiang, "Teens, Social Media, and Technology," *Pew Research Center*, May 31, 2018, www.pewinternet.org/2018/05/31/teens-social-media-technology-2018.
11 Donna E. Alvermann, *Adolescents' Online Literacies: Connecting Classrooms, Digital Media, and Popular Culture* (New York: Peter Lang Publishing, 2010).
12 James Dashner, *The Maze Runner* (New York: Delacorte Press, 2009).
13 National Governors Association Center for Best Practices, Council of Chief State School Officers, *Common Core State Standards for English Language Arts & Literacy in History/Social Studies, Science, and Technical Subjects* (Washington, DC: National Governors Association Center for Best Practices, Council of Chief State School, 2010).
14 Haynes-Moore, 38.

16

Capturing Flash Fiction: Utilizing Graphics, Family, and Friends to Engage ELL Students

Mark Esperanza
Northwest Vista College and Northside Independent School District

In the early springtime of San Benito—a deep south Texas borderland city between the United States and Mexico—I would muse over the rolling waters of the Resaca channel. In a city of many tongues, mothers and fathers placed their trusting children on a swing and pushed them forward and everlastingly. This memory reminds me of the responsibility I am entrusted with as an English educator. I am reminded of the obstacles many face when it comes to creative writing and language acquisition. I am reminded of the pauses students take to negotiate translation in communicating with their English-speaking peers, pauses Laura Gonzales calls "the translation moment—instances in time when individuals pause to make a rhetorical decision about how to translate a word or phrase from one named language to another."[1] As many educators along the Rio Grande River know, we must embrace our students' complex and multilayered relationship with language, utilizing collaborative creative writing approaches, supplemented by visuals, in ways most accessible to the community.

Demographics of Classrooms in Borderland San Benito, Texas

When last surveyed, San Benito High School identified 19.7 percent of students as bilingual and/or English as a Second Language (ESL) learners.[2] The poll surveyed the student population in 2019, a year after I taught seniors and juniors at this location, but I doubt the demographics underwent drastic changes. After all, the same survey concluded that 18.9 percent of students in all of Texas were bilingual/ESL. Make no mistake, the average percentage is higher in borderland cities. At San Benito, my regular English III and English IV class sizes ranged from thirty to thirty-six students. More often than not, the range of English language learners surpassed the 6–7 student per-class average.

As you might imagine, teaching students with various language backgrounds is challenging, especially when compared to the instruction I received in high school more than ten years ago. Strategies used were based on assumptions about the student population, which in turn advanced those already strong with the English language. In "Teaching in Multilingual Schools," authors Lawrence Baines and Anastasia Wickham list these assumptions as follows:

> The student body is monolingual. Students have established their competence in the content areas. Students can readily read, write, listen, and speak in English. Students have access to a stable family life, friends, and money. Students share an enthusiastic, positive disposition toward school.[3]

As a public school teacher, I have witnessed firsthand that these qualities do not apply to the average English language learner. It is for these reasons we must implement creative writing assignments and curricula that involve collaboration and visual learning.

The ELL Need for Collaboration

Academic collaboration among students is vital in education and applicable to their future careers. The ability to work in groups or partnerships enables to practice socializing as well as building an environment of trust and commitment. Moreover, academic collaboration allows English language learners to use their communication skills to practice in groups of heterogeneous students. Exposure to students who may be more fluent in one language than the other benefits those who are less fluent, allowing them to navigate more translation moments and strengthen their ability to communicate using English. Translingualism, which "argu[es] that all languages are constantly evolving,"[4] can only enhance the language acquisition of diverse speakers. English, after all, has borrowed wording from languages worldwide. In fact, "no modern European language has received so many words from so many languages as has English."[5] The linguistic exchange gives English the ability to adapt and further develop.

Collaboration also offers students the experience of establishing a safe and friendly environment, a critical component in their educational success. An important study found "dropout rates for ELLs are more than double those of native speakers of English, which may be attributable to weak support networks at school."⁶ If we as teachers can foster connections between students that otherwise might not have existed, we can strengthen those support networks desperately needed by English language learners. Those networks, and the feeling of not doing it alone, can also increase enthusiasm in their classroom environment. Collaboration offers students the ability to learn that this atmosphere, which fosters reliance on a group of peers, will create the trust needed to discuss writing topics and plot ideas.

Visual Communication

As part of the negotiations that happen when deciding how to translate language (Gonzales's "translation moment"), visuals become "rhetorical strategies enacted to navigate ... translation moment[s]."⁷ Applying visuals allows students to connect linguistically with others through multimodal communication. Multimodal strategies, such as the use of visuals, enhance the educational experience of all students. Not only do visuals satisfy the needs of students with multiple intelligences, but their use supports English language learners because they can participate without the stress and pressure of finding the written translation. By using visuals, English language learners gain competency in their ability to read graphics, as well as actively engage within the classroom environment.

Understanding Linguistic Usage

The socio-emotional aspects of ELL student competency in English must be addressed. As high school teacher J. Arias writes, "[M]any of my English language learning (ELL) students suffer from low self-esteem because they compare their language skills to those of native English speakers .... Their analytical language skills may be undervalued or unnoticed by their peers or teachers."⁸ For this reason, teachers must understand that when assessing English language learners, the focus should be on stylistic composition. For example, ELL students might use different diction or syntax than native English speakers, so it's important to assess the style rather than specific grammatical rules. It's advised that "attention to stylistics only occurs in Advanced Placement Language and Composition .... Ironically, ELL students perform similar tasks in multiple contexts but do not garner the same degree of recognition."⁹ Teachers must be aware that students will engage in code-mixing and code-switching—employing words or phrases from a student's dominant language for English terms they find either untranslatable or unidentifiable—in all student populations.

To clarify, code-mixing is an element of the translation moment responding to a students' uncertainty and communicative need, most often occurring as part of a shared linguistic identity. Teachers of ELL students should know "the key difference between code-mixing and code-switching is indeed that code-switching has a special, social pragmatic consequence while code-mixing does not."[10] For example, when speaking with another student, the English language learner who applies code-mixing might say, "Can you pass me the *lapiz*?" as a quicker communication of their needs. The phrase stems from a linguistic need to communicate with another based on immediateness rather than identity. Code-switching, on the other hand, will occur when speaking to people who share the same dominant language. An example of this would be when linguistically homogeneous groups form and communicate as a part of their shared identity or culture. Conversations will switch from one language to another depending on their context or the surrounding people. As it pertains to writing, code-mixing might appear when the student does not know the translation, or the word simply does not translate. Code-switching might happen if the narrator is addressing a new audience, either as a form of culture or language solidarity, or when there is a shift in speaker within a creative piece.

Therefore, when assessing creative compositions, code-mixing and code-switching should be viewed as a stylistic decision, not an inability to correctly use the English language. By changing perspectives on how diverse language is being utilized, teachers will appreciate the usage and students will find their dominant language can be employed as a tool to strengthen their writing. Valuing and validating other languages encourages students to continue exploring the possibilities of writing confidently in English.

Embracing Language Diversity

English language learners are articulate writers. As teachers, we must honor the complexity, sophistication, and nuance that English language learners bring to their writing. We must listen carefully to the stories they want to share: neatly woven tales of culturally relevant and personal narratives that must be explored and valued. Collaboration allows the exchange of ideas as well as the facilitation of language exchange and acquisition. Visuals also play an important role in communication, providing a multimodal opportunity for ELL students to participate in classroom assignments and group work. Lastly, educators of translingual students must value linguistic choices, like code-mixing and code-switching, as a stylistic approach to writing creatively. These three concepts will guide the activity I present in this chapter, which encourages writers to explore topics and narratives inspired by family and friends.

Capturing Flash Fiction

Capturing Flash Fiction is a visual and collaborative writing activity that benefits translingual students while applying Bloom's Taxonomy and addressing Texas Essential Knowledge and Skills secondary standards for students. The objective is for a group of students to work unilaterally to create one flash fiction narrative with decisions and discussions encouraging each student to learn from one another's use of language, both verbal and written.

Capturing

The 90-minute collaborative writing assignment—one block class or two traditional classes—begins with a homework assignment. Students are asked to think about a family member and a place that inspires them in a positive manner and bring a photograph of each. If they have more than one family member or location, they may bring additional photos as well. Preferably, this task should be given over the weekend or at least over a long enough time for students to reflect and capture the images. An important note here is that the term "family" must be applied liberally. To English language learners, many of whom come from socioeconomically deprived homes, "family" is a less rigid term than it often is in a nuclear family structure, since "those who do not have traditional family structures often create their own with other members of their community .... These families may not share biological bonds but they do share values, language, and experiences."[11] Therefore, it is important that the teacher acknowledges and appreciates the family selected by students.

Location is another factor toward which teachers must show understanding. Although students who come from a financially stable home might have pictures of family vacations abroad or throughout the state, many economically disadvantaged students might choose something a little closer to home. It may well *be* their home. In 2015, when I taught sophomore classes in Progreso, Texas—a location known for its bridge into Mexico—there were clear differences in what students from different economic backgrounds defined as location. We released a benchmark test, which prompted students to write about a Texas attraction. Many chose typical, middle-class southern vacation spots like Six Flags Over Texas or the Corpus Christi Aquarium. Some even wrote about the South Padre Island sands—a nearly two-hour drive from their hometown. But one student chose the neighborhood park. When I asked about it, he admitted two concerns regarding his choice: first, whether his definition of a Texas attraction qualified as something to write about, and second, whether I, as the teacher, would agree with his definition. Students need to understand that the choice in location is truly up to them. Additionally, this could be an opportunity for them to articulate the reasoning behind their choice. Of course, allowing students to find locations within a magazine or through computer searches should be permissible, so long as the student is allowed to cut or print these sources.

Flash

The first forty-five minutes of the activity consist of groups of three or four students sharing their pictures with each other. Groups of three are most effective because the assignment provides enough responsibility for each member to participate fully. Moreover, three students accommodate any extra students who might be joining the activity late, such as absent or new students. I would discourage pairs in this situation because an English language learner might not be as confident to share if they happen to be paired with a proficient English speaker. Groups can be selected randomly or strategically to create heterogeneous language groups, an approach Arias prefers because in "heterogeneous language groups … students employ their communication strategies to speak English."[12] Either method of grouping allows the teacher to take advantage of the ways "small-group discussion is much less intimidating than whole-class discussions [for English language learners]."[13] I found this to be true in my classroom. When utilizing whole-group discussions, either the same few students will respond or nobody will. Small groups allow open dialogue without fear of "looking bad" in front of the entire class.

After groups are formed, students fan out their photos so that every group member can see them. From the photos, the group of students will decide which family members will be their characters and which locations will serve as settings in their stories. If students brought extra photographs, they may either suggest those as well or share with a different group that might lack photo options. This assignment also allows for flexibility with phone usage policy. Since many students possess camera-enabled phones or participate in social media, photographs might be easily available through phone usage. Moreover, "[i]n research done it is widely accepted that 'engaging in various forms of social media is a routine activity that benefits children and adolescents by enhancing communication, social connection, and even technical skills.'"[14] This is also an opportunity for students to share a part of their home life and experiences with others, creating social bonds and a network of supportive peers.

Utilizing these visuals, students will then verbally articulate their story ideas with each other. This is another opportunity for English language learners to exercise translational moments and negotiate narrative devices with peers. As a group, students will choose which photographs they will be using and how those characters will engage within the setting. Given the fact that these photographs will be personal family members, the art of characterization will come easier to students of all backgrounds. This helps to specifically address standards to "plan a piece of writing appropriate for various purposes and audiences by generating ideas through a range of strategies such as brainstorming, journaling, reading, or discussing and develop drafts into a focused, structured, and coherent piece of writing in timed and open-ended situations."[15]

After developing a plan, students visually outline their narrative by creating a storyboard accompanied with short, summarized texts of what is happening in each scene. I have found that requiring six to eight scenes works best for a flash fiction narrative, defined as "stories under 2000 words,"[16] though I suggest nothing over 500 words for this assignment. If available, a poster-size board is ideal so that multiple students can work on it at once. If not, hand out two blank sheets of paper to each group member so that they may individually work on two scenes—groups of three will have six scenes, and groups of four will have eight. For English language learners, this provides the opportunity to rhetorically illustrate their ideas through this translation moment, which is important, because "if a student [feels] like they weren't able to express themselves in writing, this will give them a chance to graphically represent their thinking …. There's a literacy with images that's as critical as literacy with words."[17]

Fiction

For the second forty-five minutes, or the second day of a traditional schedule, students will collaboratively write the narrative they discussed. The most beneficial aspect of collaborative writing for English language learners happens during this process. In an article by Merrill Swain and Sharon Lapkin, there are instances of language-related episodes (LREs), defined as "any part of a dialogue where the students talk about the language they are producing, question their language use, or correct themselves or others."[18] This benefit is compounded when heterogeneous groups have the opportunity to share their language and learn from each other. Discussions can be facilitated by having a list of objectives needed to reach 500 words (see Appendix 16.1). From the perspective of sociocultural theory, "Learners, *novices*, construct knowledge in collaboration with more capable individuals, *experts*. Language is the semiotic tool mediating this process."[19] By communicating with others, English language learners can identify word usage, dialects, and pattern of speech within a heterogeneous group, reinforcing their competency by either acquiring new terminology and usage or cognitively recognizing mastery over written English.

This assignment should be completed using an online writing platform such as Google Docs. Many school districts utilize various Google applications, meaning students might already have a Gmail account. If not, setting students up with an account is relatively easy. Once logged in, one group member can start a document in Google Docs and share it via email. When all students are logged in, they should work together to bring their storyboard to life.

During this stage of the process, their storyboard and photographs should be on full display at all times. By having the pictures of their family members, students will more easily acquire appropriate characterizations, and in doing so, they address the state mandate that "[t]he student uses genre characteristics and craft to compose multiple texts that are meaningful," as well as one of my favorite standards, participating "collaboratively, building on the ideas of others, contributing relevant information, developing a plan for consensus building, and setting ground rules for decision making."[20]

Capturing Flash Fiction

The final product will be a collaborative two-page story about the people and places that inspire the students. The work will be fictionalized so that effective collaboration between all students occurs, and they must include at least one of their people and one of their places. Each student will work simultaneously as writer and editor to ensure communication throughout. Time permitting, students can share their stories either verbally, through Google Classroom, or if teachers have the resources, by printing and displaying them in the classroom or library.

In a larger sense, there are three immediate benefits to the Capturing Flash Fiction experience for English language learners in the classroom. They can engage multimodality through English in a situation that values their existing code-mixing or code-switching abilities; they benefit from being able to address translations visually and collaborate with their heterogeneous peer group; and finally, they will feel competent and part of something greater than themselves: a family, if you will, of supportive peers.

Notes

1. Laura Gonzales, *Sites of Translation: What Multilinguals Can Teach Us about Digital Writing and Rhetoric* (Ann Arbor, MI: University of Michigan Press, 2018), 2.
2. Ryan Murphy and Annie Daniel, "San Benito CISD," *Texas Public Schools*, April 5, 2019, schools.texastribune.org/districts/san-benito-cisd/.
3. Lawrence Baines and Anastasia Wickham, "Teaching in Multilingual Schools," *English Journal* 107, no. 6 (2018): 15.
4. Anatoly Liberman, *Word Origins ... and How We Know Them: Etymology for Everyone* (New York: Oxford University Press, 2005), 156.
5. Ibid.
6. Helen Duffy, Lindsay Poland, Jarah Blum, and Cameron Sublett, "The District Role in Graduation Rate Improvement: Promising Practices from Five California Districts," *Air.org*, American Institutes for Research, November 2015, https://www.air.org/sites/default/files/downloads/report/District-Role-in-Graduation-Rates-Nov-2015.pdf.
7. Gonzales, 2.
8. J. Arias, "Multilingual Students and Language Acquisition: Engaging Activities for Diversity Training," *English Journal* 97, no. 3 (2008), 38.
9. Ibid.
10. Payal Khullar, "Difference between Code Mixing and Code Switching," *LanguageLinguistics*, February 19, 2018, languagelinguistics.com/2018/02/06/difference-code-mixing-code-switching/.
11. Christopher Emdin, *For White Folks Who Teach in the Hood ... and the Rest of Y'all Too: Reality Pedagogy and Urban Education* (Boston: Beacon Press, 2017), 59–60.
12. Arias, 40.
13. Ibid.
14. Emdin, 195.
15. 19 TAC Chapter 110.36, Texas Essential Knowledge and Skills for English Language Arts and Reading: (2015), retrieved from http://ritter.tea.state.tx.us/rules/tac/chapter110/ch110c.html.
16. Becky Tuch, "Flash Fiction: What's It All About?" *The Review Review*, Gonzaga University, www.thereviewreview.net/publishing-tips/flash-fiction-whats-it-all-about.
17. Ibid.

18 Merrill Swain and Sharon Lapkin, "Interaction and Second Language Learning: Two Adolescent French Immersion Students Working Together," *The Modern Language Journal* 82, no. 3 (1998): 326.
19 Ana Fernández Dobao, "Collaborative Writing Tasks in the L2 Classroom: Comparing Group, Pair, and Individual Work," *Journal of Second Language Writing* 21, no. 1 (2012): 41.
20 19 TAC Chapter 110.36.

Yours, Mine, Ours: Collaboration and Differentiated Learning in the Creative Writing Classroom

Tanya Perkins and Josh Tolbert
Indiana University East

A frequent writing challenge for our students, admittedly shared with even seasoned educators, is how to get started. One way to address this hurdle in the creative writing classroom is through "individualized collaboration,"[1] a concept borrowed from online gaming that describes how shared environments can be personalized by an individual, even as they participate in gameplay with other users.[2] In many multiplayer online games, an individual can not only change their avatar's appearance but also manipulate ambient sounds, camera angle, and other visual settings within a game, thus altering their own experience while they group-chat or engage in other group activities within the game environment.[3] With this perspective, the line between independent player and collaborator becomes blurred; a player is able to differentiate their experience as an individual while still actively collaborating. Although the term "individualized collaboration" focused on digital platforms, the concept invites educators to reevaluate the role of collaboration in the brick-and-mortar classroom. Specifically, there exist opportunities for students to use the collective power of collaborative creativity to jump-start their own independent creative work.

Writing is often considered a private activity, even though it has always been a social act. M. Thomas Inge notes that "[t]here has seldom been a time when someone did not stand between author and audience in the role of a mediator, reviser, or collaborator."[4] Similarly, others assert that "[w]e make our meanings not alone, but in relation to others' meanings, which we come to know through reading, talk, and writing."[5] The challenge becomes integrating collaboration seamlessly as an integral part of writing assignments, especially since collaborative writing does not necessarily replace the independent creative work we want to see from students. Rather, productive movement between collaboration and individual work can help students use the dynamics of teamwork as a springboard for their own creativity. This parallels Wendy Bishop and David Starkey's notion that "writing is not entirely a social activity, nor is it a provably solitary one. It is at once an act of individual cognition but also always an act of intellectual and social negotiation with other thinkers."[6] Even if most of our students might not become working authors, the salient point is that *both* solitary/independent work and collaborative sessions are useful in helping students develop as creative writers.[7]

Differentiated Learning

Integration of differentiated learning strategies provides multiple ways for students to explore concepts, based on students' strengths, abilities, and interests.[8] As a pedagogical approach, it recognizes what many educators already know: a one-size-fits-all instructional approach doesn't always work. Within the assignment sequence described below, students demonstrate learning via multiple avenues, both collaboratively and alone, thus making the most of their personal strengths and interests, a key factor in intrinsic motivation.[9] In our adaptation of "individualized collaboration," student agency is embedded in meaningful choices they make as part of their personalized learning within the collaborative process, including how and to what degree they employ the group output. One tool instructors have in this regard is grouping students flexibly based on learning needs. In order to do this grouping well, instructors can create a learning profile or "interest inventory" of their students.[10] Later in the sequence, group makeup shifts so that students with similar interests work together for a time, while still developing individual craft skills like use of imagery, detail, and character development.

Assignment Sequence

The sequence that follows is adapted for the standards-based high school classroom from an introductory creative writing course taught by one of the co-authors at Indiana University East, a regional four-year university. The course introduces fiction, nonfiction, and poetry with an emphasis on exploration of broader craft skills. A significant amount of classroom time is spent reading and discussing both published works that offer examples of course concepts and student work in development. Students are organized into cooperative groups of three or four, which they remain in for multiple sessions in order to build trust and collegiality, thus lessening anxiety when it comes time to share their own work. As we will show, the small group arrangement makes collaboration easier, leading to shared or co-authored products, while "individualized collaboration," to return again to Thomas B. Ward and Marcene S. Sonneborn's phrase,[11] lays the groundwork for further independent writing. The intent is that group output becomes the raw material students are able to make use of on their own to revise, rework, or manipulate as they personally desire. The sequence is described in terms of class periods but could be extended further across multiple class sessions. The readings referenced as examples can be found online or are taken from the third edition of Sellers's *The Practice of Creative Writing*,[12] which includes an excellent anthology. Instructors are encouraged to supplement the examples with additional readings and, in fact, have an opportunity to introduce students to regionally significant work, as well as to writers of color and other marginalized groups.

Aligning Assessment with Goals and Standards

A persistent concern in K–12 has been that students are not meeting grade-level standards for writing, which can hamper writing proficiency in postsecondary endeavors.[13] Students need structured practice to develop writing skills, meaning that feedback and growth opportunities provided by formative assessments merit more attention than finished products where feedback may be overshadowed by a grade.[14] Furthermore, while teacher feedback can have a positive effect, feedback from peers or other adults can have even greater impact.[15] The sequence of assignments presented here offers multiple opportunities for student-to-student feedback, self-assessment and reflection, and direct feedback from the instructor, as well as reasonable flexibility in choosing and completing tasks that provide evidence of progress on grade-level content standards. The sequence focuses on skills related to image-rich writing, as well as learning about and practicing generic features of poetry and fiction. Specifically, students will (1) use vivid and precise language in imaginative ways, (2) create a convincing fictional character, and (3) apply methods from fiction and poetry to develop and revise creative works. These learning objectives are intended to promote formative assessment and provide evidence of progress on the following Common Core standards for Grades 11 and 12:

- CCSS.ELA-LITERACY.W.11-12.3.D: Use precise words and phrases, telling details, and sensory language to convey a vivid picture of the experiences, events, setting, and/or characters.
- CCSS.ELA-LITERACY.W.11-12.5: Develop and strengthen writing as needed by planning, revising, editing, rewriting, or trying a new approach, focusing on addressing what is most significant for a specific purpose and audience.
- CCSS.ELA-LITERACY.W.11-12.3.B: Use narrative techniques, such as dialogue, pacing, description, reflection, and multiple plot lines, to develop experiences, events, and/or characters.

This particular set of standards has a recursive quality that is mirrored in this assignment sequence, with explicit attention initially given to the first standard, then the second, and then to the application of all standards together. Finally, as the unit proceeds, the third standard works to augment the preceding two. Instructors are thus able to shape their pedagogy in ways that reflect the same engaged and recursive process their students will practice—and that we may practice ourselves as writers.

Class One

Students are introduced to the distinction between an image, which is sensory and tangible, and a "thought," or abstraction.[16] This is a fundamental concept informing creative writing across genres, and so is worth spending some time on. Together, we read Dylan Landis's prose/list poem, "In My Father's Study upon His Death," as an example of an image-rich work that describes a room but, at the same time, offers clues about not only its occupant, the speaker's father, but also the relationship the speaker had with him.[17] In their groups, students co-author a similar kind of list poem based on a physical setting. Sometimes a picture helps; if needed, students can research images as starting points, using a Creative Commons photo-sharing site.[18]

Class Two

Each team appoints a member to read aloud their co-authored poem to the entire class. The nature of the poem as a product of collaboration, and thus not specifically identified with any one student, helps relieve the anxiety that often accompanies reading one's own work aloud. Listeners are tasked with writing down one image they found effective and one abstraction that could be replaced by an image. These are handed over to the teams, who together use the rest of the class time to consider the suggestions and revise the list poem. The purpose of this first assignment is to help students see the power of tangibles—vivid, concrete images rather than abstractions and generalities. A list poem of related objects awakens students to the possibilities of the assemblage—how groups of things can invoke personality—and leads into the next set of activities. As a form, montage, with its "[reliance] on context and contestation ... the layers of voice"[19] and viewpoints, is a useful first collaboration as students work together to identify crucial elements as part of the revising or rewriting process. Of course, feedback by peers and the instructor can also play a role in formative assessment.[20]

Class Three

We read together two dramatic monologues—Denis Johnson's "The Boarding" and Joanie Mackowski's "The Larger"[21]—and discuss each speaker as a character based on language, physical gestures, description, and setting. Each team then creates a character connected in some way to the list poem they created together in the previous class. The character sketch involves various tasks from which group members can choose based on their interests. These include finding a visual image representing the character, completing an employment application on behalf of the character, diagramming a family tree or a timeline of key dates for the character, or compiling a playlist of the character's favorite songs. As they do this, students can be guided to reflect on the composite portrait that is forming, negotiating among themselves how to make sense of what might be disparate personal details. Can they explain why, for example, Ava Max's "Sweet but Psycho" would appear alongside Lil Pump's "Gucci Gang" on the character's playlist? What do their choices suggest about the character's personality? Her background or motivations? It's important for students to understand that nothing is fixed yet; together, they are working through ideas and the character will absolutely evolve. The goal is to help students see how *real* a character needs to be—idiosyncratic, detailed, and dimensional.

In essence, this class activity is where the first two standards are beginning to merge. The approach is bringing in some new details for the former and is still process-oriented enough to give some evidence of the latter. The intention here is to create a natural scaffold in which students are exclusively attending to narrative writing and use of details first, followed by explicit practice with revising and presenting their writing. After developing both skills explicitly in the prior two classes, class three is where the instructor can give more direct guidance in bringing these skills—and relevant standards—together and assess students' progress toward mastery.

At this point, each student has their team's list poem, which offers a setting, and the team character sketch. These two documents now shift from being shared creative products to raw material for each student's independently written persona poem. This can be in the voice of the team character or a different character who addresses the team character in line with the genre characteristics of dramatic monologues. Each student now has material they helped create, but each is also responsible for deciding how and to what extent to use that material, free to determine which elements are crucial to include and which to ignore, thus supporting the individual student's emerging aesthetic.

Class Four

Students share their persona poems in their groups. They are usually interested in seeing what their peers have done with the common raw material. After this, we regroup as a whole class to identify further differences between a dramatic monologue in poetic form and a scene of prose with some kind of sequential action and/or dialogue between one or more characters, reading together examples of these two genres. As a class, we consider elements that differentiate them, as well as shared elements such as imagery, tension, voice, etc.

Back in their groups, each team chooses one member's dramatic monologue and, together, they rewrite it as a prose scene, drawing on the conflict, issue, or desire at the core of the poem. Thus, there is recursive movement from "mine" to "ours" as the artificial boundary of ownership fades to allow the poem to become common property. This reflexive shifting early in the writing process helps develop a revision mindset, since it discourages students from seeing any one piece of work as "finished" too early in the writing process. This is critical to the kind of re-visioning we want our writing students to develop.

As homework, each student takes their group-written scene and extends it further on their own, changing it up, adding to it. It's useful to provide students with a list of ideas such as introducing a new character who demands or breaks something, having the character receive an unexpected visitor, adding more dialogue, or rewriting the scene from a different point of view. Students once again use the group collaboration as a springboard for their own personal creative impulse. However, if a student wants to rewrite using their own dramatic monologue as the basis for the scene, that works, too, since the goal is for students to produce two drafts—a persona poem and a prose scene.

Class Five

Students can choose to keep working with either their persona poem or their prose scene. Those who want to keep working in poetry are now grouped together, while students who prefer fiction are also grouped together. Students interested in drama might be grouped together to act out their scenes. In their new groups, students can be provided with genre-specific revision ideas and/or workshop their pieces in order to further revise, edit, and polish their work. This kind of flexible grouping builds on students' interests and strengths, while still accomplishing the overall learning goals; it also opens up further collaborative learning possibilities.

The strategy as described here cultivates a foundation of deliberate word choice and imaginative detail, which is organically refined into more elaborated works. As a deliberately scaffolded approach, it seeks to ensure students learn and practice key elements and that relevant skills from specific identified standards[22] can be accurately assessed. The final class in the sequence has students creating different products, which not only can provide evidence of their progress on multiple standards, but also their ability to apply their earlier practice with word choice, imaginative detail, and narrative elements in an authentic way.

It should be noted that, as the product of group work shifts from collaborative to individual, from "ours" to "mine," and thus becomes the object of independent development, the instructor needs to be clear about the scope of the work expected from individual students. Just tweaking grammar or adding a couple of new lines is not sufficient for students to realize the benefits of this learning sequence. However, instructors can determine scope based on their knowledge of students at the particular progression point. This, again, offers an excellent opportunity to apply differentiated learning strategies. For example, an instructor might create a "menu" of diverse revision ideas from which students can choose in order to fulfill this part of the assignment.

The Need for Reflection

Aside from the creative benefits already discussed, our adaptation of "individualized collaboration"[23] supports students' development of knowledge about themselves as socially situated writers. Collaboration itself can be a meaning-making activity as collaborators bring together multiple elements: individual participants' own background and abilities; environmental artifacts such as laptops, books, and cellphones; and the discursive object(s), whether an idea, theory, or, in the case at hand, creative construct(s).[24] Inevitably, collaborators discover challenges, as well as new connections between and among the object(s) that make up the collaboration.[25]

Introducing guided reflection into the assignment sequence is therefore crucial in order for students to articulate how all of these disparate elements are functioning within the interaction and what it means for them as individual writers. We suggest that "individualized collaboration," with its recursive movement between group and independent writing, invites student reflection at key stages, such as at transition points between team and solitary writing, with the goal of fostering metacognitive awareness of the challenges encountered and how the student personally, and the group collectively, handled them.

Note that there are both group *and* personal/individual benefits resulting from reflection on the interaction. In fact, individual writing can be part of a collaboration, since by its very nature, collaborative writing calls upon writers to come up with various ways to complete a writing task, which inevitably will include at least some solitary composition, even if temporarily.[26]

Conclusion

The strength of the approach discussed in this chapter is that students are developing craft skills by *doing*—they write either collaboratively or on their own continuously and recursively, sharing and then revising and then writing some more. Students use and reuse ideas in different forms which is, in itself, a kind of rewriting. As a process, the assignment sequence lends itself organically to integration of differentiated learning strategies, since students can demonstrate learning via multiple avenues, both within a group and on their own, thus making the most of their personal strengths and interests. Moreover, as collaboratively produced work becomes the starting point for independent rewriting, and vice versa, students begin to see how early drafts inevitably need further/deeper development and how their own role as collaborators contributes to this process. Along the way, they begin to get a sense of themselves as socially situated writers and to understand how "individualized collaboration," as we have repurposed Ward's term, can be part of a creative writing process.

Notes

1. Thomas B. Ward and Marcene S. Sonneborn, "Creative Expression in Virtual Worlds: Imitation, Imagination and Individualized Collaboration," *Psychology of Aesthetics, Creativity, and the Arts* 3, no. 4 (2009): 32.
2. Ibid., 33.
3. Ibid., 44.
4. M. Thomas Inge, "Collaboration and Concepts of Authorship," *PMLA* 116, no. 3 (2001): 624.
5. James A. Reither and Douglas Vipond, "Writing as Collaboration," *College English* 51, no. 8 (1989): 862.
6. Wendy Bishop and David Starkey, *Keywords in Creative Writing* (Logan, UT: Utah State University Press, 2006), 33.
7. Carol Archer and Christopher Kelen, "Dialogic Pedagogy in Creative Practice: A Conversation in Examples," *Pedagogy, Culture & Society* 23, no. 2 (2015): 188.
8. Diane Heacox, *Differentiating Instruction in the Regular Classroom* (Minneapolis, MN: Free Spirit Publishing, 2012).
9. Mariana Norel and Daniela Necşoi, "Valorisation of Students' Individual Potential using the Multiple Intelligence Theory. Examples of Good Practice," *Journal of Educational Sciences and Psychology* I (LXIII), no. 1 (2011).
10. Heacox, *Differentiating Instruction in the Regular Classroom*, 21.
11. Ward and Sonneborn, Creative Expression in Virtual Worlds, 211.
12. Heather Sellers, *The Practice of Creative Writing: A Guide for Students*, 3rd edn. (Boston, MA: Bedford/St. Martin's, 2016).
13. Steve Graham, Karen Harris and Michael Herbert, *Informing Writing: The Benefits of Formative Assessment* (New York: Carnegie Corporation of New York, 2011).
14. Nancy Frey and Douglas Fisher, "A Formative System for Writing Improvements," *English Journal* 103, no. 1 (2013): 6671.
15. Graham, Harris, and Hebert, *Informing Writing*.
16. Sellers, *The Practice of Creative Writing*, 137.
17. Ibid., 161.
18. Sites like Flickr and Unsplash offer royalty-free, user-friendly, high-quality, creativity-whetting choices.
19. Linda Tomoi Pennisi and Patrick Lawler, "Without a Net: Collaborative Writing," in *Colors of a Different Horse: Rethinking Creative Writing and Pedagogy*, ed. Wendy Bishop and Hans Ostrom (Urbana, IL: NCTE, 1994), 230.
20. Graham, Harris, and Hebert, *Informing Writing*.
21. Both are from the Poetry Foundation (www.poetryfoundation.org). See also the Academy of American Poets (www.poets.org).
22. The pertinent standards for Grades 11–12 addressed here are CCSS.ELA-LITERACY.W.11-12.3.D, CCSS.ELA-LITERACY.W.11-12.5, and CCSS.ELA-

LITERACY.W.11-12.3.B. These standards are taken from National Governors Association Center for Best Practices, Council of Chief State School Officers, *Common Core State Standards for English Language Arts & Literacy in History/Social Studies, Science, and Technical Subjects* (Washington, DC: National Governors Association Center for Best Practices, Council of Chief State School, 2010).

23 Ward and Sonneborn, *Creative Expression in Virtual Worlds*, 219.
24 William Duffy, "Collaboration (in) Theory: Reworking the Social Turn's Conversational Imperative," *College English* 76, no. 5 (2014): 416–35.
25 Ibid., 425.
26 Ibid., 426.

NaNoWriMo and Young Writers: Using a Novel Approach to Push Students' Writing

Erik Burgeson and Tom Strous
Worthington City School District

Scene: The Beginning of an Idea

It was a normal day in the school library. The familiar morning routine suggested the world would chug along with little or no problem. As Erik sat at his librarian's desk, Tom bounded into the room, his eyes wide and full of excitement.

"Dude! I killed off a character this morning."
"What?" Erik was a little taken aback at this.
"Yeah. It wasn't my main character, but I had to do it." Tom's response was not remorseful. In fact, he almost seemed happy about it. "I didn't think I would do it, but then it happened. It was almost like I had to write it that way."
"I know what you mean," Erik said. "It's almost as if the novel takes control and writes the story for you. So how many words are you up to now?"

The conversation continued on that early November day as the two educators—a school librarian and a teacher at Kilbourne Middle School in Ohio—discussed their ongoing writing project using National Novel Writing Month (NaNoWriMo) to teach creative writing, encouraging young writers to hone fiction writing skills while meeting Common Core standards.

Backstory

This story began in 2011, when Tom approached Erik to propose that we write our first novels together. After a few years of batting the idea around, it seemed like the right moment to begin. We both wanted to write in the same way

Chris Baty and a community of novelists in San Francisco had begun writing together in November 1999, when they decided they'd each write at least 50,000 words in thirty days. According to the NaNoWriMo website,[1] Baty called the event National Novel Writing Month or NaNoWriMo for short.[2] Eventually, the project grew from the original participants to over 325,000 writers, including 81,311 students and educators through an extension of the original event called the Young Writers Program (YWP).[3]

We'd love to say we both wrote 50,000-word novels that year, but the truth is neither of us cracked 250 words, making zero progress beyond previous attempts. After reflecting on our initial results, we realized we had neglected the most important first step of NaNoWriMo, telling people what we intended to do. Beyond our spouses and children, almost no one knew what we were doing. The following year, we made a fateful decision: tell everyone at school, students and colleagues alike. This added accountability changed our lives as writers and writing coaches.

In a serendipitous coincidence, many of the KMS parents had indicated through parent-teacher conferences that they wanted their children to do more writing. In response, Tom decided to involve all of his seventh-grade ELA students in the program. To prepare, he combed Common Core ELA standards and reviewed past lessons to see how everything would fit together. After assembling a list of rationales and a basic outline of the project, he shared the plan with the principal and received the green light. Then the real planning began as we created an ambitious writing journey that would ultimately benefit students by pushing them to work at the "creation" level of Bloom's Taxonomy.

We designed lesson plans to prepare the young writers to plot out ideas, characters, and story elements in the days or weeks leading up to November. We met often to put together the worksheets and activities to engage the writers in the process. On the YWP website, we found a shared workbook to use with our students.

Making use of the YWP website, which provides various online resources for educators to help students achieve their own writing goals, KMS students and teachers wrote more than 670,000 words by the end of November 2012. Additionally, we both wrote more than 50,000 words and felt an incredible sense of satisfaction after completing a challenge we would not have finished without including our students. In turn, we were meeting a need. Students need guidance and a directed experience to work on creative writing at an advanced level; more, we discovered, than a club without mandatory attendance could provide. Bringing NaNoWriMo into the classroom met this need and their parents' desire that they do more creative work. And we have refined the process over time. The first year, Tom mistakenly assumed the workbook started on Day One, but the lessons were intended to be done at least a week before kickoff. In similar ways, each year we've learned something new and adjusted to make the program more effective.

Each year, we hold a small launch party after school to commemorate the beginning of novel writing and generate excitement with the kids, and the library becomes a hub of NaNoWriMo action. At our first party, approximately fifteen students jumped into the process of completing a novel in thirty days together as if it were the start of a race. We handed out laptops to those who needed them and started a countdown to launch into typing. Students hovered over the computers in anticipation. Some had notes and ideas; others just made it up as they wrote. For some teachers, this might seem a chaotic mess, but it worked. Kids were excited to write and had a lot of fun, working for almost two hours that first afternoon.

Once underway, we employed several resources the NaNoWriMo program provides teachers and groups. The YWP section of the website was particularly useful, providing an online word count tracker, print resources, and the Dare Machine, an online tool that encourages student writing by challenging them to incorporate a randomly selected plot element into their novel (e.g., having a character suddenly begin speaking in a foreign language). Tom liked the Dare Machine's random, often wild ideas. They may or may not have fit with what we were writing, but we could use these ideas for our own work and to challenge each other. One prompted Erik to make his protagonist leave something important behind, which resulted in dropping his backpack as he fled a bully, an unexpected action that propelled Erik's plot forward.

Each Tuesday in November, we met student writers after school in the library, usually for a couple of hours of freewriting. We offered snacks and drinks and turned word sprints into prize-winning opportunities, their excitement growing as we gave away NaNoWriMo "swag" like pins and bookmarks. Surprisingly, kids went nuts for them. Erik also hosted Free-Write Fridays in the library, during which students—with passing grades, completed homework, and permission from their teachers—could come down during any class period and write. These sessions felt like a mixture of after-school writing club and local coffee house.

Meanwhile, with Tom's classroom located on the second floor overlooking the library, it was not unusual for him or his students to lean out a window and issue a word sprint challenge to anyone working in the library. We created an incentive sticker for students who won that read, "I bested Mr. Burgeson!" One thing we both realized early in that first year is that, if we (and the students) were going to have a realistic chance of meeting our word goals, we all had to write whenever possible. There were no limits to writing outside of school.

To encourage this work, we introduced a "Secret Noveling" badge, a prize awarded to students who wrote when they weren't "supposed to." One colleague told Tom shortly into the month-long project that a student asked to use in-class work time to write because their homework was completed. She agreed after finding the request was to work on their novel. The theoretical structure for this incentive program is based on Purpose-Driven Learning, or classroom gamification, as proposed in Michael Matera's book *Explore like a Pirate*.[4] The basic premise of classroom gamification is to mimic the motivational mechanisms from board games and video games, including but not limited to progress bars and achievement badges. This method inspired Erik to gamify his elective classes in the library, and many of the ideas and methods of KMS's NaNoWriMo program were borrowed and modified from existing lessons and ideas from the classroom.

While the only ELA class to take part that first year was Tom's, many teachers in the building supported the project. After a few years, he convinced the other seventh-grade teachers to join in, increasing the program's reach to half the school and almost 200 students at its peak. He also created several different tools and promotional materials through brainstorming sessions with Erik and suggestions from other teachers. The idea, in part, was to have students spend free time during class writing after finishing other work. Teachers were also encouraged to allow passes to the library for novel work.

The Writing Project: Making It Work

The goal of NaNoWriMo is to write a novel in one month, but what are the length expectations for students? For general participants, 50,000 words is the goal, but outcomes can range widely based on the interest and ability of student participants. Tom decided the best way to calculate their goal was to have students write a timed response. We then counted the sample's words and multiplied the total by the number of days they expected to write in November. For some, the word count goal was 1,000 words, while others reached as high as 35,000. The focus is on personal, attainable goals for each student, and the key is having students set a daily challenge goal to work toward. Without one, they write less, procrastinate, or lack motivation to advance their story. While not everyone will achieve their word count goal, teachers must promote and encourage the process.

Tracking students' progress is done through a Google spreadsheet shared with all participating teachers. (The original document was a Microsoft Excel spreadsheet, but we found it difficult to share.) Every couple of days, teachers hold a check-in with students and record current word counts (Figure 18.1).

These "touch points" motivate students and classes through friendly competition. Overall, it is important to establish a specific timeline for writing. Table 18.1 was developed combining our experiences and the basic outline from the YWP.

Student check-ins were part word count, and part conference, helping Tom keep track of the numbers that lent validity to the project as a teaching tool. More importantly, the dialogue helped him address any writing problems or needs of our young writers. Tom also reviewed completed worksheets and

Period 2

Name	word count	Goal	Percentage	Words per day
Mary	4,725	15,000	32%	157.50
Melody	2,018	13,500	15%	67.27
Brian	1,004	12,000	8%	33.47
Deliah	2,836	21,000	14%	94.53
Sarah	549	8,400	7%	18.30
Hannah	207	7,500	3%	6.90
Dillon	1,759	20,000	9%	58.63
Skylar	5,268	13,000	41%	175.60
Amy	2,935	25,500	12%	97.83
Ethan	1,148	15,000	8%	38.27
Sydney	2,897	30,000	10%	96.57
Clayton	2,876	14,000	21%	95.87
			#DIV/0!	0.00

	Class Total	Class Goal	Percent Reached	
	28,222	194,900	14%	
Strous Classes	Total Words	Total Goal	Percent Reached	
	28,222	1,728,397	2%	
Mr. Burgeson	17,238	50,000	34%	
Mr. Strous	20,257	50,000	41%	
KMS Total	65,717	1,828,397	4%	

Figure 18.1 The individual class tracking sheet providing information for each student and a status for the total school word count.

Table 18.1 NaNoWriMo writing timeline

Time	Activity	Who
Mid-October	Pre-writing exercises inspired by YWP resources, goal-setting, registration on YWP website, lessons and writing worksheets for story development from NaNoWriMo and teacher-created resources	Students
October 30 or 31	All Hallow's Read and NaNoWriMo Kick-off Party	Librarian
November 1–30	Novel writing	Students/Teacher
Tuesdays in November	Meet with student writers after school in the library for "write-ins"	Librarian
November	Students use lunch/free time to write in their ELA classroom or the library	Students
November 30	Verify individual word counts and submit to YWP website for recognition and prizes	Teacher
December	Students select a passage or chapter for editing and presentation to the class	Teacher

assignments he'd assigned in a skills packet at the beginning, and later, they walked through the steps of the writing process to develop their story, one part at a time.

In addition to individual student goals and progress, class and school goals were tracked and shared as positive feedback that created a sense of pride and accomplishment within the writing community and across classes. At the end of each word count, each class compared their progress with the other classes' data via a spreadsheet with running tallies (Figure 18.2). Tom even challenged one of the participating feeder elementary schools to write, comparing goals and progress each week. Tracking goals by percentage of total word count is an effective and positive indicator as each student works to complete their individualized word count goal. It gives a standardized view to individualized ability-based goals to which students can relate.

Resources and Worksheets

The success and rigor of this program lies in the way it covers many of the ELA standards established by Common Core.[5] The YWP, as mentioned previously,

	Class Total	Class Goal	Percentage	Words per day (30)	Words per student
1st Period	86,127	246,000	35%	2,870.90	3,445.08
3rd Period	169,552	401,652	42%	5,651.73	10,596.98
5th Period	78,884	342,000	23%	2,629.47	3,155.36
6th Period	186,739	490,500	38%	6,224.63	9,336.97
7th Period	71,183	305,500	23%	2,372.77	2,965.96
	Total Words	Total Goal	Percentage		
All Classes Students Only	592,485	1,785,652	33%	19,749.50	5,386.23
Mr. Burgeson	50,734	50000	101%	1,951.31	
Mr. Strous	51,015	50000	102%	1,700.50	
KMS Total	694,234	1,885,652	37%	23,141.13	6,198.52

Figure 18.2 Tracking class and student progress using a shared spreadsheet.

offers a set of workbooks[6] as an educational resource, covering many writing and literary concepts in middle school curricula. Many of the concepts and worksheets focus on brainstorming to prepare ideas that help launch students' projects. After starting late first year, Tom adjusted his schedule and began two weeks before the NaNoWriMo kickoff. This allowed students to plan and work on key concepts in the novel writing process. During our second year, Tom also discovered that a sixth-grade class from a feeder elementary had used the program, making the current worksheets repetitive. Modifications to the worksheets, resources, and activities throughout the program's first four years rendered a more usable and student-friendly curriculum.

Incentives

One of the most common questions asked during our NaNoWriMo program is "Did you get a sticker today?" Everybody loves a reward, and these incentives help to push writers forward. Stickers are the most common tool for this, acting as badges for milestones reached. Themes include writing goals, social gatherings, or simply being silly or creative. "Wrimos" (participants) take on challenges and score badges throughout the month, many placing them on binders or journals. Others apply them to NaNo Shields, a personalized mini poster we found on the

YWP website for students to decorate with pictures or ideas or they share them on the Brag Board, a chart for students to share their progress. Tom took kraft paper from the school paper cart and hung a long sheet in the hallway for this. Many badges on the Brag Board are silly or simply a project milestone, while percent stickers are also awarded to detail writers' progression toward goals. Because each writer's goal is based on their ability, students with differentiated cognitive abilities might be just as successful as those from Extended Projects Program classes.

Overcoming Roadblocks

When sharing this idea with teachers, one roadblock to navigate is a concern that the program disrupts an entire month in the classroom. In the age of constant testing, high-stakes assessment, and student mastery, juggling time for lessons can be a struggle. With NaNoWriMo, students have the opportunity to learn about writing, literature, collaboration, editing, and much more. Furthermore, Common Core standards are met repeatedly. For example, many students experience an increase in keyboarding skills due to the sheer volume of typing they complete. Many who hunt and peck keys soon find a rhythm, increasing word counts and meeting a standard for increased writing stamina.

For example, students must "[a]nalyze how particular elements of a story or drama interact."[7] By reading samples of their own peers' writing and studying plot, students understand this concept in detail. In addition to the literacy components, standards regarding narrative production are explored, including one required the creation of stories using effective technique, details, and sequencing.[8] The supporting elements following the standard go on to address a variety of concepts including but not limited to introducing narrators, characters, using dialogue, pacing, writing stamina, using technology, and editing just to name a few, and all of these elements are addressed by our activity.[9]

One of the most important and tangible ways teachers can support students' writing is to provide time outside of the classroom to write. Imagine the reaction of many students when challenged to write the YWP-recommended 15,000 to 30,000 words in one month. As mentioned earlier, students can choose their own goals for the month, but even *seeing* these numbers can be daunting. Neither of us ended up writing as much as one student, Ellen, who wrote more than 65,000 words and took advantage of every opportunity to write in and out of class. Additionally, KMS students have a lunch period paired with a free period, totaling forty-eight minutes, during which we opened the library to provide a quieter writing atmosphere and available technology. Some students brought their own devices and used them at the technology bar where they could charge while working.

Another important idea to stress with students is that they must silence their inner editor. NaNoWriMo is a project that often upends the rules of writing and grammar or, at the very least, temporarily sets them aside. This causes great stress, particularly for students in accelerated classes. We tell them not to throw away their writing. To help with this, Erik suggested creating a "parking lot" document for "ideas in need of rehabilitation." Nevertheless, one student deleted more than 10,000 words and two weeks of work because, in her estimation, it was a "mess" and wasn't working. In contrast, students who are most "freed up" to write are often more average in their ELA abilities. Turning off autocorrect and avoiding the delete key are essential parts of the NaNoWriMo process, privileging quickly written words and ideas. The thought process is fast—and often messy. Editing comes later.

In this regard, putting together a program for your school may present some challenges, given the way this philosophy is at odds with many traditional ELA curricula. However, getting started is easier when you are clear and honest with staff, parents, and administration. Some students will achieve their self-selected goal while others will not reach that mark, but all will learn about novels, fiction writing, and accompanying skills. As a teacher, recognize what you are trying to accomplish and be a helpful part of the process. It is *not* a time to grade other papers or create lesson plans. Teachers must write, share, and edit as a part of the group. Their participation will enable students to accept and take part in the process.

Along the way, explain the concepts to the students and share examples from personal writing or popular novels. Baty suggests that students keep a model novel by their side to look at when they experience writer's block.[10] Provide worksheets to students and allow practice writing. Use the workshop model and peer editing to give the class many opportunities to work together and share ideas. Conference with the students and discuss their progress during the month and after its conclusion. Use editing projects and excerpts to showcase passages from the students' work.

Proof of Concept

Despite instructional roadblocks and some occasional lack of buy-in or enthusiasm, the program proved valuable to parents and students. Parents commented during conferences held during the NaNoWriMo timeline that their students were having fun and really working hard on their stories. A few even joined in and worked alongside their students. In the second year, the whole seventh-grade class at KMS took part in the program, which included eight ELA classes. Additionally, Erik led a group of volunteer eighth-grade writers who wanted to participate. Within the first two weeks of writing, the school achieved a word count of one million and ended with more than 1.2 million words. Our experience developing and revising this program has shown it to be a valid teaching tool for many reasons, including the following:

- NaNoWriMo meets many Common Core standards for writing, reading, and technology.
- Students practice multiple twenty-first-century skills, including writing with Google docs and using web resources to record progress and communicate with the greater NaNoWriMo community.
- Students develop writing stamina and improve keyboarding skills.
- Creative writing is foregrounded with a significant curriculum project, thus fulfilling the "creation" level of Bloom's Taxonomy.

The amplification of creative work through this NaNoWriMo project is a necessary response to districts and teachers focusing on nonfiction expository writing, largely to the exclusion of creative and narrative writing. Such curricular single-mindedness ignores the fact that students often yearn for creative outlets, and the use of NaNoWriMo in the classroom not only addresses Common Core (and other similar) standards, but also boosts student morale and interest in novels. With so many writing and literacy standards being met, the question isn't whether we can justify teaching ELA through large-scale creative writing activities, but rather, why *shouldn't* we use NaNoWriMo in the classroom?

Notes

1   nanowrimo.org.
2   Chris Baty, *The No Plot? No Problem! Novel-Writing Kit* (San Francisco, CA: Chronicle Books LLC, 2014), 13.

3   ywp.nanowrimo.org.
4   Michael Matera, *Explore Like a Pirate: Gamification and Game-Inspired Course Design to Engage, Enrich, and Elevate Your Learners* (San Diego, CA: Dave Burgess Consulting, Inc., 2015), 81–3.
5   National Governors Association Center for Best Practices, Council of Chief State School Officers, *Common Core State Standards for English Language Arts & Literacy in History/Social Studies, Science, and Technical Subjects* (Washington, DC: National Governors Association Center for Best Practices, Council of Chief State School, 2010).
6   "Educator Resources," *NaNoWriMo Young Writers Program*, https://ywp.nanowrimo.org/pages/educator-resources.
7   CCSS.ELA-Literacy.RL.7.3.
8   CCSS.ELA-Literacy.RL.6.3.
9   Additional Writing standards addressed include CCSS.ELA-Writing.6.3, 6.3A, 6.3B, 6.3C, 6.3D, 6.3E, 6.4, 6.5, 6.6, and 6.10.
10 Baty, 13.

19

Beyond Brick Walls and Computer Screens: The Story of a University/Middle School Writing Partnership

Erica Hamilton
Grand Valley State University
Dana VanderLugt
Hudsonville Public Schools

Creative writing can be a lonely endeavor. The cursor, blinking mockingly on an empty screen to fill, can feel a little too much like its name, like a curse. Though we long for our students to be awake to the possibility and promise of a new writing piece, most find the blank page daunting. However, as writers ourselves, we have peers who support us through the gift of readership, encouragement, and honest critique. We show up for each other throughout the writing process, making it less isolating and allowing more room for creativity, risks, and growth. Unfortunately, as developing creative writers, most secondary students don't experience this type of peer support.

This fact led us to ask, "What if?" For us, this question—paired with our own experiences as writers—was an invitation to consider what would happen if we partnered middle school students and preservice teachers to support developing writers and teachers. While most secondary writing teachers work hard to ensure students receive authentic, helpful feedback on their drafts, these experiences often come up short. Given the ratio of one teacher for every 20+ students in a secondary classroom, attempting one-on-one writing conferences can feel more like an exercise in putting out fires than fueling writing development. And even when routines are structured to support students' peer feedback in small groups or partnerships, it's challenging to build on those conversations.

As a secondary educator, Dana wished for ways to make feedback timelier and more authentic. As a university teacher educator, Erica recognized that preservice teachers' time sitting in college classrooms talking about education often lacked substance and application. Collaboratively, we wondered how preservice teachers might have more opportunities to directly apply their classroom knowledge to secondary students in schools and if both of these needs—secondary students' need for more meaningful feedback and preservice teachers' need for more meaningful application of learning—might be fulfilled working directly with each other.

Ultimately, our answer to these wonderings resulted in a semester-long partnership between nineteen preservice teachers enrolled in a state-required secondary content-area literacy course from Grand Valley State University (GVSU) and twenty-nine eighth-grade Honors English students enrolled in Hudsonville Public Schools (HPS). Utilizing Google Docs to facilitate weekly creative writing exchanges, Erica's preservice teachers (i.e., mentors) provided regular feedback to their assigned HPS eighth-grade students (i.e., mentees). Additionally, these two West Michigan schools were close enough in proximity that Dana's eighth-grade students were able to participate in a university field trip at the start of the partnership to meet their college mentors and explore GVSU's campus and surrounding area. Throughout the semester, as they provided feedback on their mentees' writing, preservice teachers, who represented all content areas (Table 19.1), practiced writing assessment strategies and gained insights about how to use purposeful feedback to support adolescents' literacy development.

Table 19.1 GVSU Preservice teachers' majors/minors

Content Area (listed alphabetically)	Major	Minor
Applied Linguistics	0	1
Biology	3	0
Chemistry	1	1
Earth Science	0	1
English	4	0
Group Social Studies	1	0
History	0	3
Math	1	1
Music (K–12)	7	0
Political Science	1	1
Psychology	0	4
School Health Education	0	1
Spanish	1	0
Total	**19**	**13**

This experience was important for all preservice teachers, including those who were not English majors or minors. As Erica routinely emphasized, *all teachers* need to know how to provide purposeful feedback to support students' learning. Additionally, students are expected to write in all disciplines, so while creative writing may not be required in some subjects, through this partnership preservice teachers further developed their ability to read and provide purposeful, specific feedback on secondary students' ideas, writing, and creativity.

As a result, Dana's eighth-grade honors students benefited from ongoing, formative feedback Erica's preservice teachers provided on their weekly drafts, which were based on a series of ungraded "writing experiment" prompts designed to engage students' creativity and originality as compared to an expository assignment. The first prompt began with an invitation to compose an introductory fifty-word memoir. Throughout the semester, prompts included everything from poetry assignments to imitations of published pieces. Weekly feedback on these drafts took mentees and mentors on a journey together, culminating in several weeks of revisions and edits, during which the eighth-graders chose their strongest piece to publish in a class book, which reflected the results of this partnership. Not only did students purchase their own copies, but a copy of this book was also donated to their middle school library.

In this chapter, we share how this middle school/university writing partnership supported the collaborative and recursive nature of the creative writing process, provide details regarding how to facilitate a school/university partnership advantageous for everyone, and reflect on the power of partnering preservice teachers and developing writers.

What Does the Research Say?: Secondary School/University Partnerships

Field experiences support preservice teachers' professional development and serve to connect beginning teachers' theoretical knowledge and coursework with the pedagogies and practices of teaching. The purpose of these experiences, often described as "practice-based teacher education,"[1] is rooted in the belief that experience and learning should be connected directly to the field. As a result, these experiences enable preservice teachers to better understand and facilitate their own transition from student to classroom teacher.[2]

Moreover, these field experiences should be the result of mutually beneficial partnerships between teacher education programs and K–12 school districts[3] and require time, preparation, commitment, follow-through, and ongoing collaboration.[4] Such partnerships also require a shared vision based on clear, obtainable learning outcomes and a willingness to consistently improve.[5,6] Research also demonstrates that collaboration is beneficial for students of all ages and backgrounds. As such, we sought to ensure our collaboration was mutually beneficial, our work collaborative, and our partnership supportive of all students' learning.

Anchoring the Experience

One of the reasons this mentor-mentee partnership—or "M&M," as we called it—worked so well is because we worked well as colleagues. For example, months before its implementation, we met multiple times to talk and plan. We secured permissions and approval from our respective administrators. Of particular importance was ensuring that mentees and their parents/guardians knew about this partnership and also verifying that mentors completed a district background check.

Once these requirements were met, we created a group folder containing individual Google documents for each mentee, so their assigned mentor could access their work and we could regularly monitor content, feedback, and interactions. To facilitate introductions, we created two separate Google slideshows where mentors and mentees shared a picture and biographical information. To help students introduce themselves to one another before they actually met in person, we created and shared models (Figures 19.1 and 19.2). We knew that for this partnership to work well, participants needed opportunities to get to know one another first so they could begin to develop connections and rapport, which would support later dialogue and feedback.

Using an iPad, Dana recorded a short video-based "introduction" of her classroom, school, and experience as a middle school teacher. During Erica's first GVSU class, students viewed Dana taking mentors on a virtual tour of her classroom and explaining her expectations and goals for the partnership. After viewing the video, Erica facilitated a discussion about the ways this partnership was intended to support mentees' development as creative writers and thinkers as well as mentors' development as teachers.

One of the highlights for many mentors and mentees was the face-to-face field trip mentees took to GVSU's Grand Rapids campus. Although each mentor was assigned one or two mentees, we purposefully paired each M&M group with

Beyond Brick Walls and Computer Screens 221

Erica Hamilton - (THIS IS A MODEL PAGE - insert a headshot)

Where I Call Home: Zeeland, MI
My Major(s)/Minors: English (major); history (minor)
Activities I Participated in Middle/High School: swimming; volleyball; worked at Creme Curl Bakery (Hudsonville, MI); worked as a lifeguard and swim instructor; church youth group; Summer Science Institute (3-week out-west-HS class); student govt. National Honor Society

THREE Get-to-Know-Me Facts:
- I am a high energy, motivated teacher who is working on figuring out how to balance my personal and professional goals/responsibilities
- I have a 10-year old Shih-tzu, Sadie and a 3-year old cat, Grace (who has a closed head injury)
- I'm the oldest of three children; my brother, Ben is an officer in the U.S. Navy, currently the public works officer overseeing all the facilities at the Norfolk Naval Base, and my sister, Amy is a Chaplain in the U.S. Army, stationed at Ft. Drum, NY

Something I LIKED about school: I get to learn new things
Something I DISLIKED about school: Homework that didn't seem applicable and teachers who weren't knowledgeable

A good book I've recently read OR podcast I listened to: I just finished reading In this Grave Hour and I regularly listen to Rob Bell's podcast, the RobCast

One GOOD thing that happened recently: We recently had two foster children join our family.

Figure 19.1 Erica's Google slideshow model page.

Dana VanderLugt - (THIS IS A MODEL PAGE - insert a headshot)

Where I Call Home: Hudsonville, MI
My Major(s)/Minors: English (major); psychology/women's studies (minor)
Activities I Participated in Middle/High School: church youth group, Summer Science Institute (3-week out-west-HS class), National Honor Society, school plays, class president, editor of Vantage Point (h.s. student newspaper), tennis, worked at ice cream shop and greenhouses.

THREE Get-to-Know-Me Facts:
- We got a golden retriever puppy, named Murray, this past May. It was a summer of puppy training (which gave me plenty of opportunity for listening to podcasts while taking him for walks.)
- My husband, Tim and I have three boys: Caleb (11), Joshua (8), and Levi (5). They especially enjoy fishing and baseball.
- I publish a personal blog (www.stumblingtowardgrace.com)

Something I LIKE about school: The chance to be introduced to new perspectives and concepts
Something I DISLIKE about school: Sitting still and listening too long

A good book I've recently read or podcast I listened to: "For the Love with Jen Hatmaker: Interview with Brene Brown" (podcast) and *The Kitchen House* by Kathleen Grissom (historical fiction)

One GOOD thing that has happened to me this week: I had the chance to play Family Feud as part of our HPS District Kick-off this week, and my staff team won! (We have a very creative superintendent!)

Figure 19.2 Dana's Google slideshow model page.

another M&M group so that if any complications arose (e.g., a mentor was absent, ill), mentees would always receive weekly feedback. To facilitate introductions, conversations, and connections between mentors and mentees, Erica designed an exploration-based field trip that the paired M&M groups worked together to complete, using the following instructions:

1. Engage in conversations with mentee(s) (and, hopefully, future college students) about what it's like to be a college student, while exploring campus.
2. Practice OWL (observation, wonder, learn) as you walk around, looking and talking about what you observe, wonder, and learn. When possible, connect OWLs to Unit One's driving question.
3. Enjoy this face-to-face M&M time with your mentee(s). Take at least one picture with you and your mentee(s) and tweet out that picture using our #EDR321 hashtag.

We also used actual M&M candies (Figure 19.3) to highlight the M&M partnership. These were distributed to mentors and mentees during the GVSU field trip experience as well as a few more times during the semester, including a final debriefing with Erica's GVSU mentors (Figure 19.4) and Dana's mentees.

Figure 19.3 M&Ms for mentors and mentees (beginning of the semester).

Figure 19.4 M&Ms for mentors (end of the semester).

Using Google Docs, Dana provided weekly directions for mentors regarding the mentees' current creative writing assignments, expectations, and other contextual information (Figure 19.5). Noted earlier, these directions and the ongoing mentoring they received from Erica were helpful, as most GVSU mentors' majors were in content areas other than English.

Each week, Dana also included expectations to guide mentors' feedback and support their growth as beginning teachers. These expectations included language such as "remember to use the 'suggestion mode' in the Google Doc to provide feedback connected to grammar/mechanics so that your mentee has to 'act' on your suggestions" and "respond to mentees' specific questions with the text, either as comments or you can type your responses at the end of their piece."

At the beginning of each class, Erica and mentors collectively read through Dana's directions, discussed relevant information and questions, and then mentors spent time reading through, commenting on, and reviewing their assigned mentee writing experiment(s). At times, mentees also included specific feedback requests (Figure 19.6).

During class, Erica answered mentors' questions and provided suggestions and ideas for potential responses as well as technical support. When necessary, Erica also reviewed and provided feedback on mentees' creative writing experiments.

10.12.17

Hello again, GVSU Mentors!

Thanks for your continued commitment to my students! It's so helpful for them to have your specific, individualized feedback each week. I wish I had a mentor for each of my 143 students! I checked in with each student yesterday and made sure his/her experiment is saved in the right place. Sorry to those of you who didn't find an experiment last week. We should have those snags worked out now.

Current Unit Question: Who am I and how do I fit into this world?"

Background on Creative Writing Experiment assignments:
As mentioned last week, we are currently working with Narrative Poetry. Our focus has changed from reading, studying, and analyzing poetry to writing it. The students have done several free-write drafts and are narrowing down to which poem they'd like to choose to revise and (eventually) turn in. This Creative Writing Experiment is one of those free writes. You may want to ask the student if they are thinking of making this particular Experiment their final draft or not.

Some specific writing techniques we've been focusing on in class include:
- Line breaks and spacing
- Show don't tell, specifically:
  - Vivid verbs
  - Specific nouns
  - Figurative language

Also, help the student to consider if his/her poem is actually narrative. For example, *Is there a conflict? Can the reader see the setting? Is there some kind of resolution (though not necessarily a "happily ever after" ending)?*

This Week's Creative Writing Experiment Prompt: If You're Not...You Don't Know
We are exploring who we are, what we care about, and what makes us unique. We're also starting to work on Narrative Poetry in class -- how can we tell a story about ourselves (in the form of a poem) and make it come alive with vivid verbs, specific details, and figurative language?

Examples: Students had access to this Google Slides document with a variety of student examples, as well as Mrs. V's brainstorm and poem.

Figure 19.5 Excerpt from "Directions from Dana" (October 17, 2017).

> Three questions I have for you are:
> 1. What do you think of my line breaks?
> 2. Is there anything that doesn't make sense in my poem?
> 3. Is there a different word I could use for "girl" besides "female"?
>   a Woman, lady, damsel
>
> My answers for your questions are more easily made as suggestions in your poem. I like the line breaks. It almost leads the reader into the quotes you used. I'm the oldest, but I'm the only girl, so I can relate to the poem well. I have older male cousins that I would want to hang out with and was handed a Barbie doll instead. Great topic!

Figure 19.6 Mentee questions and mentor responses on a poetry-based creative writing experiment.

Drawing on their various disciplinary backgrounds and experiences as readers and writers, mentors practiced giving supportive feedback to developing middle school writers. Through this partnership, mentors could directly apply their learning and engage in specific teaching practices (e.g., formative assessment, building relationships and rapport with students). Similarly, mentees wrote for a real-world audience and received regular feedback on their creative writing. Realistically, no one teacher can be expected to read everything their students write (nor should everything be read). Partnering with Erica and the GVSU mentors, Dana's eighth-grade mentees received timely, specific feedback—much more than Dana, an instructor of more than 140 middle school students, could provide on her own.

Yet, more than comments on a draft, this collaboration provided authenticity and a real-world connection to someone outside the walls of a classroom—the eighth-graders gained a writing coach and preservice teachers gained skills providing formative feedback. Mentees experienced a recursive process of writing and made real-time decisions about their work. Through this partnership, they weren't pretending to be writers; *they were writers*. Similarly, mentors weren't abstractly learning about teaching; *they were teachers*.

The Challenges and Benefits of Productive Struggle

Nurturing a growth mindset[7] means resisting the urge to remove challenges that allow for productive struggle, independence, and resilience. Throughout this M&M partnership, Dana's eighth-grade students encountered challenging situations and expectations. From adhering to deadlines, navigating technology, and accepting that mentors' styles differed, this partnership gave Dana opportunities to coach her students, including stretching them to become responsible and responsive. For example, there were times when, due to mistakes and misunderstandings, Dana called students out of other classes to fix an issue so that their writing could be accessible to their mentor. Although colleagues were supportive and issues were resolved relatively quickly, this created additional work. And because students were balancing their M&M creative writing projects on top of other English curriculum and assignments, this opportunity challenged them to manage their time and energy.

Perhaps the clearest sign of the partnership's ability to make room for productive struggle came when middle school students received feedback. Because the writing process was authentic and directed more by mentees than Dana, eighth-grade writers grappled with revision in a way not often possible when assignments are one dimensional and written only for teachers. As a result, days when mentees opened their Google documents and read their mentor's comments revealed differing reactions and emotions. Students were not shy about expressing excitement, gratitude, pride, confusion, frustration, and even some indignation—emotions not unlike those writers feel when receiving editorial feedback.

Dana's role during these moments of receiving feedback was vital: here was an opportunity to coach young writers through questions and uncertainties. Unlike times when students received comments on papers or writing assignments and then tucked them back in their folders—or threw them in the trash—now students had opportunities to process and think hard about what to do with the feedback. Due to the "live" nature of Google Docs, middle school students considered how to act on their mentor's feedback, including when not to do so. When reacting to mentors' feedback, mentees asked questions such as "What isn't clear about this intro? What kind of detail would make this section come alive? What word fits here? Do I have to change this? Is this finished?" For Dana, balancing when to jump in and assist students and when to push them to think for themselves about their creative writing was its own kind of productive struggle.

Similarly, Erica and her students experienced different productive struggles. Instead of knowing *about* formative assessment, this partnership provided real-world opportunities for engaging *in* formative assessment. Given mentors' various disciplinary backgrounds, Erica sought to highlight and support mentors' identities as "more experienced"[8] readers and writers. During class, Erica sometimes modeled giving feedback, projecting a selected mentee's Google document, and she shared resources such as examples of formative feedback and potential prompts and questions mentors could use. Each week, Erica also debriefed with mentors who shared observations, asked questions, provided evidence of feedback they had shared, and discussed how to support their mentees' creative writing development.

As mentors, preservice teachers functioned as external, "more experienced readers," which meant asking mentees questions, offering suggestions, sharing what they liked and connected with, and when asked to do so, making editing suggestions. Initially, this was intimidating for some mentors, especially those who didn't feel as comfortable because "they weren't going to be English teachers someday." Erica often reminded mentors that all teachers need to be able to give clear, purposeful feedback to students—no matter the content area or assignment. Erica and the mentors regularly talked about how to balance praise with critique, making sure to identify what mentees did well and providing clear feedback about what could be improved and developed. An important part of Erica's role was helping preservice teachers understand the importance of authentic audiences for secondary students' work, while also providing mentors opportunities to learn more about and practice giving formative feedback. The fact that this partnership focused specifically on secondary students' creative writing was important because creative writing is intended to be accessible to readers across disciplines. Additionally, as noted previously, teachers must be skilled at giving feedback to students, no matter the genre, and this experience provided another opportunity to develop these skills.

Lessons Learned

In response to the "what if?" question we asked ourselves before collaborating, we found that there are logistics to consider when linking students through a partnership such as ours (Table 19.2).

In addition to logistical considerations, we also have recommendations based on our experiences, such as ensuring the partnership is a "win-win," communicating regularly with partners, utilizing available resources to support student learning and growth, and maintaining flexibility and a willingness to adjust or change based on learners' needs. We also suggest integrating partnership experiences directly into classes and/or programs, which lessens "extra" work that may be required. Finally, these partnerships should serve to support curriculum and learning outcomes and participants should have time to get to know one another and build rapport so they can readily engage in the work.

Table 19.2 University/secondary school partnership logistical considerations

University/College Logistical Considerations	Secondary Logistical Considerations
Ensure permissions from stakeholders (i.e., administrators, colleagues, and program directors)	Ensure permissions from stakeholders (i.e., district/building administration, parents/guardians, colleagues)
Communicate clearly and often with stakeholders (i.e., administrators, colleagues, K–12 partner(s), students)	Communicate clearly and often with stakeholders (i.e., administrators, parents/guardians, colleagues, university partner(s), students)
Identify details, including resources needed to support/facilitate partnership (e.g., technology, school facilities, transportation, schedules, curriculum connections)	Identify details, including resources needed to support/facilitate partnership (e.g., technology, transportation, schedules, required curricular outcomes)
Monitor students' assessment, feedback, and interactions	Monitor students' submitted work and interactions
Elicit feedback from students regarding partnership experiences and learning	Elicit feedback from students regarding partnership experiences and learning

Difficult, but Worth It

According to the National Center for Education Statistics,[9] only about one-quarter of US students in Grades 8 and 12 are proficient in writing. Perhaps it's because students don't yet value writing, or maybe they have limited opportunities to get feedback from and share their work with outside audiences. However, one fact remains: writing takes time and requires work. Through this partnership, middle schoolers understood and experienced the hard work of writing and preservice teachers learned the value of providing specific, timely feedback that intentionally supported mentees' writing and development.[10] Middle school students already know writing can be difficult. What they hadn't experienced before, though, was the importance and power of formative feedback and real-world audiences. Similarly, as preservice teachers read through and responded to their mentees' writing, they learned to engage with their mentees' stories and ideas, sharing feedback about what they read. This feedback was intended to give mentees additional suggestions, thoughts, and language to express themselves. Equally important, preservice teachers also practiced identifying and applauding excellence and growth, which all writers need.[11]

Similarly, we want future educators to recognize and embrace the challenge of providing purposeful, clear feedback that supports students' learning. This partnership is proof that asking the question "what if?" can be powerful. Creative writing paired with ongoing, authentic, real-world feedback doesn't have to be limited to the brick walls of classrooms and individual screens. It can be a vehicle to support learning and partnerships across disciplines and educational contexts.

Notes

1 Deborah Loewenberg Ball and David K. Cohen, "Developing Practice, Developing Practitioners: Toward a Practice-Based Theory of Professional Education," in *Teaching as the Learning Profession: Handbook of Policy and Practice*, ed. Gary Sykes and Linda Darling-Hammond (San Francisco, CA: Jossey Bass, 1999), 3–32.
2 Tina Heafner, Ellen McIntyre, and Melba Spooner, "The CAEP Standards and Research on Educator Preparation Programs: Linking Clinical Partnerships with Program Impact," *Peabody Journal of Education* 89, no. 4 (2014): 516–32.
3 Kate Eckert, "Clinical Practice in Education: Performance Assessment in the Third Space" (paper presented at the Interprofessional Education and Leadership Conference, Forest Grove, Oregon, 2019).
4 Robert Bullough, Roni Jo Draper, Leigh K. Smith, and James R. Birrell, "Moving beyond Collusion: Clinical Faculty and University/Public School Partnership," *Teaching and Teacher Education* 20, no. 5 (2004): 505–21.
5 Lorena Guillen and Ken Zeichner, "A University-Community Partnership in Teacher Education from the Perspectives of Community-Based Teacher Educators," *Journal of Teacher Education* 69, no. 2 (2018): 140–53.
6 Robert E. Lee, "Breaking Down Barriers and Building Bridges: Transformative Practices in Community- and School-Based Urban Teacher Preparation," *Journal of Teacher Education* 69, no. 2 (2018): 118–26.
7 Carol S. Dweck, *Mindset: The New Psychology of Success* (New York: Ballantine Books, 2008).
8 L. S. Vygotsky, *Mind in Society: The Development of Higher Psychological Processes* (Cambridge, MA: Harvard University Press, 1978).
9 National Center for Education Statistics, *The Nation's Report Card: Writing 2011*, Institute of Education Sciences (Washington, DC: US Department of Education, 2011).
10 Patty McGee, *Feedback That Moves Writers Forward: How to Escape Correcting Mode to Transform Student Writing* (Singapore: Corwin, 2017).
11 Katherine Bomer, *Hidden Gems: Naming and Teaching from the Brilliance in Every Student's Writing* (Portsmouth, NH: Heinemann, 2010).

Beyond the Desk: Fostering Community Engagement through Authentic Writing Experiences in and out of the Classroom

Justin Longacre
Toledo School for the Arts

Although I enjoy seeing my students grow as writers in the classroom, one of the unexpected joys of teaching high school creative writing has been witnessing the writing community of my classroom slowly fold into the larger writing community of my city. When I scan the list of local literary contest winners, I find the names of my students. When I attend readings, I see my students both in the audience and on the stage. When I read the bylines in local publications, my students are among them. This is a testament to the hard work of my students, but it is also the direct result of a deliberate program of engagement, one that has been mutually beneficial for my classroom, the school, and the local literary community of our city.

The old adage is that "writers write." While this is fundamentally true, writing is not *all* writers do. Writers also participate in the culture of the literary world, a culture with its own customs and expectations. As such, writing is not a solitary endeavor—it happens in the context of community. For our students, community begins in the classroom, expands to the local scene, and eventually engages the global literary world writ large. Unfortunately, these concentric communities often feel closed off to young writers and especially those from historically disadvantaged backgrounds. Admittance can seem intimidating and exclusive, something reserved for grown-ups with MFAs and a network of social and professional connections. How, exactly, does one enter this world? Secondary school writing instructors are uniquely situated to help our students understand and navigate these social conventions and practices in a safe, supportive way.

By empowering our students to participate in literature as a communal activity, they can gain a sense of their place in a culture that reaches far beyond the boundaries of the classroom and extends into the future long after they have a diploma in hand. Students discover they can actually play an active, participatory role in building and perpetuating that culture. With some careful consideration, student participation can be curated in a way that satisfies Common Core standards, increases students' personal investment, and helps foster vibrant communities.

This chapter will presuppose that students are already writing. I will focus on what to do with that writing once it has been drafted, workshopped, and edited. Students should be familiar with this process before they begin to think about making their work public, but the prospect of such public engagement can lend a sense of urgency and focus to the process. I have organized this chapter into sections covering three of the most common literary practices: performance, publication, and contests. This is by no means an exhaustive list, but I hope it will provide a basic framework for further exploration.

Hot Mics: Student Writing in Performance

One of the most direct and impactful ways for writers to interact with the community is through performance. There is nothing quite like hearing a piece come alive through a microphone and watching a room full of people hang on every word. It can be a life-changing experience. Educator Pablo C. Ramirez found that incorporating poetry performance into his English classroom "gave [the students] a space and an opportunity to express their views about life, school, and society in a powerful manner and via their creativity."[1] This space is important, especially for students from backgrounds traditionally denied a voice. For these writers especially, literary performance can be a powerful tool for social engagement and empowerment. Maisha T. Fisher also found that public performance "not only exposed students to other writers and poets, but it also showed them they were part of a larger network of wordsmiths."[2] The invitation to participate in this "network of wordsmiths" can give students a sense of writing as a lifelong practice of processing and interacting with the world around them in thoughtful and deliberate ways.

Though performance can be a valuable experience, it can also be an extremely volatile endeavor emotionally. On the page, writers can meticulously plan, rethink, and revise. The page is a controlled environment. The stage is less so. There, one must contend with variables such as audience, sound systems, time constraints, and nerves. Much can go wrong. Therefore, it is incumbent on instructors to guide our students' performance experience in safe and supportive ways. Performance can take a number of forms that should be scaffolded to help students get comfortable performing their work for others. Public performance is daunting, and it can be a site of serious vulnerability. Students should be asked to stretch their comfort zone, but never to a point that endangers their emotional well-being. Teachers should be mindful of students' limits and remember that the person always comes before the performance.

The first place to establish the expectations of performance is in the classroom. One way to do this is to integrate workshopping into your curriculum. For my class, students read their pieces aloud before receiving feedback from their peers and the instructor. We spend at least one day a week workshopping; receiving genuine, supportive feedback from the instructor—and especially from peers— can do wonders to build a student's confidence. As part of a collaboration between Cleveland State University and John Marshall High School, participants found

> the performance dimension of the workshop was essential to make this work because in performance, writers bring words to life. Students in the workshop could see the person and hear her poem and share the experience and respond appropriately. The poem comes alive as the utterance of the poet, literally a creation of her breath and body, and students hear what is said in that context.[3]

Context is important for both performer and audience, and the workshop introduces students to the conventions, expectations, and demands of that form. This routine workshop process, if done carefully, can acclimate even shy students to the process of presenting their work.

Once students are comfortable with reading, consider getting out of the school and into the public. Schedule an offsite public performance in the late fall, once students have each had a chance to experience the process of presenting their work in the classroom. When they are prepared, the next step is to find a venue. If the school is located in a major metropolitan area, there will likely be at least one venue already hosting readings on a regular basis. In a mid-sized city or smaller, you may need to get creative. Consider public spaces: libraries, art galleries, restaurants, pizza parlors, farmers' markets, or places of worship. The physical space is less important than the support of the people involved.

Once a location has been secured and scheduled, consider the performance parameters of the reading. Is this venue big enough to require a sound system? If so, will it provide one? If not, find out if your school has a portable PA system you can use and familiarize yourself with its operation. One way or another, make sure readers are audible. Nothing can squash a student's confidence more than not being heard. In preparation for this first performance, I partner with one of my school's drama instructors to provide a lesson about vocal projection and microphone technique. I even bring a PA system and microphone into my classroom so students can practice. Once they know how to perform, consider the material they will be performing. For this first performance, it is a good idea to keep the parameters fairly loose. Students should be expected to read between one and three pieces, no more than five minutes of material. Encourage them to read something they have already workshopped or submitted for an assignment. Also, have students submit what they would like to read a week in advance so you can look it over.

The focus of this first performance should be creating a fun, welcoming environment. Encourage interaction and a robust crowd response. Both students and the audience will take their cues from the instructor. This sort of low-stakes, supportive performance environment provides a safe space for less-confident students to make their work heard. When my class first began these reading years ago, attendance was mostly relegated to the students, myself, and a few parents. After about a decade, we now pack our local coffee shop to standing room only. The convivial culture around these readings draws people in and creates an important bond among the students, as well as between them and the broader community.

In addition to the fall reading, we also present a more structured spring program. If the fall reading is about bringing the students' work out into the community, the spring performance is about bringing the community into our space in order to showcase the students' best work. We hold this performance in our theater and it is always comprised of pieces drafted around a central theme selected specifically for this event. In preparation, students spend a significant amount of class time considering the theme together and planning how they might present their work. The entire performance is written as one cohesive unit comprised of many parts. This involves a great deal of group work and cooperation among the class. As part of these summative performances, consider opportunities for collaboration with other departments. This can be an excellent way to enhance the performance while encouraging cross-curricular connections and multimodal creativity.

In addition to the benefits discussed earlier, these performances can also be a valuable way of satisfying the goals of the Speaking and Listening strand of the ELA Common Core. Many of the standards are addressed in preparation for performance. In deciding a theme and establishing performance parameters, students will be deeply involved in collaborative discussion.[4] In the process of group writing, students engage in democratic discussion to work toward a shared goal.[5] When performing, students necessarily "adapt speech to a variety of contexts and tasks."[6] As we see, performance can be an excellent way to get students personally invested in content standards while introducing them to a foundational practice of the literary community.

Getting the Word Out: Encouraging Student Publication

In many ways, publication is the common currency of the literary world. For young writers, wading into the world of publication can be an exhilarating experience. It might also lead to a flurry of questions. Which publications are right for my work? What is a simultaneous submission? Exactly what belongs in a cover letter? Questions like these can present a significant barrier to participation. Consider all of the brilliant work that never found an audience simply because the writer was never introduced to the means of publication or was too confused and intimidated to try. If we want our students to become practicing, publishing writers beyond the limited time they spend in our classroom, our job is to help familiarize them with the process.

The first and most accessible outlet for most students will likely be internal school publications such as school newspapers and yearbooks. If your school is of sufficient size, these platforms are probably already in place. Talk with the editors of these publications about publishing a creative writing spotlight in each edition of the newspaper or a dedicated spread in the yearbook. Most editors of student publications are hungry for quality content, and if they can be guaranteed a carefully selected and edited piece every month, they will likely be amenable to that collaboration. The easiest way to provide a piece for such a spotlight is to hand-select it yourself from the pool of student work produced in class or club. Of course, always check with a student before publishing their work.

The next step is to establish a dedicated literary publication. There are a number of options based on budget, perhaps the simplest, least expensive of which is creating an online journal. If your school has a website, speak with the webmaster about adding a tab for student writing. While digital media is increasingly popular, pixels rarely match the tangibility of a physical product, which can range from the humble photocopied packet to professional, perfect bound trade paperbacks. There are many self-publishing options available at reasonable prices. By selling the books for a small fee, you should be able to keep this process cost-neutral.

In-house publishing can help students understand the process and value of publication in a safe, controlled environment. Because you are directly involved in selection and production, you can ensure that every student who wants to be published is afforded the chance. There are few experiences more encouraging for young writers than seeing their work read and enjoyed by peers. In addition, producing a journal helps build a sense of community within your building and provides students a sense of ownership by directly involving them in the process. As educators DiMarzio and Dippre found:

> The anthology experience created a sense of community in our combined classes. The students were together for a specific purpose, and they worked with each other to complete that purpose independently. While the writing experience gave students the chance to express themselves, the anthology experience gave them the opportunity to see the personal expression of others and organize those expressions according to their personal preferences. This social interaction added depth and importance to the work of our students and increased their focus throughout the anthology sessions.[7]

This reflection is indicative of the publication experience in general. The cooperation required to produce a finished product often brings students together in new, unexpected ways and encourages them to view their own work and others' within a broader context. Writing becomes less of a solitary activity and more of a collective one.

At some point, you will probably want your students to branch out into publishing beyond the school environment. First, consider opportunities in your immediate community. The local newspaper is an excellent place to start. You might also consider alternative presses that focus on the arts or a specific sub-community. For example, this year my students supplied monthly articles about local issues for a newspaper that serves our homeless population. It has been a great way for them to practice writing and editing skills while researching social issues that often go unnoticed.

Once you have identified some local options, familiarize students with the concept of literary journals as the basic forum for publishing single pieces in the literary world. It is likely that many of your students are unaware this world exists. Begin by directing students to some of the most storied names in publishing, such as *Poetry*, *The New Yorker*, and *The Paris Review*. Many of these publications have web content accessible for free. *Poetry*'s website, *Poetry Foundation*, in particular has an entire section especially designed for teens.

The nearest major university can also be a valuable resource. Major universities often publish a literary journal, and it is a good idea to familiarize yourself with it. Reach out to its editor about making a field trip, or ask about someone coming in to speak to your class. In my experience, university creative writing departments often welcome this partnership because it serves as a recruiting tool. Over time, the relationship between your classroom and the university can grow in many valuable ways. Our university partner sends second-year MFA students into the classroom to conduct lessons throughout the spring semester. The lessons themselves are valuable, but so is the opportunity to talk with diverse voices pursuing creative writing as a lifestyle.

Next, introduce students to common online resources. For example, the website for *Poets & Writers* hosts a database allowing users to search for publications based on specific genres or areas of interest. With some creative use of the filters, students will be able to find journals publishing whatever niche they happen to work in.

Once students understand what a literary journal is, help them understand how to send their own work for consideration, beginning with journals that welcome work from emerging writers. Choose a journal (or several) with which you are familiar and use their submission guidelines as an example. Discuss the importance of familiarizing yourself with the journal before sending anything and of following the submission guidelines' directions. Discuss how to write a concise cover letter and an author bio. Don't forget to frame rejection as part of the process. Students must understand that rejection is the rule rather than the exception, and they must handle it with professionalism. As fiction writer and essayist Kim Liao says in her excellent article, "Why You Should Aim for 100 Rejections a Year":

> My ego resists mustering up the courage to submit writing to literary magazines, pitch articles, and apply for grants, residencies, and fellowships. Yet these painful processes are necessary evils if we are ever to climb out of our safe but hermetic cocoons of isolation and share our writing with the world.[8]

Breaking out of those cocoons is the point of submitting work for publication. Even if students don't immediately get published, they can learn valuable skills such as resilience, determination, and dedication to the process.

In my class, students research and identify five literary journals to which they might send work at the beginning of the year using the *Poets & Writers* database. They are required to read an issue of their selected journals and summarize their style and focus, as well as provide basic information about submission requirements. Then, students are required to provide proof of submission to at least one journal or contest quarterly. Not all students will get published, but they will familiarize themselves with journals, approach their own work with a critical eye, learn how to format a submission, and learn how to deal with rejection. At least a few students will likely get published throughout the year. Make sure to celebrate these publications!

The process of publication neatly aligns with Common Core Writing 11–12 Standards 4–6. Identifying the style of a journal and tailoring one's writing submission guidelines is an excellent way to demonstrate that students are able to produce writing that is "appropriate to task, purpose, and audience."[9] The process of polishing a piece for submission ensures students are engaging in the process of editing and revision.[10] Overall, the goal is to use technology to produce and publish their work, as explicitly directed by the standards.[11] Many writing assignments can hit these same standards, but writing for publication enhances the pursuit of mastery by providing a clear objective.

From Writing Papers to Making Paper: A Guide to Literary Contests

Another mainstay of the practicing writer is the contest. Like publishing, contests come in a wide variety of flavors based on genre, theme, and experience level--from local flash fiction for elementary students to nationwide contests for full-length books. Contests often have a specific focus or set of requirements. Some contests charge a fee, and most have some kind of prize for the top three pieces in a given category.

For students, it is best to start small, local, and free. I advise students against submitting to contests that require a fee. Some of these are completely legitimate options for more experienced writers, but some less-scrupulous organizations take advantage of young, inexperienced writers to generate a profit. By starting small, local, and free, students are more likely to avoid paying out fees and target their work to markets where they are likely to be the most competitive. The best contests categorize entries by age, allowing students to compete with other writers of their age and ability level.

Seek out literary contests in your area. They are often held by community organizations such as newspapers, universities, libraries, museums, and clubs. In our city, for example, we have an annual essay contest sponsored by the library system, an ekphrastic poetry contest sponsored by the art museum, and a ZIP code-based poetry contest sponsored by the Fair Housing Center. Each of these contests offers cash prizes and a specific category for students. My own students are required to write and submit poems to these contests as an assignment. We discuss the forms in class and draft, workshop, and revise together. If you do this, your students will already have an edge over the competition. This is a huge confidence boost for the winners and an excellent way to see what is achievable for everybody else.

If your community does not already have a few contests in place, encourage local institutions to create one. Libraries are an excellent option, as well as museums, historical societies, or philanthropic organizations. Offer to help organize and advertise. You can even solicit donations from local businesses for the prize. The important thing is to create a sense of community involvement. Announce the winners at a ceremony where contestants read their work. Invite stakeholders to judge. A few hours of time and a small gift certificate could provide a lifetime of confidence.

Simply, Writer: The Importance of Authentic Writing Experiences

One common error in secondary creative writing instruction is a tendency to position students as *potential* writers rather than *actual* writers. On the one hand, we work to prepare them for their future as writers. On the other, it is important for students to understand they can be writers right now. They don't have to wait. Angela Wiseman says of her experience encouraging poetic practice in her class that "an important aspect of learning an artistic craft, such as poetry, is that workshops take on authentic purposes."[12] In an environment often governed by hypotheticals, standardized tests, and preparations for an abstract future, students crave authenticity.

One benefit of creating opportunities for authentic engagement is it moves student writing from the potential to the actual. In front of a crowd, students take their place alongside the bards and griots of history. When they see their piece in a journal next to the work of experienced adults, they take their place alongside Sappho and Claudia Rankin and anyone else who mustered the courage to write it down and send it out. Suddenly, they see themselves as part of that conversation. When they cash that prize check, they take their place alongside the long line of those who have been able to eke out an existence through words. Suddenly, they see that a literary life might just be sustainable for them too.

Of course, not all of our students will win contests, get published in prestigious journals, or deliver earth-shaking performances, but they will all be invited to participate as actual writers. In this respect, the role of the instructor is to extend an invitation our students might not otherwise receive. In doing so we confer the status not of *potential* writer, but, simply, *writer*.

Notes

1. Pamela J. Hickey and Pablo C. Ramirez, "Lingua Anglia: Bridging Language and Learners: Engaging Culturally and Linguistically Diverse Youth through Performance Poetry," *The English Journal* 103, no. 6 (2014): 76.
2. Maisha T. Fisher, "From the Coffee House to the School House: The Promise and Potential of Spoken Word Poetry in School Contexts," *English Education* 37, no. 2 (2005): 128.
3. Ted Lardner, Barbara Sones, and Mary E. Weems, "'Lessons Spaced by Heartbeats': Performance Poetry in a Ninth-Grade Classroom," *English Journal* 85, no. 8 (1996): 65.
4. CCSS.ELA-LITERACY.SL.11–12.1. Standards taken from National Governors Association Center for Best Practices, Council of Chief State School Officers, *Common Core State Standards for English Language Arts & Literacy in History/Social Studies, Science, and Technical Subjects* (Washington, DC: National Governors Association Center for Best Practices, Council of Chief State School, 2010).
5. CCSS.ELA-LITERACY.SL.11–12.1.B.
6. CCSS.ELA-LITERACY.SL.11–12.6.
7. Erica DiMarzio and Ryan Dippre, "Creative and Critical Engagement: Constructing a Teen Vision of the World," *English Journal* 101, no. 2 (2011): 29.
8. Kim Liao, "Why You Should Aim for 100 Rejections a Year," *Literary Hub*, June 28, 2016, lithub.com/why-you-should-aim-for-100-rejections-a-year/.
9. CCSS.ELA-LITERACY.W.11–12.4.
10. CCSS.ELA-LITERACY.W.11–12.5.
11. CCSS.ELA-LITERACY.W.11–12.6.
12. Angela Wiseman, "Powerful Students, Powerful Words: Writing and Learning in a Poetry Workshop," *Literacy* 45, no. 2 (2011): 74.

Appendix 3.1: Workshop Procedure

The goal of the workshop day is to provide the author with a snapshot of the reader's experience of the text. It is not primarily an advice session but should sound more like a close reading of a poem.

Before Workshop

1. **Distribute** copies or share pieces in advance. **Tell** your readers what questions you have about your piece or what kind of feedback you're looking for. Readers **write this down** on your paper.
2. **Read** carefully on your own and **annotate** for meaning. Line edits are okay to make if desired. You may choose to give this paper back to the author or not, depending on what the author wants.
   Other things to notice and mark in your annotations:
   - related or repeated images
   - structure (number of lines per stanza, number of syllables per line, rhyme scheme, etc.)
   - favorite or confusing lines
   - possible edits (remove unnecessary words, unnecessary lines)
   - deeper meaning of the piece
   - how you felt while you were reading different parts
3. **Write half-page interpretation** of the piece. You may answer the following questions or not. But your feedback should be phrased in a supportive way; it should provide an interpretation; it could give ideas for revision. You will use this to prepare for the workshop and then you will give this to the author after the workshop. What story did it tell? What did it mean to you? What did it make you feel? What bigger issues or thematic subjects came up as you were reading? Which lines or phrases were your favorite? What do you want to know more about? What is the heart of this piece, the most interesting thing about it?

Workshop Day

1. **Preparation**: Determine how much time will be allotted for each writer. Designate a timekeeper. Designate a chairperson to ensure everyone is following the procedure.

   Participants are **prepared** with feedback (half-page interpretation and annotated copy). If you do not have this feedback, you get a zero for the day and may be prevented from participating in the workshop.

2. **Author reads** the piece aloud once or twice, depending on length. (Read an excerpt if it is prose more than two pages long.)

   * Cone of Silence *

   The author *cannot talk* from steps 3–6. The readers should discuss the story as if the author isn't there, BUT you must continue to be kind. Throughout these steps, the author must MAKE NOTES about what everyone says. This prevents the author from telling readers information about the work mid-workshop that isn't coming through on the page.

3. **The story.** Discuss what story the piece tells. Literally what did you think was happening?

4. **What you noticed.** Discuss your annotations. How would you describe the style it's written in? What other kinds of writing or movies did it remind you of? What did you notice in terms of sound devices, form, and so on?
   "I was struck by _____"
   "This piece makes me think of _____"
   "I think the most interesting part was when _____"

5. **Deeper meaning.** What is the deeper meaning of the piece to you? Make sure to address theme and take-away.
   "To me this piece was really about_____"
   "This piece made me think about_____"
   "I felt like this piece was actually talking about_____"

6. **What If Session.** Discuss what would happen to the piece if various edits were made. What might make this piece stronger? You could also share line edits if the author wants. Use the following phrases to frame your suggestions:
   "What would happen if you_____"
   "I wonder how it would read if_____"
   "If you _____, maybe the reader would_____,

"I was curious what we thought about_____"
"I kept wondering _____"
"I got lost when_____"
"I found myself wondering if we wanted to hear more_____"
"I don't know if you need the part where _____ What if you cut that?"

7. **Remove cone of silence.** Author can answer any questions posed by the group or ask questions.
8. **Next steps.** The author should share what they might do in the next draft.
9. **Thank-yous** and pass your half page of comments to the author. If the author wants the line edits on the papers you annotated, they can ask for them.

After the Workshop

Using the notes from your workshop and your own gut, revise your piece.

Appendix 3.2: Flash Fiction Assignment

Goals:
- Use varied sentence structures (syntax) for specific effects.
- Follow or adapt a traditional plot diagram.
- Include many prepositional phrases, compound sentences, adjectives, and adverbs.

Requirements:
- Must be written in **third person (limited, omniscient, or simple)**.
- Characters must remain **unnamed** (use pronouns). This will force you to describe them instead of just naming them.
- Must include a **conflict**.
- Must follow a **plot**.
- Must have a distinct syntax style. (See below.)

Prewriting
1. Select conflict type:
   - ❏ Man vs. Man
   - ❏ Man vs. Self
   - ❏ Man vs. Society
   - ❏ Man vs. Nature

   Describe conflict here:

2. Select syntax style:
   - ❏ Mostly short, simple sentences with a climax of long, flowery, descriptive sentences.
   - ❏ Mostly long, flowery, descriptive sentences, with a climax of short, simple sentences.

3. Sketch out plot (does not have to be well developed at this time).

4. Sketch out characters. You may have as few or as many characters as you like. Characters can be animals or objects as well as people. **The narrator cannot be a character. Remember, no names!**

Who?	Who?	Who?	Who?
Strengths?	Strengths?	Strengths?	Strengths?
Weaknesses?	Weaknesses?	Weaknesses?	Weaknesses?
Something that happened to them in the past that's important:	Something that happened to them in the past that's important:	Something that happened to them in the past that's important:	Something that happened to them in the past that's important:

5. Begin writing.

Complete rough draft due Tuesday, January 24.

Honors: Rough draft should be at least one page, typed, double-spaced (or two pages handwritten).

Regular: Rough draft should be at least half page, typed, double-spaced (or one full page handwritten).

Final draft due Monday, January 30. Must be typed, double-spaced, with appropriate MLA-formatted header and a **title**.

Appendix 8.1: Sample Materials

Assignment 1: Narrative Self-Portrait
(3–5 pages, excluding photos, tables, citations, etc.)
Rough Draft Due: February 2
Final Draft Due: February 5

How odd I can have all this inside me and to you it's just words.
—David Foster Wallace, *The Pale King*

Who are you? An athlete, a poet, a student, a daughter or son, an activist, an astronomer, a scientist, dancer, teacher, book-lover, dreamer, animal-lover, writer, citizen. Are you brilliant, sensitive, tough, hilarious, moody, creative, flighty, logical, irrational, mercurial, grounded, caring, strong? Are you an eternal optimist? A cynic?

Most likely you are all of the above at one time or another ... and much more. When faced with questions of identity, we inevitably turn to words: they make us up and let us convey portions of ourselves to each other, because we are not only communal animals, but we are symbol-using animals. Our words let us define who we are in complex and ever-changing ways ... and that is your first assignment: **to define yourself via words, specifically via narrative**.

Narratives are some of the earliest linguistic definitions of self—after all, who doesn't love a good story? Achilles personified valor for ancient Greeks, Solomon wisdom for the ancient Hebrews, Gilgamesh strength for the ancient Sumerians. For this assignment, you will write a narrative that paints a portrait of yourself ... a deceptively easy task!

To do so, you will draw on the various skills and concepts you have been learning this semester: we are each walking supercomputers made of history, psychology, biology, chemistry, technology, and numbers (with a dash of photographic evidence). Now, to put it on the page!

Appendix 8.1: Sample Materials

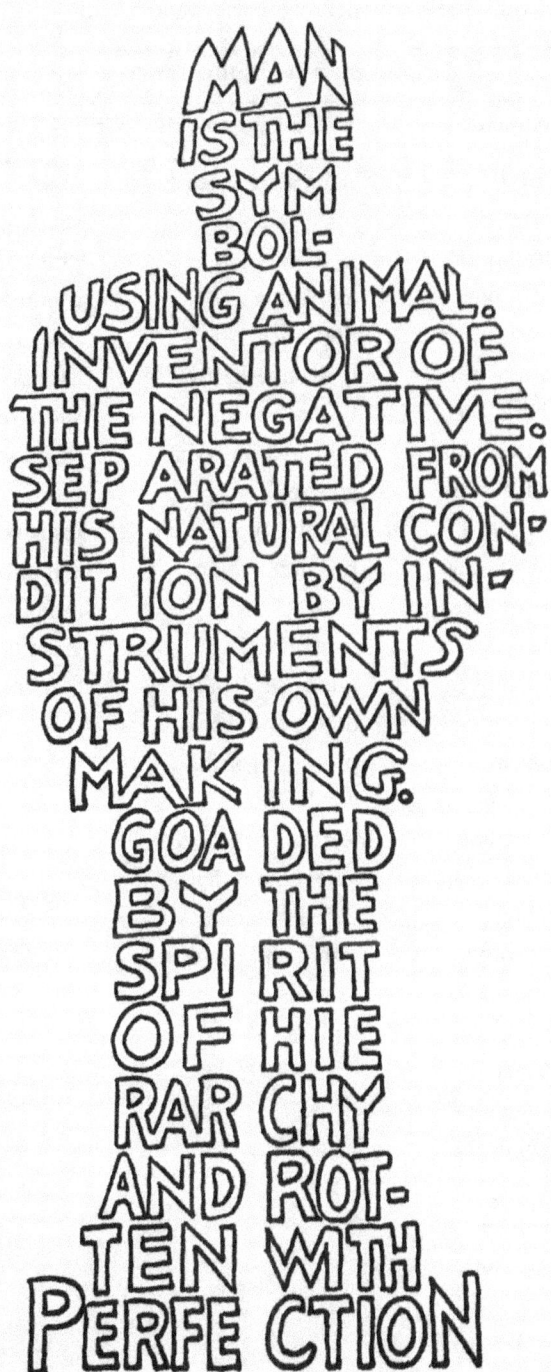

Figure A8.1 Frontispiece, *Late Poems, 1968–1993*, Kenneth Burke.[1]

Table A8.2 Narrative Self-Portrait Assignment Requirements

	Assignment Requirements				
Genre Requirements		**Technical Requirements**		**Writing Requirements**	
1.	**Argumentative:** Your narrative self-portrait is an argument about who you are—your conception of self is your thesis, the points of your story the evidence. What do you want to convey? And how best to convey it?	1.	**Appeals:** (At least) one example each of ethos, pathos, and logos	1.	**One stunning semicolon**
		2.	**Statistics:** (At least) one statistic that conveys information about yourself	2.	**One comma + a coordinating conjunction**
				3.	**One powerful short sentence** (< seven words)
		3.	**Formatting:** The posture of your essay is in the formatting! You must use all of the digital and word-processing skills you have been learning to create a document that visually stands proud and projects its message	4.	**One exceedingly long, yet effective sentence** (> 20 words and grammatically flawless)
2.	**Chronology:** A good narrative need not be chronological, though it should have a chronology				
3.	**Descriptive:** An engaging story uses both concrete language and metaphor to move the reader along. And good description need not be flowery or overdone to be effective (for an example of this, see the detailed descriptions you write in lab reports)				

Reflective Cover Letter Prompt

When submitting your Narrative Self-Portrait, please include this cover letter addressing the following questions:

1. Which criterion from the assignment sheet do you feel you achieved most successfully? Why?
2. Which criterion from the assignment sheet did you find most challenging? Why?
3. Which paragraph of your essay are you most proud of? Why?
4. Which paragraph did you find most challenging to write? Why?
5. What else would you like me to focus on as I comment on your work?

Note

1 Kenneth Burke, *Late Poems, 1968–1993* (Columbia, SC: University of South Carolina Press, 2005), frontispiece.

Appendix 16.1

Example Flash Fiction Discussion Questions

1. Prewrite: Which point of view will the story be written in?
2. Prewrite: Which photo(s) will serve as the main character(s)?
3. Prewrite: Which photos will be the first, second, and third settings? Will there be more settings?
4. Prewrite: Which photos will serve as antagonist(s), confidant(s), and foil(s)?
5. Prewrite: What major conflict do(es) the main character(s) have to resolve? What smaller obstacles will appear before the major conflict?
6. Act 1—Exposition: How would you describe the main character(s) (personality and appearance)?
7. Act 1—Exposition: What motivates the main character(s) to act towards his or her goal?
8. Act 2—Rising Action: What obstacles are in the main characters' way?
9. Act 2—Rising Action: What drawbacks do(es) the main character(s) face due to these obstacles?
10. Act 2—Rising Action: How do(es) the main character(s) respond to each drawback?
11. Act 3—Conflict: What lessons did the main character(s) learn that help them with the main conflict?
12. Act 3—Conflict: What exactly happens to the main character(s) as they solve the conflict?
13. Act 3—Resolution: What is the new normal for the(se) main characters?

Contributors

Oona Marie Abrams is a teacher of English Language Arts at Chatham High School in Morris County, New Jersey. She is an active member of NCTE, ALAN, the Council on English Leadership, the New Jersey Council of Teachers of English, and ASCD.

Amy Ash is an assistant professor of English at Indiana State University and director of the ISU Creative Writing Program. She specializes in poetry and poetics, collaborative writing, and creative writing pedagogy. She is the author of *The Open Mouth of the Vase*, winner of the 2013 *Cider Press Review* Book Award and the 2016 Etchings Press Whirling Prize post-publication award for poetry.

John Belk is an assistant professor of English at Southern Utah University where he directs the Writing Program. His poetry has appeared in *Sugar House Review, Crab Orchard Review, Salt Hill, Kestrel, Worcester Review, Crosswinds, Sport Literate, Poetry South,* and *Arkansas Review* among others. His work has been selected as a finalist for the Autumn House Rising Writer Contest, the Cathexis Chapbook Contest, the Autumn House Poetry Prize, the Barry Spacks Prize from Gunpowder Press, and the Comstock Writers Group Chapbook Contest. His scholarship can be found in *Rhetoric Review, Rhetoric Society Quarterly, Composition Forum,* and edited anthologies.

Erik Burgeson serves as the library media specialist and teaches reading electives at Kilbourne Middle School in Worthington, Ohio. He has held National Board Certification in World Languages other than English since 2005. Erik published his first NaNoWriMo novel, *5ive Sundays in February*, on Amazon in February 2018. He also co-presented the NaNoWriMo project from his chapter with Tom Strous at the National Council of Teachers of English Conference in November 2015.

Heather J. Clark has been an English teacher, primarily in Southern California, for the past twenty years, working in a wide variety of settings from middle school to college composition in both urban and suburban areas. Serving students ranging from English language learners and at-risk freshmen to AP, Clark has held the leadership roles of literacy lead and department chair at the high school level. She is constantly looking for new methods to incorporate into her curriculum to best meet her students' ever-changing needs.

Michael Dean Clark is an associate professor of writing at Azusa Pacific University near Los Angeles, California. An author of fiction and nonfiction primarily, his work has appeared in *Pleiades, Jabberwock Review, The Other Journal, Angel City Review*, and a number of other publications. Formerly an award-winning journalist, he is also the coeditor of *Creative Writing in the Digital Age* and *Creative Writing Innovations* (Bloomsbury).

Amanda Clarke is the Dr. William Turner Levy Endowed Chair for Inspired Teaching at Viewpoint School in Calabasas, California, where she teaches AP English Literature and Composition and World Literature Honors, a post-AP research course.

Nan Cohen is the English department chair at Viewpoint School in Calabasas, California. The author of two books of poems, *Rope Bridge* and *Unfinished City*, she is also the longtime director of poetry programs at the Napa Valley Writers' Conference.

Chris Drew is an associate professor of English at Indiana State University, where he supervises the English teaching program and teaches creative writing and teaching methods courses. He previously taught ELA and theatre at Heritage Hills Middle School and Mater Dei High School, both in Indiana. His work has appeared in publications that include *English Leadership Quarterly, The Journal of Creative Writing Studies, Minnesota English Journal, Wisconsin English Journal, Mad River Review, Bellevue Literary Review*, and *Quarterly West*. He is a coeditor of *Dispatches from the Classroom: Graduate Students on Creative Writing Pedagogy* (Bloomsbury).

Mark Esperanza is an adjunct professor at Northwest Vista College in San Antonio, Texas, and a teacher at Progreso High School in Progreso, Texas. He's lived near the Mexican-American border his entire life and enjoys writing about this special region.

Alexa Garvoille is a National Board–certified teacher who has taught secondary ELA and directed the creative writing program at Durham School of the Arts in North Carolina. She holds an MFA in Poetry from Virginia Tech.

Erica Hamilton previously taught high school English and now works as an associate professor in the College of Education at Grand Valley State University in Grand Rapids, Michigan. An advocate for community-based partnerships, Erica welcomes opportunities to partner with K–12 teachers and their students. Erica holds a PhD from Michigan State University in Curriculum, Teaching, and Educational Policy.

Stacy Haynes-Moore is an adjunct lecturer in the College of Education at the University of Iowa and the Content Lead for Secondary English Language Arts in the Cedar Rapids Community School District. Stacy's research interests include adolescent literacies and digital literacies, with a particular focus on teaching and learning language arts within blended spaces.

Trent Hergenrader is an associate professor of English at the Rochester Institute of Technology in Rochester, New York. He is the author of *Collaborative Worldbuilding for Writers and Gamers*, coeditor of *Creative Writing in the Digital Age* and *Creative Writing Innovations* (Bloomsbury), and editor-in-chief of the peer-reviewed, open-access *Journal of Creative Writing Studies*.

Kelli Krieger is a department chair in English at Union-Endicott High School in Endicott, New York. Kelli specializes in teaching creative and analytical writing and has a special interest in graphic novels and the intersection of STEM and English.

Justin Longacre teaches English and creative writing at Toledo School for the Arts. His poetry and fiction have been published in *Word Riot*, *Spartan*, *Rabble*, *Great Lakes Review*, and elsewhere.

Sara C. Pendleton currently teaches English and writing at Grace Brethren High School in Simi Valley, California, where she also serves as the English department chair. In addition to teaching, she is a freelance editor and has worked for Fitbit, Inc. and other health and wellness companies.

Tanya Perkins is an assistant professor and chair of English at Indiana University East, where she teaches fiction and professional/technical writing.

Jennifer Pullen is an assistant professor of creative writing at Ohio Northern University. She received her PhD from Ohio University. Her publications include her chapbook, *A Bead of Amber on Her Tongue*, which won the Omnidawn Fabulist Fiction Award. Her research foci include creative writing pedagogy, science fiction and fantasy literature, folklore and fairy tales, gender studies, and environmental writing. She originally hails from the forests of Washington State but now lives and works in Ohio.

Tim Staley has been unruining poetry with humor and humility since 2001 in the public high school classrooms of Southern New Mexico. From New Mexico State University he earned a Poetry MFA, a Special Education license, and a General Education license. He was born in Montgomery, Alabama, in 1975. He founded Grandma Moses Press in 1992 and continues to serve as editor and primary caregiver. His most recent poetry chapbook, *The Most Honest Syllable is Shhh*, was released by NightBallet in 2017. His debut collection, *Lost on My Own Street*, was released by Pski's Porch in 2016.

Tom Strous is currently a middle school technology teacher with Worthington Schools in Worthington, Ohio. He has been teaching for eighteen years in public schools and has taught outdoor education, English Language Arts, gifted ELA, and technology electives. He co-presented the NaNoWriMo project described in his chapter at the National Council of Teachers of English Conference in November 2015 with Erik Burgeson. He published *The Portage*, his first novel written during NaNoWriMo, on Amazon.

Josh Tolbert is an assistant professor of special education at Indiana University East. His current research interests include strategies for teaching Spanish to students with learning disabilities and the multicultural perceptions of preservice teachers.

Dana VanderLugt is a former middle school English teacher who recently became an instructional coach for Hudsonville Public Schools in Hudsonville, Michigan. She has a master's in Education and has taught first-year composition classes at a local liberal arts college. She also writes, blogs, and is pursuing an MFA in Creative Nonfiction from Spalding University in Louisville, Kentucky.

Stephanie Vanderslice is a professor and director of the Arkansas Writer's MFA Workshop at the University of Central Arkansas. Her most recent books include *The Geek's Guide to the Writing Life: An Instructional Memoir for the Rest of Us* and *Can Creative Writing Really Be Taught?*, both from Bloomsbury. She also writes novels, creative nonfiction, fiction, and creative criticism.

Index

21st century learning/skills 143-4, 150

Adsit, Janelle 24, 39, 42, 54-5
advanced placement 3, 153-63, 165, 187
analytical writing 44-5, 63-5, 80, 86, 150, 154, 165
assessment 19, 39, 43, 86, 100, 103-7, 145, 153, 168-9, 177, 197, 199, 212, 218, 225-6, 228

Bishop, Wendy 11-12, 52-4, 196
Bloom's Taxonomy 101, 145, 189, 206, 214

California Common Core State Standards 143-4
canonical literature 26, 41-2, 53, 73, 79, 154
career readiness 18, 24, 30, 57, 131, 186
character 30, 42, 44, 66, 69-70, 80, 88, 91, 145-9, 156, 158, 162-3, 175, 178-82, 190-2, 196-200, 206-7, 212, 244-5, 250
collaboration 25, 52, 55, 113-17, 132, 176, 182, 186-8, 192, 195-202, 212, 220, 225, 233-5
Common Core State Standards 2-4, 7, 17-33, 49, 74, 80-1, 87, 102, 119, 124, 128, 139, 144-5, 151, 154-6, 158, 160-1, 178, 197, 205-6, 210, 212, 214, 232, 234, 238
Composition Studies 61, 99
constructionism 63, 72
creative nonfiction 3, 20, 27-8, 113-20, 137, 196
Creative Writing Studies 2, 7, 37, 53-4
critical thinking 61-71, 80, 114, 117, 119
curriculum maps 19, 154

demi-rubrics 3, 86, 99-109
Depth of Knowledge (DOK) 145-8

ekphrasis 161-2, 238
English language learners (ELLs) 4, 186-92

facilitator 56, 87, 113, 166
failure (productive) 3, 40, 85-7, 89, 90, 92, 95-6, 147
feedback 4, 24-5, 39, 42-5, 52, 54, 56, 58, 64, 104, 116, 118, 147, 150, 169-70, 176, 181-2, 197, 199, 210, 217-20, 222-3, 225-9, 233, 241-2
fiction 3-4, 19-20, 27-8, 43-6, 63-6, 69, 73-83, 90-1, 132, 145, 162-3, 176, 191, 196-7, 201, 205, 213, 237
flash fiction 4, 43, 46, 162, 185, 187, 189, 191-2, 238, 244-5, 250
Foerster, Norman 25, 53
freewriting 43, 118, 126, 207
Frost, Robert 44, 124

Gallagher, Kelly 41, 169, 172
genre 3, 19-21, 27-28, 30, 40, 42, 44-5, 47, 65, 73-82, 88, 117, 155, 158, 162, 167, 171, 192, 198, 200-1, 227, 237-8, 248
grading 2-3, 43, 86, 99, 102-7, 116, 118, 147
growth mindset 40, 225

Hunger Games, The 3, 66, 175, 177, 179, 180-1
Hunley, Tom C. 23, 27, 30

Iowa Writers' Workshop 11-12, 25, 42, 52-4, 73, 75-6, 79, 81
Ishiguro, Kazuo 74, 81, 153, 163

Kittle, Penny 15, 40, 167, 169, 172

Leahy, Anna 12, 31, 51, 54-5
literary community 4, 74, 231, 235
literature 1, 24-5, 27, 29, 30, 54-5, 63, 67, 73-81, 87, 91, 126, 129, 143-7, 150, 153-4, 165-6, 175-8, 182, 212, 231
lore 7, 37, 41, 53, 73

Mad Libs 21, 94–5
marginalized/marginalization 1, 41, 51, 55, 59, 73, 155, 197
Mayers, Tim 12, 27, 30
Morrison, Toni 10, 153, 157, 163
Moxley, Joseph M. 12, 52, 54
multigenre writing 3, 165–72

NaNoWriMo 4, 205–14
National Writing Project 8, 14, 46
New Jersey Student Learning Standards 165, 171
nonfiction 3, 20, 27–8, 80, 91, 113, 116–20, 132, 137, 196, 214
novella 86, 88, 90–1

Orwell, George 27–8, 76, 79

Poe, Edgar Allen 26, 133
poetry 3, 19–20, 22, 27–8, 31–2, 41, 45–7, 57, 94–5, 100–1, 104, 123–9, 133–4, 136, 155–6, 158–62, 196–7, 201, 219, 225, 232, 236, 238–9
point of view 20, 26, 30, 68, 146, 149, 200, 250
preservice teachers 4, 10, 217–19, 225, 227–8
process-based 21, 29–30, 86
product-based 3, 29

public reading 4
publication(s) 30–1, 38, 46, 53, 91, 231–2, 235–8

revision 8, 26, 29, 38, 40, 42, 45, 52, 58, 90, 101–2, 118, 179, 200–1, 226, 238, 241
role-playing 146
rubric(s) 93, 100–7, 143, 147, 165, 169

scaffold, scaffolded, scaffolding 43, 103, 105–6, 114, 118, 199, 201, 233
Shakespeare, William 10, 26
STEM 18, 131–3, 139–40

Texas Essential Knowledge and Skills 189
Twitter 41, 92–3, 166

Vanderslice, Stephanie 2, 32, 37, 54

Wikipedia 67–9
workshop 3, 7, 12, 23–6, 29, 39, 42–3, 45, 51–9, 63, 73, 75, 79, 81, 114, 144, 146, 150, 166, 168, 201, 213, 233, 239, 241–3
worldbuilding 3, 44, 63, 65, 68–9, 71, 80
writing process 3, 11, 22, 29, 38, 40–3, 47, 51, 90, 106, 113, 116, 118, 169, 200, 202, 210–11, 217, 219, 225

www.ingramcontent.com/pod-product-compliance
Lightning Source LLC
Chambersburg PA
CBHW072130290426
44111CB00012B/1847